New Times in Modern Japan

New Times in Modern Japan

Stefan Tanaka

PRINCETON UNIVERSITY PRESS

PRINCETON AND OXFORD

Library of Congress Cataloging-in-Publication Data

Tanaka, Stefan.
New times in modern Japan / Stefan Tanaka.
  p.   cm.
Includes bibliographical references and index.
ISBN 0-691-11774-8 (cl : alk. paper)
1. Japan—History—Meiji period, 1868–1912.   I. Title.

DS882.T336 2004
952.03'1—dc22   2003066411

British Library Cataloging-in-Publication Data is available

This book has been composed in Electra
Printed on acid-free paper. ∞
pup.princeton.edu
Printed in the United States of America
1 3 5 7 9 10 8 6 4 2

For Kyoko

———————————

CONTENTS

ACKNOWLEDGMENTS

Writing the acknowledgments, a sort of biography of this book, is one of the true pleasures of the final stages of preparing a manuscript. It is one of those rituals that gives me a sense—no doubt mythical—that completion is near. In our discipline such senses of completion are rare at best and, at times like this, fleeting. (Books are not completed, they are moments along an intellectual journey.) Thus it is a chance to review the long process that has led to this book; it is a reminder of one of the best parts of history, the serendipity of following data and ideas whose import, as well as "mere" interest, are often unanticipated.

This project began long ago after what seemed then as an odd request. In talking to John Gillis about a paper for a conference on memory, he asked that I come up with a topic that dealt with something tangible. My work on art history began; more important, it directed me more toward an inquiry into what I now see as the materiality of ideas. Two other conferences were especially and unexpectedly pivotal, again turning this project away from what I thought it was going to be. I am thankful to Sally Humphreys for stimulating what has become my work on childhood. Another unexpected turn arose when Kevin Doak refused my initial suggestion for a paper. A paper on the Hōryūji came out of what at the time, I thought, was a throwaway line. The ideas in this book developed through contact with many colleagues who invited me to present my preliminary work at the University of Chicago, Washington University, the German Historical Institute, Tokyo National Research Institute of Cultural Properties, University of California at Los Angeles, and the Exploratorium in San Francisco.

This project was supported by many institutions. A research fellowship from the National Endowment for the Humanities was very important in getting it off the ground. An Andrew Mellon postdoctoral fellowship at the University of Southern California gave me some conceptual room to allow for reading and thinking. I thank Clark University and the University of California, San Diego, both of which provided research support. An International and Area Studies Fellowship from the American Council of Learned Societies, Social Science Research Council, and National Endowment for the Humanities in 2000 allowed me to spend a year pulling all the parts together.

This book is a reformulation of some previously published materials, the result of conferences that stimulated me to explore new issues. I am thankful to the publishers for allowing me to use the following essays: "Imaging History: Inscribing Belief in the Nation," *Journal of Asian Studies* 53 (1994): 24–44; "Childhood: the Naturalization of Development into a Japanese Space," in S. C. Humphreys, ed., *Cultures of Scholarship* (Ann Arbor: University of Michigan Press, 1997); "Discoveries of the Hōryūji," in Kai-wing Chow, Kevin M.

Doak, and Poshek Fu, eds., *Constructing Nationhood in Modern East Asia* (Ann Arbor: University of Michigan Press, 2001); and "Nature—the Naturalization of Experience as National," in Michele Marra, ed., *Japanese Hermeneutics* (Honolulu: University of Hawai'i Press, 2002).

Most important, I have had some wonderful colleagues who helped me to work through many of the ideas that have found their way into this book. Above all, I am indebted to Harry Harootunian and Tetsuo Najita for their continued support and friendship; their comments on a draft reminded me that there is so much more to think about than is here. Masao Miyoshi has been a wonderful colleague and friend: very challenging and very supportive whenever the need has arisen. Through the electronic realm, Doug Howland has been a constant source of feedback and support; George M. Wilson has generously shared his thoughts over many fine meals and wine. At Clark University I was lucky to teach courses with Jim Wertsch and Sally Deutsch, who both forced me to read texts and think about issues that I probably would not have otherwise. Marc Steinberg, Jim Gee, Sarah Michaels, and Paul Ropp all made important interventions in my intellectual growth, as well as helping me survive in Worcester. At UCSD an opportunity to teach with Geoffrey Bowker added substance on the topic of time that was not always there, and I think (hope) thoughts are more clear as a result of many long rides with Stan Chodorow. Dain Borges and Luce Giard helped me work through virtually all of the ideas in this book (as well as many other topics) over many cups of coffee. And Kazuhiko Endo, with whom I inflicted my ideas upon graduate students, pushed me to think more about the materiality of ideas. Thank you also to Shigeki Sekiyama, Gerry Iguchi, Mie Kennedy, Shawn Bender, Matt Johnson, George Solt, Tomoyuki Sasaki, and Rika Morioka.

In this moment of increasing angst about academic publishing, the staff at Princeton University Press has been very professional—a delight to work with. Brigitta van Rheinberg has been very supportive of this project, and I am thankful for her engagement, patience, and curiosity in what has not always been a readily graspable idea. Alison Kalett and Gail Schmitt have kept things (me) on track, Anita O'Brien's judicious editing will save me from several embarrassing moments, and Maria denBoer prepared the index—at last, bringing this decade-long (and continuing) inquiry to another existence.

Finally, this project has followed another temporality: that of our home. Not only has Kyoko remained supportive, but her sense of visuality has infiltrated the way I have approached my scholarship. Alisa and Keenan have contributed to this project in more ways than they know; they help me realize the abstractness of modern time and rejuvenate my interest in stories. Thank you.

New Times in Modern Japan

TIME, PASTS, HISTORY

Time is everything, man is nothing; he is at the most the incarnation of time.

—Georg Lukacs (1971)

The great revolution introduced a new calendar. The initial
day of a calendar serves as a historical time-lapse camera.
And, basically, it is the same day that keeps recurring in the
guise of holidays, which are days of remembrance. Thus the
calendars do not measure time as clocks do; they are monuments of a historical consciousness of which not the slightest
trace has been apparent in Europe in the past hundred years.

—Walter Benjamin (1968)

Time-keeping passed into time-serving and time-accounting
and time-rationing. As this took place, Eternity ceased gradually to serve as the measure and focus of human actions.

The clock, not the steam-engine, is the key-machine of the
modern industrial age.

—Lewis Mumford (1934)

I HAVE LONG BEEN STRUCK by the statement of a Japanese elite, reported through
Erwin Baelz in 1876: "We have no history. Our history begins today" (quoted in
Wilson 1980, 570).[1] The absence of history in an archipelago that abounds with
traces of its long past (at that time believed to be around twenty-five hundred years,
and over fifteen hundred years if one begins from the tumuli) seems odd. But this
statement roughly coincides with the reform of calendrical and clock time in
1872. The beginning of history coincides with the adoption of a modern time; it
recalls Mumford's statement that time is the key machine of the modern age.

A new reckoning of time was one of a series of events of Meiji, beginning with
the *Ishin* in 1868, which brought about a truly remarkable and revolutionary
transformation of the archipelago.[2] The myriad communities that existed at the

---

[1] Wilson's inquiry into historical time is a remarkable essay from which I have learned much. It is a
joy to discover such insightful and adventurous essays but depressing to know that this has been
largely ignored in the profession.

[2] I use the Japanese word rather than the normally translated word "restoration"; the characters for
ishin suggest renewal rather than restoration. More important, my examination of this period of
transformation suggests a shift in epistemology from renewal to revolution. The word "restoration"
is more reflective of the political desires and certainly does not encompass this shift.

start of the era were completely reconfigured both spatially and temporally into one society, Japan. A new temporality is fundamental to this new society. While the *Ishin* marked the inherited as old and the hereafter as new, the transformation of time not only punctuated that separation but ensured a wholly different way of thinking about the present.

The purpose of this book is to inquire into this reconfiguration of society around a modern time, what several German historians call *Neuzeit* (new time).[3] In a sense, academics and scholars have long recognized this *Neuzeit*, usually characterized as civilization, modern, first world, and so forth, and opposed to barbaric, traditional, and third world. Establishing this "new time" was one of the dominating themes of the Meiji period—enlightenment or *bunmeikaika*. In his terse, elegant essay, "What Is Enlightenment?" Kant defines it as "mankind's exit from its self-incurred immaturity." Finding and mapping that exit from what Japanese intellectuals believed to be their self-incurred immaturity is not linear. My invocation of Koselleck's new time is to highlight the different conceptions of time that underlie this juxtaposition between old and new and that make up modern society.

The epigraph above from Lukacs encapsulates some of the key temporalities that were new in Meiji. The most obvious is that the Meiji period ushered in a new government, economic system, and conceptual structure. It truly was a new time that broke from the old. Second, clocks were adopted and became the principle timekeepers that marked the units of the day. They brought mechanically regular time—the time of a progressive society. The time of the newly adopted Gregorian calendar was also new, but this time signified (and continues to signify) the "monuments of a historical consciousness." This constantly recurring time has gained a transhistorical status, a temporality removed from time to transmute objects and relations into natural conditions. Finally, with regard to Benjamin's perceptive comment above that the absence of traces of this monumental time (and I would add chronological time) is another part of modern temporality, the historical consciousness of the modern person is built upon fragments of the past that are now remembered as quaint, romantic, and/or primitive conditions prior to the better life of modern society. The transformation itself is naturalized as a passing, inevitable condition of all societies that seek to develop and become modern. These different temporalities were all part of the transformation where, by the end of the Meiji period, a historical consciousness emerged that had transmuted the heterogeneous communities of the archipelago into a unified nation-state, Japan.

As the different temporalities suggest, the process of transformation to the modern is not just how society was transformed, but how people conceived of a society where a historical understanding of one's world is necessary to one's

---

[3] For a description of *Neuzeit*, see Koselleck (1985), especially pp. 231–66.

liberation. A study of the transformation of time is a history, in the commonly used sense, of the transformation of the Japanese archipelago in the Meiji period. It was quite evident to a wide range of people on the three main islands (in 1868 Ezo was "foreign," soon to be colonized into Hokkaido) near the end of the Tokugawa period that the inherited knowledge no longer coincided with their experiences. The various movements that eventually resulted in a modern, capitalistic nation-state were attempts to reunify knowledge and experience. These multiple times force us to recognize that "time is no longer simply the medium in which all histories take place; it gains a historical quality" (Koselleck 1985, 246). This study is also historical in another sense, that is, history as representation by both contemporaries and present-day scholars. It is not my purpose to engage in a defense of what has been called the linguistic turn nor to point out the simple-mindedness of those who defend an objective historical truth. Others have done this better than I can.[4] My hope is to bring out some of the ways that intellectuals, everyman, and scholars have given meaning to those changes.

My focus on history is driven by an old desire in our profession: to write a historically accurate account of the past. This is quintessentially modern. But unlike many positivists and empiricists, I approach this endeavor by including history itself as a part of that past; it, too, should be an object of our inquiry, for our understanding of history today emerged at the same time as modern nation-states. The historicity of history is empirically verifiable. When history, too, is included, this moment of transformation is not just some stage of an evolutionary process. Instead, it is a historical moment when the very ideas, forms, and structures of modern society are being formulated and constructed. In his brilliant reappraisal of Marxism, Moishe Postone encapsulates this modern capitalist society as "a directionally dynamic society structured by a historically unique form of social mediation that, though socially constituted, has an abstract, impersonal, quasi-objective character" (1993, 5). It is the combination of a linear time and transhistorical temporalities into a unifed nation-state as if they are all universal and/or natural conditions.

Time is at the root of this social mediation. One of the characteristics of modern society is the synchronization of various temporalities into a unified, homogeneous, and empty time. That this abstract, empty time has to be put into place shows it is social and historical. This synchronization occurs on several levels. On the one hand, the synchronization of the archipelago into the same temporal system as Europe and the United States facilitated interaction of the new nation-state into the international (and imperialistic) arena. This reconfiguration of society, the "rise of modern Japan," was driven by the desire to synchronize the archipelago with the liberal-capitalist codes of the burgeoning

---

[4] For some recent examples, see Davidson (2001); Ankersmit (2001); and de Certeau (1988).

international system. One part of this sychronization was the fear of coloniza-
tion; old and new leaders struggled to learn about and deal with the very different demands (unlike the Dutch at Deshima) of this new West.

As a part of this synchronization, the new leaders reformed the calendar,
adopted the twenty-four-hour clock, changed the practice of reckoning years
to coincide with reign, and reconfigured the archipelago into a Japan. The
epigraphs, however, suggest that the change in reckoning of time involves more
than a mere technical adjustment. Just as the French Revolutionary calendar
connected the new political system with a new temporality, this reform connected a new time with a new politico-economic system, the Meiji government,
under the slogan *fukoku kyōhei* (rich country, strong military). In contrast, anything old and connected with the previous temporality becomes potentially
anachronistic.

But as so many contemporaries and subsequent scholars have already
noted, modernization requires the reformulation of the archipelago so that its
components can also function as a unit. This brings up another form of synchronization: time provides an organizing framework that allows for a different flow of people and goods (more conducive to capitalism) that reorganizes
the diverse regions of the archipelago into the unit of Japan. Here it is important to remember that history, the state, and the capitalist economy emerged
at the same time. This framework is comprised of what Nico Poulantzas calls
the materiality of the state: "It is, in fact, a specialized and centralized apparatus of a peculiarly political nature, comprising an assemblage of impersonal,
anonymous functions whose form is distinct from that of economic power;
their ordering rests on the axiomatic force of laws-rules distributing the
spheres of activity or competence, and on a legitimacy derived from the
people-nation" (2000, 54). An important part of this materiality are not only
the laws-rules that go beyond the formal laws of the state but also encompass
the norms that organize people and places. Here, we must seriously consider
Postone's statement that this materiality is historically specific, abstract, and
impersonal. In this process, various ideas, institutions, and timeforms are formulated to reestablish those codes that hold society together, especially amid
the centrifugal tendencies of this new modern world. These forms structure
society in ways that facilitate the productive processes of capitalism and seek
the obedience of the actors, the inhabitants turned into citizens. But they are
forms that gain an abstract, but seemingly specific, character by being located
in a different temporality—often called culture. In short, this book is about the
way that a new reckoning of time is at the root of the politico-economic reformulation of the archipelago.

The remainder of this prelude is roughly divided into the two fundamental
components of the historical craft that informs this work: history as discourse
and history as practice.

TIME

A place to begin my history is the reform of the lunar calendar in 1872. This seemingly mundane reform brings out the historical character of time and the "sacrilege" that its alteration evokes.[5] On the ninth day of the eleventh month of the fifth year of Meiji (December 9, 1872, according to the Gregorian calendar), the *Tokyo nichi nichi shimbun* (as well as other newspapers) reported on the imperial edict announcing the change to the solar calendar. The paper announced that the third day of the twelfth month would thereafter be January 1 according to the new solar calendar:

> The customary calendar of our country calculates months from the waxing and waning of the moon, and an intercalary month must be added every two or three years to adjust to the movement of the sun. Thus, the seasons are early or late and it produces uneven measurement of the heavenly bodies. Just as among the middle and lower levels, it belongs to arbitrariness and ignorance, and impedes the achievement of knowledge. But the solar calendar calculates months in accordance with the movement of the sun. Even though there is a little variation in the days of the month, there is no fluctuation of the seasons, only one intercalary day every four years, and an error of no more than one day in 7,000 years. It is much more accurate than the lunar calendar, and debate whether or not it is convenient is unnecessary. I, hereby, abolish the old calendar, adopt the solar calendar, and order the realm to obey for eternity. (Okada 1994, 117)

This edict cited the greater accuracy of the solar (Gregorian) calendar and appeared with little comment, as if it were a rather minor administrative change. Perhaps political exigency was a reason for the suddenness as well as limited publicity; Okada cites the desire to reduce the new government's expenditures. By eliminating the twelfth month and the intercalary month, the Dajōkan (Council of State) eliminated two months of stipends to samurai and daimyo (Okada 1994, 181–82). Katō Shūichi, for example, described this as a simple matter of synchronizing Japan to Europe—it was a simple course correction, that of rationality and efficiency (Katō and Maruyama 1991, 353–54). Indeed, the new government was concerned that the lunar calendar made interchange with Westerners more difficult and smacked of backwardness.

It is hard for us today to imagine such temporally heterogeneous worlds. Yet, prior to this reform, time was not unified: several calendars (all lunar) existed on the archipelago. Throughout most of the Tokugawa period, both the court and the bakufu (governing structure headed by the shogun) employed astronomers to

---

[5] E. G. Richards describes the transformation of time in religious terms: "To change the calendar is therefore a sort of sacrilege and all too frequently, it would seem, its reformation has resulted in bloodshed, or, one might be tempted to infer, divine retribution" (1998, 110).

determine the proper calendar.[6] Many of these early astronomers were familiar with Copernican heliocentric theory, Newton's physics, and Kepler's laws of planetary motion. They did not, however, apply this knowledge until social and cultural conditions made it suitable (Nakayama 1969; Postone 1993, 186–225). To limit the temporal transformation to a new scientific knowledge, greater accuracy, and bureaucratic convenience enforces the separation of science from politics and of politics from culture. It overlooks the importance of social decisions to whether or how knowledge is to be utilized.

As difficult as it is to imagine worlds of heterogeneous temporalities, it is even more difficult to grasp the transformation of one's world when the reckoning of time is changed. The impact of this calendrical reform went well beyond cost savings. The time of the solar calendar was completely alien to the inhabitants, unsettling the knowledge and practices that revolved around the lunar calendar. Those inherited ideas and customs that explained the connection of humans to humans and to the environment now became anachronistic. Although the solar calendar is also "natural," that is, determined by the cycle of the sun rather than the moon, this new time seemed empty; it was located in the physical universe, not always seen, but more regular. The significance of this new time is that it is abstract; it opened up the possibility for the transformation of myriad communities that had somehow coalesced into a "Japan" into a unified nation-state that is rational, scientific, and efficient.

The heterogeneity of the archipelago and problems that such multiplicity created for the simple announcement of an administrative rule can be illustrated through the process of disseminating this edict. The Dajōkan's 1873 estimate of duration necessary for directives to reach different regions of the archipelago was as follows: news would circulate in Tokyo by the next day; people in Kanagawa, Mie, Aichi, and Fukushima would find out three days later; those in Kyoto and Osaka would be out of the loop for as much as eight days; and those in Nagasaki would not received news for two weeks (Okada 1994, 132–33). This gap between announcement and transmission is true of this edict, illustrating the lack of uniformity and centrality, not to mention the difficulty of managing a system using highly imperfect modes of communication. For example, on 11/12, Kikuzawa Tōzō, an official at the Kyoto branch of the calendar distribution office established by the Ministry of Education, wrote in his diary that the rumors from Osaka of the new calendar were baseless.[7] Kikuzawa learned the next day that the change was true, but official word from the Kyoto government was not re-

---

[6] In 1868 the new government abolished the astronomy offices that were connected to the bakufu, and a monopoly on calendar making was granted to the Tsuchimikado family, which then selected astronomers who had been tied to the court. On 2/3/Meiji3 (March 11, 1870), jurisdiction over calendar making was transferred to the university (*daigaku*), and Tsuchimikado Kazumaru was placed in charge. His office was in Kyoto. Six months later the office was moved to Tokyo, and in 1871 the Kyoto office was closed (Nakayama 1969, 218–22).

[7] Perhaps rumors were spread by the new telegraph line between Tokyo and Osaka, which opened in the same month.

layed until 11/17 (Okada 1994, 135–38). Officials like Kikuzawa and his counterparts in realms farther from Tokyo had only two weeks or less to implement the new calendar and clock!

Above all, this edict shows that the reckoning of time is not natural, that the passing and cycle of moments, especially marked by the body and seasons of nature as well as modern time, now synchronized with that of Western nation-states, is socially constituted. A newspaper article just a few days after the edict expressed well this separation between time and nature:

> Now, we will carry out your august will announced in the imperial edict to abolish the old calendar and disseminate the solar calendar. However, there is one matter that will most likely shock the unenlightened and ignorant: that is the roundabout way to celebrate the festival days—gosekku [jinjitsu—1/7, jōshi—3/3, tango—5/5, shichiseki—7/7, chōyō—9/9]—as well as tsuchinotomi, kanoesaru, kinoene, etc. Moreover, it is certainly difficult to anticipate the new moon on the first day of the month and the full moon on the 15th night when there is an odd number of around thirty or so days to a month depending whether it is major or minor. Will one not lose reality when the moon is rising at the end of the month and no longer corresponds to the word tsugomori [end of the month] or, on the other hand, when the fifteenth night is dark? This is laughable. (Quoted in Okada 1994, 236).[8]

This separation of time from nature opened pandora's box; all inherited forms of knowledge became suspect. The Meiji period, I will argue, ushered in a quite different notion of what came before, of the present, and of what will come. Reinhardt Koselleck describes the nonmodern as a space of experience in which many layers of pasts are present. He writes: "It makes sense to say that experience based on the past is spatial since it is assembled into a totality, within which many layers of earlier times are simultaneously present, without, however, providing any indication of the before and after" (1985, 273). In contrast, the new temporality imposes a unilinearity (progress or development) with a "horizon of expectations" in some unknown future, determined from the certainty of past experience. This contrasts to earlier temporalities in which the ideal was located in some mythical past.

---

[8] The five days of gosekku were among the most important holidays on the archipelago. Their origin is from China. In the Tokugawa period, jinjitsu was a day of/for people. It was observed, from the bakufu down through the peasants, by eating a rice gruel of seven vegetables (nanakusagayu). Jōshi originated as a day for ablution, but as people began to perform the act symbolically using paper dolls, it gradually turned into a doll festival among the townspeople of Edo. Tango was originally connected to the power of plants such as the iris (shōbu) and mugwort (yomogi). When brought to Japan, these plants were hung from the eaves, and chimaki and kashiwamochi (sweet rice cakes) were eaten. Among samurai families, the iris was transformed into a martial spirit, and this festival became marked by the flying of koi kites and by military dolls. Shichiseki was a festival of the stars and took on several forms in different areas. Chōyō was originally connected to the auspiciousness of the number 9 in China. In the Tokugawa period it became a festival connected to the chrysanthemum and awagohan (rice with millet) among commoners. For more detail, see Okada and Akune (1993, 102–6).

One of my favorite statements exhibiting the dislocation created by the new calendar is this lament of the abolition of the lunar calendar in 1873: "Why did the government suddenly decide to abolish it? The whole thing is disagreeable. The old system fitted in with the seasons, the weather, and the movement of the tides. One could plan one's work or one's clothing or virtually anything else by it. Since the revision . . . nothing is the way it should be" (Yanagita 1957, 258). This lament not only describes the connection between time and nature, but it also demonstrates the centrality of time in the way that societies organize (and are organized by) that understanding. When the reckoning of time changes, one's very relation to the world is both disoriented and altered.

This potential to employ time as a tool to transform society was recognized by the new government and is suggested in the directive enumerating the new calendar and clock that accompanied the edict (Okada 1994, 119):

- The abolition of the lunar calendar and the adoption of the solar calendar will occur on the third day of the twelfth month. That day will be January 1, Meiji 6 [1873].
- The year will be divided into 365 days, with twelve months and an intercalary day every four years.
- The keeping of time had been divided into day and night with each having roughly twelve hours. Hereafter, day and night will be equal, and a clock (*jishingi*) will determine the twenty-four units. The period from *ne* (rat) *no koku* to *uma* (horse) *no koku* will be divided into twelve hours and called *gozen* (morning); the period from *uma no koku* to *ne no koku* will be divided into twelve hours and called *gogo* (afternoon).
- The telling of time [lit: ringing of bells] shall be in accordance with the schedule below. When asking about the time of a clock we have used *nanji* [the character for time (*ji*) is *aza* (section of a village)]; this will change to *nanji* [using the character *toki* (time)].
- Days and months of all festivals will be adjusted to the new calendar.

These reforms make sense to us today—they describe the timekeeping method we use. But that only indicates the extent to which modern time imbricates our lives. Each clause leads to substantial social transformation (or, more accurately, transmutation), and if we think of Benjamin's statement that calendars are "monuments of a historical consciousness," then we must also recognize the ways that the state uses time to orient or regulate how people think. The first directive is straightforward: there is an abolition of the lunar calendar and the adoption of the solar calendar. But embedded in this simple change is a new relationship of people to their environment and inherited practices. As the lament of the townsman indicates, the new calendar no longer marked the seasons in his mind. The new year no longer coincided with beginning of spring but was in the middle of winter; the phases of the moon no longer corresponded to the days of the month; and so forth.

This act of change—the denigration of the previous form as old in favor of an implicitly better "new"—is a common practice and not necessarily tied to modernity (O'Brien and Roseberry 1991). The new calendar fit a political rhetoric, that of legitimizing the new regime as compared to the previous, Tokugawa rule. The message transmitted by the solar calendar was that the lunar calendar, which had guided people, was arbitrary, connected to ignorance and backwardness, and an impediment to the achievement of wisdom. And since the Tokugawa bakufu used the lunar calendar, it was an example of the backwardness of its rule. In this way, rhetoric combined with a political act that had been seen as an obvious, natural part of change. Indeed, many people began to call the lunar calendar the Tokugawa calendar. The connection of this separation of past and present to the desire to synchronize the archipelago to the temporality of the West is evident in the Charter Oath, issued in the fourth month of 1868, just after the change in political power. The fourth article stated: "Evil customs of the past shall be abandoned, and actions shall be based on international usage."[9]

Regardless whether the lunar or solar calendar is better or more accurate, the change placed the very organization of people's lives as "evil customs of the past." The lunar month (twelve in a year, with an intercalary month approximately every third year) was either thirty days (major) or twenty-nine days (minor). The month was further divided into ten-day units (tōka). According to Tang practices, from which this calendar was adapted, officials took the tenth, twentieth, and thirtieth day of every month off. In the first month of 1868, the new Meiji government declared the first and sixth days as official days of rest. In treaty ports, however, foreigners insisted that Sunday be a day of rest, and in the second month of 1870, the Dajōkan declared sakujitsu (first day of the lunar month) and Sunday as days of rest. In short, daily rhythms were not divided according to the week as we know it, and inhabitants did not enjoy a weekly day of rest. (There were numerous holidays, which will be discussed below.)

The lunar calendar describes a particular relation to a received knowledge that is organized around lunar rhythms that are cyclical and constantly recurring and supports a "space of experience" where one's surroundings reinforce the idea of recurrence. Keith Thomas's description of medieval Europe, similarly based on agriculture and organized into local communities, fits Japan well:

> But, essentially, these beliefs about the unevenness of time were the natural product of a society which was fundamentally agrarian in character, and relatively primitive in its technology. They reflected the uneven value which time inevitably possessed for those engaged in agriculture or simple manufacturing operations in

---

[9] I use Robert M. Spaulding, Jr.'s, translation (1997, 11–13) rather than the more commonly used version from the Sources of Japanese Tradition. Spaulding's exegesis of the Charter Oath is a terrific example of a history that examines the event in its various manifestations and is then able to show how subsequent historical writings have molded the meaning of the event according to interests of the various histories. I am indebted to Doug Howland for bringing this essay to my attention.

which the weather was a crucial factor. The sundry doctrines about unlucky days, saints' days, climacteric years, leap years, etc., were all more easily acceptable in a society dependent upon the seasons for its basic living pattern. (1971, 622)

The new calendar broke this uneven time, the rhythm of daily life on the archipelago. Basic to this new solar calendar that upset the inherited practices was the seven-day week. As Thomas is well aware, the seven-day week marked the uneven time that he was describing. But the difference for Japan is that the new calendar not only rearticulated the new months, it also transmuted what had been the auspicious days of the year, those connected with the seven planets, into the days of the week. In the Edo period, the seven stars had the following connotations (present day of week in brackets):

nichiyō (sun) [Sunday]: Generally a positive day: profitable for those in commerce, but the dishonest might become sick. A bad day to build a house.

getsuyō (moon) [Monday]: Generally a positive day: but nonbelievers should be wary of fire and floods, and the nose, mouth, or stomach might become afflicted.

kayō (Mars) [Tuesday]: Not a good day for travel. If in the second, third, fifth, seventh, ninth, and eleventh months, illness or calamity is likely.

suiyō (Mercury) [Wednesday]: Believers should be pleased on this day. A good day to increase assets; but for the average person, be careful of flood or illness. A good day to enter school.

mokuyō (Jupiter) [Thursday]: Generally a positive day: honest people will increase their assets, and minor calamities will decrease. Bad day to enter school.

kinyō (Venus) [Friday]: Generally a day of misfortune: propensity for debate and argument. Believers will gain. In spring, a bad day to travel, and disaster likely.

doyō (Saturn) [Saturday]: A day prone to argument. Men likely to get boils, women to become pregnant. In the first, third, fifth, and sixth months, possibility of illness, accusation, calamity. Bad day for marriage. (Okada and Akune 1993, 159–60)

A close look at the new printed calendar shows a similar transformation away from the old knowledge and beliefs toward an empty, linear time. At the beginning of most old calendars, just after the column listing the year (both by period name and sexagenary cycle), one finds the position of the gods of misfortune, Konjin and the eight warrior gods (*hasshōjin*), as well as a compass graphically displaying the inauspicious days of the year.[10] The new calendar was not yet structured into the familiar twelve-month grid; in place of these warnings, one finds the new clock, removing the spirits and natural cycles from time. This new calendar also connects a new temporality with the new government. This emptying of time is also evident in the French revolutionary calendar (and Auguste Comte's new calendar). Like this Meiji calendar, they, too, sought to break the

---

[10] The eight gods, and their connection to a particular star, are Daisaijin (*mokusei*); Daishōgun (*kinsei*); Daionjin (*dosei*); Saigyōshin (*suisei*); Saihashin (*dosei*); Saisetsushin (*kinsei*); Ōbanshin (*rakōsei*) [imaginary star]; and Hyōbishin (*keitosei*) [imaginary star]. For further information, see Okada and Akune (1993, 198–203).

connection with old beliefs, in those cases God and the saints connected to the Catholic church (Richards 1998, 113–14, 257–64). The revolutionary calendar, adopted in 1793, divided the month into a ten-day "decade." Each day received a numerological name: Primedi, Duodi, Tridi, Quartidi, etc. Unlike the revolutionary calendar, the reforms in Japan have lasted, and today we call the beliefs that had been associated with these words superstition, folklore, and religion, while the words now, emptied of previous meaning, are used to mark the days of the week, as if the seven-day week is natural time.

But this universalistic time did not remain empty. The new calendar connected this new time to the emperor and the state. The first line of some calendars listed the year as Meiji 6 (1873) of the solar calendar; others announced the year 2533, the number of years since the accession of Jimmu tennō, or the mythical founding of the country of Japan. This practice of counting the years from Jimmu and commemorating it on the first day of the new year was established in 1869; it was not announced, it just happened. It was the idea of Tsuda Mamichi, who argued that rather than use period names (*nengō*), it would be better to change the system of years more like that of the West. Following the practices of the Christian, Muslim, and Jewish calendars, Tsuda probably also drew from *kokugaku* scholars such as Okuni Takamasa, who was also influenced by the Western systems (Okada 1994, 255). The inherited practices of reckoning years were cyclical: one system was a sexagesimal cycle based on the Chinese calendar, and the other was the *nengō*, counting the years of an era, such as Ansei 1 (1854) or Manen 1 (1860). Emperors and empresses in previous reigns usually presided over many eras; for example, there were six eras (Kaei, Ansei, Manen, Bunkyū, Genji, Keiō) under Emperor Kōmei, Meiji's predecessor. The eras changed as a way of marking renewal: a new era was often declared after a calamity or unfortunate string of events. This practice was transmuted synchronizing the era and reign names. Iwakura Tomomi became a powerful advocate of this idea, called *"issei ichigen"* (one life, one beginning), which began with the accession of the Meiji emperor.[11] The obvious import of this new form of *nengō* is the connection of the new temporality to the emperor rather than the myriad locales, deities, and spirits.

The third and fourth directives basically imposed the twenty-four-hour clock to divide and measure the day. The reform, however, shifted from a habitual world to an accurate, mechanical world, that of the clock. The inherited practice of "keeping time" was an amalgamation of different systems: the twelve branches of the duodecimal cycle (each unit was called a *toki*); division of day into daylight and night, each with six branches; and bells to mark the units. Even though clocks existed in the Tokugawa period, many had only one hand, were inaccurate (which wasn't a problem), and were very expensive. Instead of the *toki* being divided into fixed units, each two hours long and measured by a clock in a central location, the daily cycle of day (*ohiru*) and night (*yoru*) was

---

[11] See for example, Okada (1944, 59–67). For descriptions in English of the different systems, see Bramsen (1880).

divided into six units each, all of them animals, from rat to horse, and these units were further divided into a *shokoku* or *seikoku*. The day started approximately thirty minutes before dawn and ended approximately thirty minutes after dusk. Night began just after dusk and ended just before dawn. Obviously, these units were not even, varying by season, latitude, and horizon. Interestingly, the Japanese clock was adapted to take into account these variations, rather than to try to regularize the day according to the machine.

THE DIVISION OF THE DAY

Duodecimal Cycle		24-Hour Clock	Bells
ne no shokoku	rat	11 p.m.	
ne no seikoku		12 a.m.	9
ushi no shokoku	ox	1	
ushi no seikoku		2	8
tora no shokoku	tiger	3	
tora no seikoku		4	7
u no shokoku	hare	5	
u no seikoku		6	6
tatsu no shokoku	dragon	7	
tatsu no seikoku		8	5
mi no shokoku	serpent	9	
mi no seikoku		10	4
uma no shokoku	horse	11	
uma no seikoku		12 p.m.	9
hitsuji no shokoku	sheep	1	
hitsuji no seikoku		2	8
saru no shokoku	monkey	3	
saru no seikoku		4	7
tori no shokoku	cock	5	
tori no seikoku		6	6
inu no shokoku	dog	7	
inu no seikoku		8	5
i no shokoku	boar	9	
i no seikoku		10	4

The six intervals between sunrise and sunset were marked by bells (from four to nine rings, with the cycle repeated). The timekeeper was usually someone at a temple or the castle, and most people "knew" time from the bells or drums that punctuated the day or night.

The day divided by a clock is obviously quite different: it brings order, regularity, and predictability, and thus control. Johannes Kepler described this mechanical time: "I am much occupied with the investigation of the physical causes. My aim in this is to show that the machine of the universe is not similar to a divine animated being, but similar to a clock" (quoted in Shapin 1996, 33). The clock shows uniformity and regularity; it also begins the demystification of nature, nature as a machine rather than a place inhabited by spirits. As Steven Shapin points out, as a result of Newton's work (begun by Galileo), "All natural processes were now conceived to take place on a fabric of abstract time and space, self-contained, and without reference to local and bounded human experience" (1996, 62). It gives rise to a change in understanding, from habitual and heterogeneous worlds to an homogeneous, universalistic world. Time becomes an accurate and homogeneous form, one tied to the movement of a machine (the sun as a machine), something that is better because it is accurate, and not connected to the convenience of the people or to the vagaries of place and horizon. We can easily imagine the girls/women at the Tomioka silk filiature plant (or any of the other textile factories) operating in this temporality. Indeed, it would be difficult to envision capitalist society in heterogeneous temporalities.[12]

The fourth directive confirmed through language that this new temporality separated time from place. The same *"ji"* for *nanji* (what time) would be used, but the character was changed from *aza* (subvillage) to *toki* (time). *Aza* suggests the priority of place and locale, Koselleck's "space of experience." It highlights the immediate surroundings, one's immediate community, and the learning that is transmitted locally. Thus, we can think of many spaces of experience, a heterogeneity in Tokugawa society. Politically, the Tokugawa system was divided by domain and class. Socially, occupations, neighborhoods, and communities were relatively self-contained (this is especially so when contrasted with the situation today), and linguistically, while "Japanese" was spoken, it differed considerably by class, region, and community (Maher and McDonald 1995). Moreover, the categories and boundary mechanisms of today were not necessarily present then. For example, Karatani Kōjin points to a nature formerly veiled by diverse prohibitions and significations; it was the realm of spirits, the outside of the village or household (1993, 88). Strangers (*ijin*) — demons, spirits, ghosts, etc. — lived within and apart from communities; foreigners were those from another culture, which could have been a different region of the archipelago, a different class, or a different country; and the environment was a constituent of society, not separate from it.

The new word for time, *toki*, does not have the same spatial connotation as *aza*, and by being grounded in the temporality of the solar calendar, it became affiliated with an abstract and mechanical system. Moreover, because it was adopted at the same moment that a progressive developmental time was being implemented, this new reckoning of time was connected to a society oriented around what Koselleck calls a "horizon of expectations," a linearity where the future is some unknown better form rather than an ideal rooted in a previous

---

[12] The classic essay that describes this relation between a mechanical time and the factory is Thompson (1967).

world. In Meiji that future was an economically and militarily strong nation-state (*fukoku kyōhei*) built upon industrial development. This horizon of expectations is not diametrically opposed to the space of experience, but a dissimilar mode of existence. Both can coexist, but the horizon of expectations usually takes on a utopian quality that both incorporates and goes beyond what has already been experienced; these horizons are located in some collective singular, the future, and are always new (Koselleck 1985, 267–88).

According to most historical accounts, the transition to the new timekeepers occurred rather smoothly. To an extent, historians have overlooked the protest against the reforms of the 1870s, especially the draft and compulsory elementary education.[13] For example, in a March 1873 anti-Christian riot, protesters listed Sunday as an example of the problems. In June 1873, protesters in Tottori demanded lower rice prices, expulsion of foreigners, abolishment of the draft, abolition of compulsory elementary education, and restoration of the lunar calendar. Historians are not solely to blame for this oversight; contemporary elites and newspapers described such complaints as ignorance, conservativeness, and backwardness. Such a conclusion is rather easy when, from our perspective, we read complaints about the change:

> At a public bath in Tsukiji, an old lady over eighty complained while bathing: "This year is very strange: the head priest will not even offer a Buddhist service— nothing like it in all these years, and they say that, even though the year has not ended, on the third day of the twelfth month the new year begins. I've never experienced this!" The prostitute next to her said, "Well then, that means that yesterday was the first of the twelfth month and tomorrow is the Imperial Court's first day of January; but that means that in two days the moon will have worked thirty days. Impossible! For us the Tokugawa calendar is better." (Okada 1994, 239)

But to dismiss protests of this transformation as laments of conservative, elderly, or cranky people who were too set in their ways, that is, wedded to the evil customs of the past, is to accept the temporality of modernity—the perspective of those fostering change.[14] Such descriptions, themselves, are time markers of the process of synchronization; backwardness is a locus as a prior moment on a continuum of development. It is the acceptance of the outcome of the process—the separation of time from inherited language and of the teleology of change from primitive to advanced—without examining the process that has led to that outcome.

---

[13] For a fine study of conscription in early Meiji Japan, see Norman (1945).

[14] For an examination of the relation between event and history in the change of the calendar in England in 1752, see Poole (1998). Poole argues that the popular view—symbolized by William Hogarth's painting, "An election entertainment"—that the peasants' protests of change, "Give us our eleven days," was a sign of their backwardness is largely mythic. It is not that there was no protest, but that the adjustment to the new calendar was partial and depended on different groups, economic, religious, and regional.

The fifth directive showed the importance of maintaining this separation between the event and rhetoric of the event, even by (or especially by) contemporary actors. The adaptation of all "festivals" to the new calendars can be a simple adjustment if one is dictating change; but as discerned by the *Tokyo nichi nichi* just four days after the announcement, the connection is much deeper, and the change of the calendar will probably bring about quite drastic changes to society. The adaptation of festivals to the new calendar was much more than an exercise of converting dates; it was an act that enforced the recurrence of the new time. To recall Benjamin, the new festivals became "monuments of a historical consciousness."

During the Edo period, the principal days off and ritual days were the new year; *gosekku, hassaku* (harvest ritual on 8/1); and rituals tied to the shrine and Buddhist ritual, especially *bon* (7/15). Many other customs were connected to the lunar cycle. For example, the last day of the year, *ōmisoka*, was a day to remove the ominous signs of winter and bring in the spring, that is, to eliminate the demons of the dark and bring in the gods of light. This was marked by the spreading of beans in the house. This practice (among elites as well as commoners) of warding off demons was also connected to the belief that demons come from the northeast. Thus the temple Enryakuji on Mt. Hiei protects the ancient capital, Kyoto, and a peach tree at the northeast corner of one's house protects the house (Hirose 1993, 148). To change *ōmisoka* to the end of the solar year keeps the signifier, but not the signified. *Misoka* marks the end of the lunar month, and *ōmisoka* is the last lunar cycle of the year; December 31 can arrive at any point of the lunar cycle. Moreover, December 31 (as is January 1) is in the dead of winter; it does not mark the end of winter.

An awareness of the importance of days of commemoration is certainly not new to modernity. The new government leaders' interest in holidays predates the calendrical reform, but it, too, indicates this transformation of time from the natural and local to the symbols of the state. In the fourth month of 1869 Tsuda Mamichi proposed, in conjunction with the recalibration of the years, that the first day of the first month be commemorated as the anniversary of the accession of Emperor Jimmu. This proposal was implemented when the Dajōkan issued a circular in 1870 announcing a revision of festival days: 1/1 (new year—also the accession of Jimmu), 1/15 (little new year), 3/3 (*jōshi*), 5/5 (*tango*), 7/7 (*shichiseki*), 7/15 (*bon*), 8/1 (*hassaku*), 9/9 (*chōyō*), *and* 9/22 (*tenchōsetsu*—emperor's (Mutsuhito) birthday). This announcement combines the old and the new, adding commemorations to the imperial family and beginning the elimination of popular festivals.

This amalgamated system ended in 1873. On January 4, 1873, *gosekku, hassaku*, and other popular holidays were abolished. On March 7, 1873, the commemoration of Jimmu's accession was renamed to *kigensetsu* (the founding of Japan), and the date was changed to February 11, the adjusted solar date of 1/1/660 B.C. *Tenchōsetsu* was adjusted to November 11 (Mutsuhito was born on

9/22, Keiei 5 [1852]). On October 14, 1873, the Dajōkan published the annual holidays and festivals; most of the old holidays that were connected to agriculture and customs of the populace were replaced with days commemorating the emperors and imperial system (Okada 1994, 251–69):

Jan. 3 *genshisai* (new year's festival in the court)
Jan. 5 *shinnen enkai* (new year's feast)
Jan. 30 commemoration of Emperor Kōmei
Feb. 11 *kigensetsu*
Apr. 3 commemoration of Emperor Jimmu
Oct. 17 *kannamesai* (harvest festival at Ise shrine)
Nov. 3 *tenchōsetsu*
Nov. 23 *niinamesai* (harvest festival)

By the end of 1873, the government had completely transformed the calendar. This was a terrific opportunity: not only did it introduce the possibility that the past is old and must be changed, but it reconfigured time markers to shift attention from the spirits and gods to the emperor, the center of the emerging nation-state. Symbols of the state became those monuments of a historical consciousness. Even though *niinamesai*, the only old holiday that was part of the lunar calendar, remained, it occurred almost a month later than usual, in November. Again, the signifier remains, but without the signified. This temporal adjustment separated the festival from the harvest and reconnected it to Shinto and the emperor. (Today, it is celebrated as labor day.) But here, we must be careful not to take this reform as the marker that people changed. Hayashi Wakaki describes the public reaction to these new holidays:

> The government abolished the age-old holidays, such as the five annual celebrations [*gosekku*] and the *bon*, and instead appointed days like the emperor's birthday and foundation day, which mean nothing to the people, as national holidays. Ask any child, and he will tell you that the eighth day of the fourth month is Buddha's birthday, and that during the *bon* festival the boiling caldrons of hell are opened for the condemned souls to escape. But even an old fellow like myself will not be able to tell you why the foundation day and the emperor's birthday need to be commemorated. To exalt these days that the people care nothing about, the government makes everybody put up lanterns and a flag that looks like an advertisement for red pills. The old holidays were celebrated because the people felt them to be festive occasions. It is asking too much to make the people celebrate days they do *not* [sic] feel to be festive. (Yanagita 1957, 261)

The new calendar upset the knowledge, practices, and rituals that had oriented and guided societies organized around agrarian modes of production. It brought out the separation of time from nature; in the words of the townsman, "nothing is the way it should be." For him, the solar calendar depicts a nature severed from his surroundings; though there is recurrence, it is that of a mechanical regularity that is accurate but separated from visual cues. It is replaced by what we have called "invented traditions." As Hayashi suggests, however, those traditions were meaningless when created. If we were to stop here, we would not complete the story of how time mediates modern society. Indeed, the lunar calendar was commonly used in rural Japan up through World War II. According to a 1946 survey in which respondents were asked which new year they commemorated, in rural regions 37.6 percent followed the lunar and 48.8 percent followed some combination of the two, while 93 percent of those in urban areas used the solar new year (Okada 1994, 225). This suggests the possibility of multiple temporalities: like the ghosts that haunted pre-Meiji Japanese society (and continue to today through a much less public presence), the past is not stable and constantly shifts, threatening to destabilize the certainty of the known world. But in this case, the specters are the uncontrollable past. The domestication of these pasts depends on a structure that places them in a particular order that renders them voiceless.

History

Interestingly, this rather prosaic edict is usually ignored when histories list the revolutionary series of changes—spatial, political, and economic—that marked the early 1870s. The relative lack of attention to this transformation, both at the beginning of Meiji and today, indicates the successful naturalization of modern time in Japanese history, as well as society in general. This brings out the second way that this book approaches history: as representation. The articulation of pasts that accompanied the transformation of time not only separates pasts from the present, but also makes them absent (that is, anachronisms) (Ankersmit 2001, 11). History is then written and compensates for that absence, thereby giving meaning—a cultural identity—to that place we now know as Japan. Baelz's informer reminds us of the words of the great historian Huizinga, that historical writing "is the form in which a culture expresses its conscious of its past" (quoted in Ankersmit 2001, 1).

History becomes a principal tool for the reintegration of the past in the present. It is a technique for determining and ordering the rules through which we come to know a society. In this sense, historical representation is not perception and description, but rendering one's natural and human world into an orderly form. It creates what Arnold Davidson (2001) has called the "conditions of possibility," those statements, categories, and epistemes that make certain kinds of knowledge possible.[15] In other words, history, too, is both technology for and

---

[15] Davidson (2001) juxtaposes such conditions of possibility against conditions of validity—the techniques, using evidence, proof, and truth claims for determining whether something is true or false. In short, conditions of validity are connected with objectivistic history. See especially his preface and chapter 5.

actor or agent in the transformation of society. It is not a mere transparent descriptive medium, but an ideational form that helps restore order and meaning to a society newly emptied of prior meanings. In this sense, history has a materiality in the ideas and structures to which it gives meaning and form. This materiality raises interpretive challenges: we must ascribe a history to a place that had no history but was trying to find one. This, of course, does not mean that there was no past or that the people prior to Meiji did not have records from prior events. Nor does it mean that time is new to modern society; to recognize the historicity of our current understanding of history and time, we need only ask how people organized their lives without clocks and learned about their community and locale without books and mass media. But we must take care not to ignore the historicity of history at this time.

I hope that this focus on time and history redirects our attention to modernity (rather than modernization) and enables the examination of both the process of becoming modern and how Japanese intellectuals debated and resolved this difficult and often contradictory process. This focus on modernity, of course, is not new (an interesting study would be an examination of why we keep forgetting this point). Perhaps the most troubling issue confronting the study of Japan today remains how we discuss modernity in a non-Western place. Despite many of the excellent studies over the past twenty years, histories of Japan are still written within a teleology of development, examining the way Japan has (and has not) modernized. Our omission of inquiries into modern temporality and of the role of history facilitates the acceptance of the norms and structures of the very transformation we seek to study.

The teleology that has dominated Japanese history since the 1960s is modernization theory. Like many historical trends, fads, or movements, modernization theory has made important and lasting contributions. Even today, we often fail to see how our questions and criticisms are still framed within this influential dogma. The problem with modernization theory can be shown by going back to W. W. Rostow's manifesto, *The Stages of Economic Growth*, which has been so influential in its application to Japan:

> In short, the rise in the rate of investment—which the economist conjures up to summarize the transition—requires a radical shift in the society's effective attitude toward fundamental and applied science; toward the initiation of change in productive technique; toward the taking of risk; and toward the conditions and methods of work.
>
> One must say a change in effective attitude—rather than merely a change in attitude—because what is involved here is not some vague change in psychological or sociological orientation, but a change translated into working institutions and procedures. (1990, 20)

I agree with Rostow's focus on the materiality that economic change fostered. In modernization theory's aversion to Marxism and our more recent turn away from modernization theory, we have forgotten how central economics is to the constitution of society. The last sentence indicates my difference: Rostow and modernization theory do not examine history and civilization, but rather establish civilization (read "liberal capitalism") as a goal and history as the mode of description in its search for the implementation of science, rationality, and efficiency. While recognizing that all of society changes—the "radical shift"—Rostow goes on to separate society and culture from institutions and techniques. His "vague change in psychological or sociological orientation" denigrates ideas and culture as mere attitude. Indeed, it explains the absence of historical studies on temporal transformation as well as Katō's dismissal of the problem as simply synchronization. But this vague change, too, is part of those working institutions and procedures, what Poulantzas has called the materiality of the state. Indeed, they serve as the foundation for the more mechanical and rational forms Rostow privileges.

This prioritization of the mechanical and the abstract over human sensibilities is a problem of societies today, and a central theme of this book is to examine the process by which science and rationality have taken precedence over human sensibilities in Meiji Japan. This elevation of institutions and procedures over culture is historical—a decision to elevate certain elements of society for particular purposes. I prefer to work from Rostow's "effective attitude," for the transformations he enumerates—science, productive techniques, risk, and methods of work—all presuppose a particular, modern idea of time that organizes society differently. But in his analysis these forms assume a transhistorical status as natural or universal and require mere technical knowledge to understand and implement properly. But when we locate such categories within their historical moment, that is, when we examine those "knowable and consistent laws" as historical, we find that the dualisms that imbricate our thinking are subject to a renewed scrutiny.

In a sense, this is a moment in the creation of the international, an expanded world that coordinated diverse societies into a singular temporal order. The common way to render this synchronization has been to talk about the discovery or "opening" of nonsynchronized places, then describe them in terms of their insufficiencies and backwardness, and prescribe a path of development or progress. Indeed, this is the historiography of modern Japan. But we must remember that as Japan was adapting aspects of Western society, Europe and the United States, too, were in the process of synchronizing their own societies.[16]

---

[16] While time in these places had already become mechanical, it was not yet synchronized. Railroad time became the standard time in England, replacing local times, in 1880; the United States became effectively standardized with the adoption of a Standard Railway Time in 1883, reducing the forty-nine different railway times to four time zones; and at the International Meridian Conference of 1884, the Royal Observatory at Greenwich was adopted as the prime meridian. See, for example, Schivelbusch (1977); Bartky (2000); Chandler (1977).

Modernization theory is but one manifestation of a teleology of development that has emerged since the nineteenth century. In a sense, Rostow (and those who applied his ideas to Japanese history, Edwin O. Reischauer, John W. Hall, and Marius B. Jansen) is an easy target. Scholars who have perceived problematics in modern society have long pointed out many of these problems. Japanese historiography has a rich tradition of critiques rooted in Marxist interpretations.[17] Reactions of many Japanese scholars to the initial application of modernization theory to Japan at the Hakone conference also point to this blindness to the historicity of the idea.[18]

What is less obvious are the ways that the historical frameworks that undergird modernization theory continue to inform our understanding. Postone and Poulantzas have shown that most Marxist critiques also rely on a transhistorical idea, labor, that removes the historicity of social forms from history. My hope is that an inquiry into the temporal transformation of society frees us from such dualisms as science and culture, technical and political, modern and traditional, Occident and Orient. To be sure, they exist institutionally and in our conceptual structures, but they are historical, not natural forms. An emphasis on process shifts the object of attention away from the reasons for failure (or success) toward the ways that people interact with the overlay of abstract forms of knowledge and structures—that is, the nation-state, science, rationality—upon their everyday lives. My presupposition is that this historical time, too, is socially constituted and that our modern idea of time as separated from the human and the realm of the physical sciences is also a product of the scientific and economic transformation that began during the fifteenth century.[19]

Of course, the archive often does place the rhetoric of the problem within a dualism. Meiji Japanese did juxtapose *bunmeikaika* (civilization) against their inherited practices. It is not an invention of later historians. A dilemma for these historical actors is that new epistemological systems—liberalism, capitalism, and science—are monological systems that often provide predefined categories (as backward or static) for new places, such as the newly "opened" Japan. Thus people in the non-West who seek those internal conditions of possibility must do so from categories that define them as without those conditions (in the case of Japan, as Oriental).[20] Yet as Doug Howland (2002) has recently shown in a careful examination of adaptation of the concept civilization in the Meiji period, it

---

[17] See, for example, the debates between the two schools of Marxist history, *koza-ha* (lecture) and *ro no-ha* (labor-farmer). For a succinct description, see Najita (1974).

[18] The published version is in Jansen (1965).

[19] See, for example, Elias (1992); Toulmin and Goodfield (1965); Koselleck (1985); Luckmann (1991). For the connection of temporal reform and capitalism, see Sohn-Rethel (1975); Postone (1993).

[20] Although we still have not worked through the implications of Said's *Orientalism*, I find Hegel's *Philosophy of History*, though establishing rather than criticizing it, the best single expression of this problematic.

meant different things to people at the same moment and across time. Here, we must be mindful of the rhetorical positions of those people of Meiji who, born of one conceptual system, sought to understand another system as well as to determine how one was to transform one's own society into a modern place. They sought those internal conditions that make change possible; in this very process, they were representing the past in relation to the new in ways that made sense to their present needs.

At this point I would like to return to the 1876 lament: "We have no history. Our history begins today." The second statement is not the cumulation of the myriad events and people of earlier moments; it is a particular organization of pasts that gives form to a collective present, the "we," or what we now call Japan. In this way, history (broadly construed) gives form to places and ideas; it helps create a "conceptual space and its history." This succinct phrase by Davidson (2001, 127) encapsulates the ideas that have been important to my understanding of history, the epistemes of Michel Foucault, the history of concepts (*Grundbegriffs Geschichte*) of Reinhardt Koselleck et al., and the quest for a modern human experience in the writings of Michel de Certeau. (I am omitting here many others who are equally important and will appear throughout this study.) Among these historians, there are important differences, but they are simultaneously committed to the field of history and at the same time see the ways that history frames (and often constricts) human action.

In this sense, the struggle with one's own past in modernizing places is part of the process of modernization. Parts of that struggle of course might be nostalgia, anachronism, traditionalism, conservatism, etc., but to limit this change to some kind of reaction against the modern is both to accept the teleology of modernization and to overlook the contradictory process that non-Western places must confront as they try to become modern. Walter Benjamin confronts this transformation in his essay "The Storyteller." He writes that the decline of storytelling "is, rather, only a concomitant symptom of the secular productive forces of history, a concomitant that has quite gradually removed narrative from the realm of living speech and at the same time is making it possible to see a new beauty in what is vanishing" (1968, 87).[21] Benjamin is addressing a different relation with the past: the integration of inherited ideas and practices as a part of life is being replaced by the separation of pasts as something to be admired—as tradition, authenticity, natural, etc.—as it disappears from life but is perhaps preserved as objects. This is where inquiries into temporality must also interrogate history itself as historical, that is, as a form of social mediation that orients pasts into some systematic, both timeless and diachronic, order.

---

[21] Peter Osborne (1995, 134–35) comments on Benjamin's essay: "Yet it contains some of Benjamin's sharpest insights, not only into modernity as a destruction of tradition, but also into the production of the idea of tradition within modernity as its inescapable dialectical other."

In this sense, a central goal of the transformation of Meiji, that is, the modernization of Japan, was to discover a history and to organize a society based on civilization that would become the basis of rules that provide for stability in the international world. This idea of history is what de Certeau calls the "making of history":

> It appears to me that in the West, for the last four centuries, "the making of history" has referred to writing. Little by little it has replaced the myths of yesterday with a practice of meaning. As a practice . . . it symbolizes a society capable of managing the space that it provides for itself, of replacing the obscurity of the lived body with the expression of a "will to know" or a "will to dominate" the body, of changing inherited traditions into a textual product or, in short, of being turned into a blank page that it should itself be able to write. (1988, 5–6)

To inquire into this moment when history is being formulated, I have turned to an examination of the relation between objects and their meanings. Here, I find particularly apt Hans Blumenberg's turn to the "absolutism of reality" (1985, 3–33), which he defines as follows: "What it means is that man came close to not having control of the conditions of his existence and, what is more important, believed that he simply lacked control of them. It may have been earlier or later that he interpreted this circumstance of the superior power of what is other by assuming the existence of superior powers" (3–4). In the case of Japan, this superior power might have been the *kami* (gods and spirits) and bodhisattva (Buddhist deities); the ghosts, demons, and Westerners (*ijin*—outsiders); God; or science and rationality. The strength of Blumenberg's analysis is that he consistently avoids teleologies, such as "from mythos to logos," as well as any putative/natural "real." In this sense, both myth and logos (or superstitions and science/rationality) are representations; in Blumenberg's analytical structure, they are attempts to address this absolutism of reality. Our modern understanding of history, too, is part of this effort to overcome that absolutism of reality.

When seen this way, history is part of the formulation of a logos that allays uncertainty. Drawing from Alphonse Dupront, de Certeau brings this effort directly into the making of history:

> "The sole historical quest for meaning remains indeed a quest for the Other," but, however contradictory it may be, this project aims at "understanding" and, through "meaning," at hiding the alterity of this foreigner; or in what amounts to the same thing, it aims at calming the dead who still haunt the present, and at offering them scriptural tombs. (1988, 2)

In history, those "scriptural tombs" alter what had been a part of the present into a dead past that is separated from the present as a discrete object. The past becomes an other, a defined object of reflection, stripped of its alterity. In this sense, history, too, is a central agent that turns experience, "inherited traditions," into those "textual products" or "blank pages" that can then be molded into prescribed (and proscribed) forms. This domestication of pasts transmutes alterity. Those others that are integral to the constitution of society shift from what Michael Theunissen (1984) calls an alien-I relationship of mutual dependence to a relation of exclusivity, the self and other.[22] Strangeness in the alien-I relationship is a realization of the strange/unpredictable within human interaction and human interaction with the external world. The external worlds includes those of outsiders, ghosts, spirits, and wonders. In the self/other relation, more characteristic of the modern world, the other is reduced to the foreign, the outsider who constantly reinforces the inner as Japanese. This transformation of alterity is not a mere philosophical exercise; it is integral to the homogenization of the myriad peoples on the archipelago into Japanese. They became the Same, interchangeable units setting up a structure that facilitates the flow of commodities (here labor).

In the transformation of Japan, those inherited practices that are changed into textual objects involve the domestication of wonders and strangeness; those pasts that do not readily fit into the rules and structure of the rational are relegated to prior moments of the present, that is, timeforms with their own history that become examples of earlier moments of a Japan as if it had always existed.[23] Thus the environment filled with plants, beings, ghosts, and spirits that surround people becomes nature, folklore, religion, and so forth; children become known through the category of childhood; and icons of spirituality are organized into chronologies of art, architecture, and so on. These objects gain meaning as timeforms, establishing new rules, principles, and essences (the materiality of the state) that organize life of people as citizens, as Japanese, of a national society. In other words, history is one of the technologies of modernity: it gives form, a materiality, to abstractions, thereby making them "real." In other words, history helps create what Henri Lefebvre has called the "alternative reality" of modernity: "Within this reality an alternative reality emerges, another world within our own. What alternative reality? What other world? Technology and control over nature" (1995, 181).

That alternative reality is the world formulated according to abstract ideas and criteria, that is, modernity. History functions as a timekeeper that, like time, specifies particular functions for humans—that when one changes the other might also change. Norbert Elias's statement that the clock face directs people can also be applied to history: "The changing constellation on the face of the clock has the function of showing people the position they and others at present occupy in the great successive flow of events, or how long they have taken to get from one place to another" (1992, 14). In other words, time organizes an

[22] I use the present tense because I agree with Blumenberg that the "myths" that we identify as superstition and folklore have not disappeared from society.
[23] For a wonderful account of the centrality of wonders in the European world, see Daston and Park (1998).

understanding of the idea of the human and humankind's relationship to its surroundings, social and environmental. With this in mind, when we work through the question of the transformation of history, we have to invert the relation between humans and institutions and humans and knowledge in our understanding of the process of modernization. We would have to take more seriously issues of human life (Rostow's "effective attitude") as integral to, not autonomous from, the institutions and aggregate (abstract) categories of modern society. Not to do so means that we continue to abide by a modernist epistemology in which abstract ideas rather than knowledge gained by direct contact guide human meaning and organization. While I am not advocating some kind of nostalgic return, in our studies of modern societies we must be more mindful of how human society was completely inverted. What had been natural, that is, the "myths of yesterday," is turned into something historical, while what had been historical is removed to some abstract and detached realm, typically rendered within categories of modern, nature, and tradition, thus remaining within the epistemology of modernity. That is history.

The overemphasis on the techniques of objectivity and description in the modern practice of history has tended to overlook this history of things and to ignore the representation that often gives meaning to that moment. Davidson encapsulates well this variability of the past, made stable through history. He writes, "Some of the most remarkable moments in the history of thought are precisely those in which an old phrase or word is stabilized in a new way, resulting in the production of a new set of concepts and a new realm of statements" (2001, 186). This has been naturalized through the repetition and naturalization of categories, such as "nation," "Japan," "childhood," and "art history," which, though seen and experienced as common and natural, are conceptual spaces with a history. Just as chronology becomes the way we experience time, in numerous aspects of modern life the idea that gives meaning to the form increasingly becomes the way it is experienced.

It is clear that the problem of modernization is one of the most important (and tragic) of processes of the past century. In our examination of that process, however, we can no longer employ the categories that are themselves the goals of the process. To follow Rostow's manifesto and focus on the "working institutions and procedures" is to accept the abstract ideas that serve as the basis of modern society as normative. When applied to non-Western societies and when used to try to organize a nation-state, however, the categories used not only provide an aura of order and stability but also determine how people should experience their lives, either as "orientals" or as "citizens." But when we examine this process through time (or any other subject that historicizes the process), we find that the very categories upon which objectivity depends are embedded within the formation of the modern culture, and we must also examine the way in which thought, language, and culture themselves are imbricated within the technologies of society. This is a specter of the modern; just as ghosts are foundational in the constitution

of nonmodern societies, the specters of the modern are those previous and inherited forms that refuse to be limited to the dead categories, the scriptural tombs
(categories of history), which are created to entomb them.

NARRATIVE

There are two ways to read this book. On the one hand, it is a story of the disrup-
tion of the heterogeneous temporalities of the Tokugawa era (chapters 1 and 2)
and the formulation of a modern temporality (chapters 3 through 6). On the other
hand, it is a story of the discovery of the past (chapter 1), the reconfiguration of
those pasts into history (chapters 2 through 4), and the imbrication of that history
throughout society (chapters 5 and 6). Both are reasonable, though the first is
more likely to revert to the teleology of modern society. I have decided to highlight
these possibilities because an operating principle throughout this book is the
problematic of historical representation and the historiography of Meiji Japan.

Modern historians, including myself, have too often described the moment
prior to the modern as its antithesis. In chapters 1 and 2 I provide a few more layers, discussing the heterogeneity of society. In the first chapter I focus on the realization that nature has a history that is separate from man. This comes about
by a number of discoveries that raise the possibility of a past distinct from the
present. This chapter ranges from the *Jinshin* (1872) survey, an early exploration
of old artifacts in temples and shrines, to Edward S. Morse's discovery of the
shell mounds at Ōmori, Edmund Naumann's discovery of a geological rift cutting across the archipelago, and the demise of the Office of Topography.

The discovery of a separable past has led to a rather interesting dilemma: the
inherited forms of knowledge that had organized society were now denigrated because of a hope and promise that a better system based on science and rationality
exists. Chapter 2 takes its title from a reaction to the calendrical reform, "Nothing is the way it should be." This is a story about struggles to deal with the rupture
of time; I examine the different ways that people sought to make sense of this separation of nature from culture or past from present. In this process, the relation of
the parts to the whole was being reconfigured. Inoue Enryō turned to psychology
to exorcise the ghosts, spirits, and wonders that existed everywhere. This despiri-
tualization of nature was also evident in John Milne's description of the Ōshima
volcanic eruption. Historians like Shigeno Yasutsugu and Kume Kunitake increasingly questioned what had been the authoritative historical tales. This was
the disenchantment of the archipelago where ties to the local communities were
being severed and the ground for a unifed Japan was being prepared.

Chapters 3 and 4 examine the reconfiguration of the given and created, or nature and history, into an essential time and a chronological time of the nation.
In other words, this is the moment that history fills the void opened up with the
separation of the past. In chapter 3 I examine the extraction of a national place

from the possibilities of the past. Even though Japanese intellectuals generally agreed that a "Japan" existed, they still had to explicate its characteristics. Intellectuals such as Katō Hiroyuki, Miyake Setsurei, and Okakura Kakuzō debated what that Japan is, and in the course of that debate, they extracted aspects of the past and reorganized them into transhistorical categories that naturalize them as Japanese characteristics. These characteristics were then reinforced through the writing of chronologies. In chapter 4 I examine the debates over history, between history and national literature, and in art history to establish chronologies of Japan. In addition, the chronological structure was reinforced by the similitude of ontology. The formulation of childhood tied the human body through ontogenesis to the progress of the nation.

This newly historicized society is a necessary part of the liberal capitalist structure that was also emerging. In the 1890s intellectuals discovered a "social problem," that is, the rise of urban slums, increasing disparity of income, exploitation, and atomization. In chapter 5 I examine the ideas of men, such as Inoue Tetsujirō and Takayama Chogyū, who sought to ameliorate the new desires set off by modernity with the demands of liberalism for control, that is, civility. The resolution was the use of a national past to establish social norms that correct for those social problems.

Finally, we know that Japanese society became (and has been) a rather closely circumscribed culture. In the final chapter, I examine the idea of Japan as a museum. Different observers have noticed that the nineteenth-century museum both destroyed culture and preserved it (often destruction occurred in the act of preservation). At the very least, there is a fixity to the museum. I look at the Hōryūji and childhood to examine the ways that they serve as mnemonics of pasts that symbolize norms that fix the present.

Chapter 1

DISCOVERY OF PASTS

> Morse in Japan remains what he has been all his life—a man
> locked in a silent struggle with time, one whose days are filled
> with a pursuit of practical truths that can be shared with a
> world hungry to understand itself.
> —Robert A. Rosenstone (1998)

WE ARE QUITE FAMILIAR with the Meiji period as one of considerable transformation of all aspects of life on the archipelago. But its characterization as a move from old to new—as simply exiting from its self-incurred immaturity—obscures the historicity of modernity, that process described above by Rosenstone: a "pursuit of practical truths" for a "world hungry to understand itself." Several steps are necessary to begin that process: first, the idea of immaturity suggests that one's present society is incomplete and living in the past. In other words, there is a recognition of a progressive time and a separation of pasts from present. Second, one must recognize that the world of inadequacy is man-made, not because of a degeneration from some originary ideal, but because of the artificial constructions posed by such primitive ideas and institutions. And third, any attempt to explain this level is dependent upon a different configuration of the whole, a "struggle with time." Now, inherited ideas and men that were the subject of chronicles became the past, which reflected recognition that the aristocratic system is not natural or endowed but anachronistic. These discoveries occurred in Europe from the late medieval period to the nineteenth century.[1] During the Tokugawa period, intellectuals began the separation of humans from nature (*rangaku*) and the formulation of an alternate origin (*kokugaku*). But this discovery of the past and its separation from the present occurred principally during the Meiji period.

The discovery and separation of the past is one of the central components of the Meiji period. In early Meiji, various practices and ideas that had been connected with the Tokugawa era became the objects from which society would be emancipated. But unlike previous reform efforts, improvement would come through something new rather than a restoration of an ideal located in some pure originary moment. But this transformation of the conceptual order must

---

[1] The specific periodization depends on who one is reading and which objects and transformations are described. See, for example, the essays in Bender and Wellbery (1991); Toulmin and Goodfield (1965); Koselleck (1985); and de Certeau (1988).

not be described today within the same temporal ordering that was used to argue for the new. To do so accepts the neutrality, or emptiness, of time. That is, it fails to consider the arguments by scholars who point out that time is not external, but a constituent of and constitutes life. Thomas Luckmann writes,

> Time is constitutive of human life in society. Of course it is also constitutive of human life in nature: *all* life is in time. But as a dimension of human life time is not only the matrix of growth and decline between birth and death. It is also the condition of human sociality that is achieved again and again in the continuously incarnated contemporaneity of face-to-face interaction. (1991, 151)

If we are to take Luckmann's point seriously, as I do, then we must also recognize that when the reckoning of time changes, then human life in society also changes. Blumenberg's notion of an absolutism of reality provides an analytical structure for dealing with the centrality of time, especially in moments of change. It helps us recognize that it is crucial to separate the object of study from our analytical apparatus. In other words, we must be mindful that the temporal structures that give meaning to objects and relations, too, are historical. Moreover, as I will describe below, they came into particular use to address particular reasons, to reconcile this new temporality and the dislocation and anxiety it set off. By grounding thought in this basic condition that gives rise to a fear of one's lack of control over the social and natural environment, Blumenberg removes the hierarchy of science over myth, instead seeing both as two modes for "working up reality" (1985, 50–51). Thus myth is not exclusively past—nor is it implied that it should be—but, rather, is coexistent with science, though differentially valued. Moreover, if myth and logos function to allay fear in the unknown, our inquiry shifts to what one is familiar with, rather than pointing to sites where ignorance hindered the fulfillment guaranteed by knowledge (enlightenment).

The trope of discovery is important to the characterization of logos as the progressive separation from myth. As I hope was evident in my discussion of calendrical reform, the discovery of a past does not mean that knowledge of previous people, events, deeds, and so forth did not exist. Indeed, many of the discoveries I will discuss were well known prior to Meiji. For example, even though Edward Sylvester Morse has been credited with discovering shell mounds in Ōmori (between Yokohama and Tokyo), numerous people knew about these mounds, and collections of paraphernalia from them existed in the Tokugawa era, if not earlier (Bleed 1986). The principal difference is how those objects relate to knowledge (logos). The pre-Meiji world is characterized by multiple temporalities. Recurrence and cycles coexisted with a linearity where the past located the ideal from which society had degenerated and toward which it must return (or come to an end). That ideal was in the sages, the *Nihon shoki* (720) and, from the eighteenth century, the *Kojiki* (712). The curios from the shell mounds were understood through and in support of the belief structure at the time, rooted in the age of the gods and the spirits that pervaded communities. Thus, a stone scraper was called Tengu's rice paddles, a stone mace was a thunder club, and long projectiles were spears of the gods (Bleed 1986, 63). Today, we are amused by these labels as stories of the past, that is, as myth or ignorance.

In contrast, one of the constituent parts of modernity is the separation and denigration of the past, as something to move away from. De Certeau writes, "Historical discourse makes a *social identity* explicit, not so much in the way it is 'given' or held as stable, as in the ways it is *differentiated* from a former period or another society. It presupposes the rupture that changes a tradition into a past object" (1988, 45). One characteristic of nonmodern societies is the fluid boundaries between other periods and other societies and communities: they are both different and part of one's own society. Often what we call myth has been a principal device to establish separations from the unfamiliar, the uncanny. In contrast, in modern societies, what we consider a separate and dead past no longer has such a potential, even likelihood, of returning to the present or of returning the present to a past ideal. Instead, a historical discourse domesticates the alterity of pasts by making it into a former version of the present and into proof of the distinctiveness of oneself.

There is no single discovery that has led to this historical sense of the world. It is widespread; it is connected through intellectual discoveries, scientific observations, and sociopolitical changes. Moreover, it is gradual; numerous scholars have shown that the understanding of time has changed throughout human history (see, e.g., Toulmin and Goodfield 1965; Borst 1993; Dohrn-van Rossum 1996). Yet a major break does occur around the Enlightenment—the growing separation of God from nature and mankind brought about by scientific observations, the discovery that the Earth has a history beyond known history, and the discovery of ancient civilizations in Asia (Smith 1991; Toulmin and Goodfield 1965). In Japan one can see such a transformation accelerating during the Tokugawa period. The introduction of recent European scientific advances through the Dutch brought hints of the separation between humans and nature that led to the scientific and industrial revolutions in Europe. Tokugawa intellectuals were aware of Copernican heliocentric theory, Newton's mechanics, and Linnaeas's classificatory system (Bartholomew 1989, esp. chap. 2). Ogyū Sōrai's separation of political institutions from the sages created a break of sociopolitical institutions from the ideal structures of the sages, and Kamo no Mabuchi and Motoori Norinaga's discoveries of a Japanese origin brought out the possibility of a linear history (as opposed to the chronological and dynastic-like histories of writers such as Arai Hakuseki). But the transformation accelerated near the end of the Tokugawa period and was punctuated by the fourth article of the Charter Oath, which declared, "Evil practices of the past shall be abandoned" (Spaulding 1967, 11). This recognition of an evil past is a recognition of change but itself is not necessarily modern. *Neuzeit* unfolds as the horizon changes from an ideal located in the classics to the possibility of exiting from that "self-incurred immaturity." This separation is one of the key moments in the possibility of a historical society; the ability to relegate those inherited forms of knowledge that bind into a past potentially liberates humanity.

In this chapter I hope to show this process. To articulate the past, a new conceptualization of time was necessary—that of progress, one that separates the present from the past and then re-emplots that past as an earlier, now dead, moment of one's "experience." This is teleological: a historical understanding is necessary to give meaning to the past, while the past proves a historical understanding (see, e.g., Hides 1997, 11–13). This re-emplotment of pasts is based on criteria that are separated from social forms and knowledge. This articulation of a different time alters the meaning of space, that is, how persons interact with their human and natural environment. Inside and outside were redefined: on the one hand, space first becomes blank, an abstract notion separated from human beings; on the other hand, space is circumscribed according to national units.

DISCOVERY ONE: PASTS PRIOR TO HISTORY

One of the first discoveries of the past, one that is common in revolutionary movements, is the destruction of previous symbols of power. One of the first laws of the new government separating bodhisattva and kami (*shinbutsu kyūri*) set off widespread pillaging of Buddhist temples, many of them former sites of political and economic power.[2] Buddhist statues were decapitated; sutras and other texts burned; buildings torched, torn down, or sold; and priests and monks retired en masse.[3] Destruction at the Kōfukuji, the most powerful temple in Nara up through the Tokugawa period, was considerable. Either books were burned (the bonfire reportedly lasted for more than three months) or their pages were used as wrapping paper for lacquerware or as lining for tea boxes. The three-roofed pagoda was sold for thirty yen, and local officials proposed to burn down the five-roofed pagoda but demurred, fearing the spread of fire (Mizuki 1921, 171–73). Fortunately this pagoda was not reduced to ashes, but it was saved not to preserve an irreplaceable monument but out of the fear that nearby houses and shops would also be destroyed.

In contrast, a neighboring temple, the Hōryūji, was largely spared, probably due to its lower status, its relative isolation, and the popularity of the Taishi cult.[4]

---

[2] This law is usually translated as the Law Separating Buddhism and Shinto. I have instead followed Allan Grapard's practice, which recognizes the syncretism of what we now separate as two distinct religions. See his *Protocol of the Gods* (1992) and "Japan's Ignored Cultural Revolution" (1984).
[3] James Ketelaar describes the discovery of a graveyard of decapitated statues of Buddhist statues in Kyushu. It has now been turned into a local shrine, the Hall of the Headless Kannon (1990, 57).
[4] In contrast to the 104 pages of material on the Kōfukuji in Murakami et al. (1921), the 5 pages on the Hōryūji were essentially speculation on why it did not suffer such damage. Murakami et al. suggested that in addition to the connection of Shōtoku Taishi to the imperial line, the tutelary deity of the Hōryūji was not on the temple premises.

The local name for this temple was *bimbōdera* (poor temple). At the outset of the Meiji era, the new government cut its annual stipend to 250 *koku*, and in 1874 it reduced it again to 125 *koku*. The temple was dilapidated: many monks had retired or left, local government officials proposed the demolition of the cloister walls on both sides of the south gate (*nandaimon*), and cows and horses were housed inside the cloister (Takada 1987, 88). In other words, the years of relative obscurity throughout the Muromachi and Edo periods facilitated a for-getting of or indifference toward the temple that saved it from the rampage that beset the powerful Kōfukuji. Yet, it was not completely forgotten; it was part of that experiential space of the everyday where farmers could keep their livestock.

The difference between the Kōfukuji and the Hōryūji indicates that this dis-covery of the past was more an attack against the powerful institutions such as the Kōfukuji that served as symbols and institutions of power. The Hōryūji in this discovery is far from its current status as the originary moment of Japanese architectural history as well as of historical Japan. Indeed, it is not a discovery at all; instead, it is indicative of a limited notion of the past, an indifference to the past as past, especially to this site, which is now the archetype in the emergence of a "Japan." In fact, it shows that time, the past, was not separate from the pres-ent; the temple was indeed part of the present, but one connected to a disgraced power structure that oversaw local matters. The masses (often at the instigation of Shinto priests) who destroyed Buddhist symbols and icons were reacting to the system that enveloped them in their everyday existence; it was part of a power structure of oppression, not a past that incurred immaturity. Second, there is no Japan or East Asia here. Decisions over the fate of the Kōfukuji and Hōryūji rested in local needs and meanings: the fear of a conflagration of the town and the need to contain livestock. It would be a leap to extrapolate the lat-ter into evidence of a nation.

DISCOVERY TWO: LOSS OF FUNCTION

In the fifth month of 1871, the Dajōkan, concerned about the destruction of ob-jects from the ancient and recent past, issued an edict on the preservation of old things (*kyūbutsu*), stating in part, "There are not a few benefits of some artifacts and old things in the investigation of today's transformation from old to new and of the history (*enkaku*) of systems and customs. It is natural to hate the old and struggle for the new, but actually we should lament the gradual loss and de-struction of evil customs" (Nara kokuritsu hakubutsukan 1996, 6). This was the first official recognition of the importance of a past, what can be called "discov-ery." One of the results of the edict was that the Ministry of Education sent out an investigatory team, headed by Machida Hisanari. Machida was a key figure who recognized the continuity between modern society and its past while on a study tour in Europe. The *Jinshin* survey began in May 1872 and lasted four months, visiting Kyoto, Osaka, Kanagawa, Shizuoka, Aichi, Watarai, Sakai,

Ashigara, Shiga, Wakayama, and Nara (Tokyo kokuritsu hakubutsukan 1973 [hereafter TKH100], 73–74).[5] Machida was accompanied by Uchida Masao from the Ministry of Education and Ninagawa Noritane (1835–82), an official with the exhibition section (*hakubutsukyoku*), of that ministry.[6]

Although it was not articulated in this way, this edict was a recognition that modern society has no fixed referent.[7] One effect is the loss of previous congruence between meaning and object, or, in de Certeau's terms, the "destruction of tradition" (as custom and habit). This issue, of course, is not new; intellectuals and commoners in transforming societies have constantly searched for the limits of change, the point where society will no longer be recognizable to its anterior, rather than as another homogenized place. We must remember that the nation will fill this vacuum; but during the 1870s, it was unclear that the idea of nation will become that referent where particularities of the past—customs destroyed by modern liberal-capitalist forces—are re-emplotted as "traditions" authorizing the nation as an immanent form.

This survey designed to confirm the existence of and record artifacts was the first step in the new government's preservation efforts, that is, to establish that referent or the idea of tradition within modernity (TKH100, 75). One of the aspects that stands out most clearly is that, historical rhetoric notwithstanding, from this early date the new leadership showed concern for old things along with an insistence on transformation to the new. To best facilitate that transformation to the new, administrative personnel in the Dajōkan saw value in retaining a past, that is, old things. Ninagawa's draft report of the survey complained of "a foreigner's" observation that Japanese like novelty and shun old things, and that people were selling artifacts from the temples and shrines of the western capital (Kansai). Ninagawa then warned that if this continued, in a number of years there would be no remnants of the ancient provinces (TKH100, 77).[8]

But we must not go too far. There is an idea of history, but it is *enkaku* (closer to chronicles and accounts, *histoire*), not *rekishi* (today's developmental notion

---

[5] Many of the site visits were rushed (including those to the Shōsōin and Hōryūji) because the leaders had to return to Tokyo to participate in the decision on the location of the museum; in addition to Ueno, Oji was also being considered.

[6] Other members of this team were Kashiwagi Masanori, whose role was to copy text, Yokoyama Matsusaburo, who photographed objects, Kasakura Tetsunosuke, and Takahashi Yūichi, a painter.

[7] Drawing from Henri Meschonnic, Osborne writes, "'Modernity,' then, has no fixed, objective referent. 'It *has only a subject, of which it is full.*' It is the product, in the instance of each utterance, of an act of historical self-definition through *differentiation, identification* and *projection*, which transcends the order of chronology in the construction of a meaningful present (1995, 14).

[8] Much of the information from this survey derives from Ninagawa's diary, *Nara no settō*. Ninagawa was perhaps referring to Edward Morse, with whom he had considerable contact. Indeed, Morse's fine collection and his expertise on pottery and ceramics drew heavily from Ninagawa, a collector of antiquarian objects.

of history).[9] There is little teleology. At this point, the Dajōkan seemed concerned about destruction and neglect, but a belief in value did not necessarily correspond to an articulation of what that value is. Moreover, despite this newfound concern for the past, not all shared it, especially those such as temple officials, who were in dire need of money—why not pawn a statue or painting rather than watch a mob destroy it—for food or maintenance as well as those who quickly learned a central tenet of modern society, self-interest.

More important, this event indicates an emerging sense of separation of the present from the past. Things were becoming important because they were old, not because they were tied to some form of belief or spirituality. The materiality of the object or textual data took precedence over the idea and transmitted knowledge. Buddhist items that lost their connection to previous ideational and political structures were deemed at this moment particularly "worthless," their materiality as old not yet established. But even in the desire to save, there is a nostalgia, a fear of loss that is possible only through recognition that an object is currently of another world. Here the past is becoming foreign (Lowenthal 1985). It is a separation that is necessary for the production of history.

We must be careful not to confuse this interest in the past with our current knowledge of Japanese history. Indeed, these men have largely been forgotten. I believe that the principal reason for their demise was the lack of history, especially the history of the nation (and East Asia) as we know it today. Their past is not yet nation, national, though it is moving in that direction (TKH100, 74–75). Ninagawa's invocation of the "foreigner" can at best be read as a lament of an antiquarian that Japan is discarding its charming artifacts; the delineation of this past as proof of distinct national cultures—Japan, China, Korea, etc.—is absent. Ninagawa's interest in using artifacts to educate the inhabitants indicates both an early recognition of the importance of the past in fostering support for the new government and the still unformed idea of the nation-state. The objects that he selected in this survey are rather eclectic by today's disciplinary structures. The most important criteria were old things and objects connected to the imperial, especially ancient, lines.

The principal object of the survey's attention was the Shōsōin (Imperial storehouse) of the Tōdaiji.[10] The survey of the Shōsōin, which lasted for twelve days, is indicative of a coexistence of this transformation of time: on the one hand, the connection with the imperial family suggests the inherited idea of renewal, halting the degeneration of the world by returning to that pure originary moment of ancient emperors and empresses. But on the other hand, it is indicative of the shift from practices to pasts: a veneration of old objects not

---

[9] Doug Howland (1996) translates *enkaku* (Chinese: *yange*) as successive administrative changes of a unit. For an account of the rise of *Geschichte* from *histoire*, see Koselleck (1985, 21–38).

[10] Even though they did visit the Hōryūji, little has been written about that visit; see, for example, TKH100, 74–75. The desire to tie the past to the emperor is parallel to the rituals and pageants described by Takashi Fujitani (1996) to turn the emperor into the public centerpiece of the nation.

seen throughout this storehouse's history. From the middle part of the Heian period, its objects were largely forgotten. Tastes had changed; the Tang culture that such objects represented was passé (*tōi*), having become commonplace from frequency of intercourse as well as a changing style. The storehouse had last been opened in 1833. The transformation that the 1872 survey set off is summarized in an introduction to a recent history of the Shōsōin: "It is now always included in history textbooks and today there is nobody who does not know of the treasures of the Shōsōin. But, the attention paid to these treasures is not very old" (NHK 1990, 178).

The ambiguity of this moment is evident in the ceremony convened to open the doors of the Shōsōin. It was a great event; Uchida likened the excitement to a wedding ceremony or a meeting of a potential marriage partner (*miai*). Ninagawa's diary records the anticipation:

> We followed the procedure for removing the treasures from storage. Present were Governor Shijo and three lower officials; among the temple priests, one colored robe, three white robes, and six black robes; ten temple officials; and four carpenters and blacksmiths. At the storehouse, the previous day a platform across the front about 1.8 meters deep and a ramp were built. On a stage, the priests lined up on the left and officials on the right; they sat on chairs. After 12 o'clock we commenced the ceremony. A black-robed priest called the *yakushiin* and four carpenters went up to the platform and used a lever to remove the gate bolt from the south door, and then they removed that of the middle and north. And then the head priest (*shiseibō*), wearing a perfumed robe, removed the official temple seal from the lock on the south; next, the *yakushiin* removed the bamboo wrapping of the imperial seal from the middle and north. And then Seko [Nobuyo, the imperial envoy] went up, took the imperial seal, and showed it to all. We looked. And then the *yakushiin* took all seals from the lock. And then they inserted the key. And then they opened the door, and everyone entered. They removed ten long boxes and the temple officials carried them to the head priest. And then they closed the doors as before and removed the lock. At this time lots of people came from everywhere to look. A line formed and they opened the boxes. (THK100, 80)

The continuous use of "and then" (*tsugi*) suggests the careful ritual procedures the priests followed. The priests were conducting the ritual for the first time in thirty-nine years as they could best reconstruct it. Their ceremony indicates that the value of objects that were rarely seen was in its connection to the imperial court. For the survey team, *tsugi* suggests some exasperation at the length of the ceremony; indeed, the sudden attention of many people when the boxes were opened suggests a transformation of meaning whereby the ritual had lost significance. Value was in knowing and seeing, something to be catalogued and displayed. They were not disappointed when they finally saw the contents. Ninagawa's account marvels at the craftsmanship of the objects, especially the *koto*, flutes, *go* boards, and boxes; they returned him to the past, a sense of the eighth century. He rejoices that these objects are "sufficient to envision the ancient system" (NHK 1990, 184).

For Ninagawa, the antiquarian, the ancient period was reborn; it came alive again. But his purpose was not just to relish in the moment. He advocated its political potential, that the past and the wide dissemination of this information—the education of the population—would foster belief in the nation. In this sense, through acts of preservation or restoration, the subject had changed to the nation, making this more new than a restoration. Although Ninagawa was relishing in this imperial regalia, his efforts began the transformation of the artifacts from forgotten paraphernalia tied to the imperial families into objects that depict a national past. Ninagawa also advocated the establishment of museums as sites for preservation and display; many of the objects unearthed in this survey were placed on display three years later at the Nara exhibition (hakurankai), held in the Tōdaiji. The survey and subsequent exhibition are indicative of what de Certeau calls the transformation from "tradition into a past object" where new categories of differentiation transform the meaning of objects. A phenomenon of the new international world of the latter half of the nineteenth century was the plethora of exhibitions and world's fairs (see, e.g., Rydell 1984; Mabuchi 1997). Indeed, one of the reasons for the 1872 survey was to locate material to send to the world's fair in Vienna (another survey was conducted to prepare for the Nara exhibition). Exhibitions were one of the new organizational forms through which culture and technology could be distilled into a presentation for large audiences. Public displays, per se, were not new; these exhibits relied heavily on antecedents from the Edo period.[11] The purpose, however, was quite different.

The 1875 Nara exhibition was one of a series of public displays being held throughout the archipelago. The idea was connected to the exhibitions in the West that displayed industrial products, antiquities, nature, and cultures of the world. Meiji displays were usually public (i.e., sponsored by central and local governments), presented as new, organized by categories rather than ownership, and money making (they charged admission) (Kornicki 1994). Ninagawa envisioned a connection between artifacts and the production of a new arts industry of export items. In these early years, artlike objects were seen as an important export commodity. Much of the Nara exhibition consisted of artifacts from the Shōsōin and Hōryūji, but objects were usually arranged with little sense of historical order. The list of objects is different from today's standard inventory of important objects from that age; they fit in a category of orientalia that could be reproduced for export. There were few of the large Buddhist statues that are now canonized as Japanese art, and many smaller bronze statuettes of bodhisattva. Moreover, of the text I have seen, Ninagawa did not distinguish what was Japanese or from the continent (even subcontinent).

---

[11] For the transformation of public displays during Meiji, see Kornicki's fine essay, "Public Display and Changing Values" (1994); in Japanese, see Yoshimi (1992).

But these very acts of preservation, display, and reproduction (as export item and as a depiction of ancient society) indicate an increasing objectification of previous practices. First, the selection of the Tōdaiji shows a new significance of temple space: it was a large, enclosed site that could contain the exhibition. It no longer possessed the grandeur, spirituality, power, and wealth of the past. It was now a public (i.e., empty) space (the closest thing in 1875 to a convention center) whose meaning depended on the contents of the moment. The exhibition indicates a concern among the government to preserve important aspects of the past, especially those connected to the imperial family and art objects, such as the register of objects donated by Empress Kōken to the temple and a cushion that had once belonged to Shōtoku Taishi (Tokyo kokuritsu hakubutsukan 1959, 4). Even though the *kaichō*—temporary unveiling, or viewing, of sacred statues—served as an important antecedent for these exhibitions, religious objects no longer dominated; most of the objects, especially the large statues that now fill the art history books on Japan, were not included. Those Buddhist icons that were included were bronze statuettes of *kannon* and *nyōrai* that demonstrate the casting skills of Japanese artisans. The more famous of the 140 objects from the Hōryūji included in the exhibit were the Yakushi *nyōrai* from the main hall (*kondo*), the guardians Jikokuten and Tamonten, and the Tamamushi shrine.

Perhaps the best indication of this transformation of meaning is the removal of the Yakushi *nyōrai* from the main hall of the Hōryūji and its display among many other objects in the Tōdaiji as an important artifact of the past. Important objects that had been seen by so few people and were connected to specific temples could now be seen by the vast public (NHK 1990, 185). The value of the *nyōrai*, the principal icon of the Hōryūji, changed: it was now separated from that site and resituated as something old. The separation reflects the contradistinction of mobility and stability in modernity. Old things became a symbol of stability that grounds a changing society. Moreover, the removal of spirituality from this statue indicates an early stage at which these objects become aesthetic images that speak for an abstract idea, in this case a national past. Though not well framed yet, Ninagawa's desire to display artifacts in order to inform the masses was an early attempt at the use of aesthetics to connect the masses to the whole of the nation. The icon was now outside, something for people to see (which was not usually possible in the past), and thus it penetrated their lives. Those who went to the exhibit saw evidence of an emerging nation-state and experienced the result of a specific sequence of changes that explained the significance of what they had formerly known as a local site (Elias 1992, 76–80).

The final moment of this divestment of the objects from their function culminated in 1878.[12] Chihaya Jōchō, the head priest of Hōryūji, completed negotiations with Machida for the donation of more than three hundred temple

---

[12] For a discussion on the relation between function and the subjectivity of a divested object, see Baudrillard (1994).

objects to the Imperial Household. In return, the temple received a donation of ten thousand yen. From Chihaya's point of view, the donation would help avoid the dispersal of the temple's objects, remind the government of the temple's existence, and restore temple finances (Takada 1994, 66). This is indicative of the transformation of conceptual space. For Chihaya, the objects were part of the Hōryūji's space of experience, not an example of some history—of the imperial court or of a Japan. Not all objects were willingly relinquished; in the early negotiations in 1876, the temple proposed donating 157 objects. The number was increased after a prefectural (Sakai) survey determined that the temple's buildings were so dilapidated that they could not protect the objects. Some of the meaningful objects included on the final list were the shoes placed before the statue of a seated Shōtoku Taishi, the sword from the statue of Mochikuni in the main hall, and a brazier from the five-roofed pagoda. None of the large statues was included.[13] In short, for Chihaya, preservation was in the site itself, which gave meaning to the objects. But "to save" means the restoration of structures that were of value in an old system where lore and sacredness have power. To save that site—to pay for repairs to the main hall(kondo)—he had to relinquish many of the objects that gave meaning to the temple. It is important to remember that the temple used objects connected to Shōtoku Taishi to elevate its position among the believers of the Taishi cult (and thus earn money) during the Tokugawa period, and at the beginning of Meiji many bodhisattva had been burned, decapitated, or dumped unceremoniously in storage. From the viewpoint of Machida, the donation was important to provide a safe place to store the objects, now valued because of their connection to a past of Japan. Machida was ushering in a new system in which objects themselves have value even though they are separated from the institution that had given them their significance. This was an early moment where the nation-state would become the abstract system that determines possession, not only in terms of physical holding, but also in the criteria from which the objects gained their meaning.

The identification of old things was a key moment in the separation of pasts from present. In the process, there was the beginning of the reduction of the heterogeneity and specificity of society according to specific places into categories of a national past. The expertise that had been varied and local began to shift, where important knowledge of the old increasingly gained meaning as the past of Japan. The way that ideas and sites were identified and made known altered their meaning by differentiating them from their own local and specific sites, the space of experience, and resituating them as moments of a national past. But at this point, we must be careful that we do not overstate this common concept. This new past did not yet organize a history of Japan. The celebration of old things does not necessarily order them into a historical narrative. Indeed, the

---

[13] For a list of the donation, see Tokyo kokuritsu hakubutsukan (1959).

author of an 1880 series of photo essays, *Kokka yohō* (Glories of the country), indicates this ambiguity:

> It is a principle of nature [that works] when we see nobility in the ruggedness of mountain peaks and get a desire to study the flowing rivers and bays. More important, because we contact the spirit of ancient people in various books, pictures, and artifacts, when we come into contact and are edified, we will understand those secrets and miracles. In a country like ours, with an unbroken imperial line, we should honor more those artifacts that still exist. Last year, upon orders, I visited each prefecture and inspected books, paintings, and artifacts in the imperial treasuries, shrines, temples, and homes of samurai and merchants. I, an observer 1,100 years later, could not help but be inspired by the exquisite and elaborate details, the bequest of sages and philosophers, and products of expert artisans. . . . I have tried to animate the spirit of the ancients for [those of] the present. . . . I hope [the volumes] spread throughout the public and become a tool that nurtures the principles of patriotism and, most of all, augments (*hiho*) civilization. (Tokunō 1880)

This passage demonstrates both an emerging separation of past from present, as well as the limits of this process. On the one hand, the declaration "to animate the spirit of the ancients" as a tool to encourage patriotism indicates that separation: the past is dead and thus is able to be used (animated) for a quite new purpose. This is part of the process of becoming modern. Susan Buck-Morss writes that Walter Benjamin was struck by an "incontestable, empirical fact: Consistently, when modern innovations appeared in modern history, they took the form of historical restitutions" (1989, 110). The idea of unifying the archipelago into a nation-state is such a modern innovation. A part of that innovation is the reorganization of space from the locale to the nation-state. Indeed, in 1871 the old domains were abolished and reorganized into prefectures. The title *Kokka yohō* is instructive: the characters for *kokka* are those for country (*kuni*) and brilliance (*ka*) (not family, which combines into the more familiar nation-state), and *yohō* suggests continuity. These volumes suggest the beginnings of a shift from the importance of local places filled with lore, superstition, and magic to a new grouping as sites with a common past.[14]

But the organization of these volumes also indicates that in the restitution of pasts, the new both uses the past and is also understood through the past, that is, through inherited forms of knowledge. The organizational structure is closer to the travel guides (*zue*) of the Edo period. The content—shrines, temples, and imperial tombs—emphasizes regions and important sites. The images of these volumes are organized by region, not by time. The prefectures listed are Ise, Yamato, Kii, Izumo, Kawachi, Yamashiro, Saikio, Ōmi, Owari, Mino, Suruga,

---

[14] Luke Roberts argues that the Meiji government's use of the word *kokka*, which had signified regional domains, to represent Japan was related to its desire to transfer allegiance from those local places to the new nation-state (1998, 4–9).

Kai, Shinano, Kōzuke, Shimotsuke, and Nikko. The images are of views from distant vantage points—roads leading to the shrines, temples, or imperial tombs, bridges, and landscapes—of the temple gates, as visitors first view the site upon their arrival, and of principal buildings. Photos of statues, paintings, or artifacts from inside the temples or shrines are noticeably absent. The past that is being celebrated in this series is of sacred and meaningful sites, not historical artifacts. In short, while these sites and artifacts are now valued for their significance to a common past, they are not yet organized into a structure that orders the space of the nation.

Discovery Three: The Archipelago Has a Past

One of the limitations of the notion of old things is the dependence on the Chinese classics and the Japanese texts, *Kojiki* and *Nihon shoki*. The conceivable past is that which is tied to what was a part of the world as known through these ancient accounts. Moreover, Ninagawa's discovery of old things did not necessarily lead to the idea of development. To be sure, there were ideas of progress in Japan. But the discovery of pasts did not lead to the writing of a historical narrative of Japan. In the 1870s, progress was an idea that was evident in the West, and Japan was characterized as the past, still in the first stage. For example, Fukuzawa writes in his famous *An Outline of a Theory of Civilization*:

> Therefore, throughout the whole twenty-five centuries or so of Japanese history, the government has been continually doing the same thing; it is like reading the same book over and over again, or presenting the same play time after time. Thus when Arai Hakuseki talks about "nine stages" and "five stages" in the general spirit of the country, he is just presenting the same play fourteen times over. A certain Westerner writes that, though there have indeed been upheavals in Asian countries, no less than in Europe, in Asia these upheavals have not advanced the cause of civilization. In my opinion, this is undeniable. (1973, 142)

Later, Fukuzawa explicitly states that Japan is still at the first stage of development; that is, even though he recognizes change and the separation of past from present, it does not guarantee that Japan, too, can have a history (159).

The problem for Japanese intellectuals was that even though they were attempting to break from and separate the past, they were still working within a conceptual system in which an originary ideal determined knowledge. The distinction does not necessarily lead to the next issue, the way that the past and present interact to understand a future. In the organization of modernity in Western nations, such as France, Germany, and Great Britain, the elevation of themselves as modern innovators was built upon the old, either that of ancient Greece or an Indo-German language. Both serve as originary moments from which a narrative of development (history) becomes possible.

There is an obvious dilemma: the synchronization of Japan (or any other non-Western place) into the world at this point entailed placing Japan into that originary category. A problem for Japanese intellectuals like Fukuzawa, and I believe all non-Western societies confronting the modern, is one of history; while Fukuzawa recognizes a history in the West, there is a question whether Japan also has history. For Fukuzawa, Japan's past was twenty-five hundred years of stagnation. In this attempt to synchronize Japan with the temporality of progress, it is not a question of whether previous forms or change existed. Change was occurring throughout the Tokugawa era and accelerated during the *tenpō* and *bakumatsu* periods. But the threat and allure of the West catalyzed that change and also made impossible the return to an ideal located in some past.

It is at this point that civilization as defined by the West not only is the goal but also becomes the impediment. The possibilities seen in science and capitalism that cannot be accommodated in past ideals encouraged change. As Vico once wrote, life and nature is full of incertitude; it is dominated by chance and choice (1990, 34). But as is hinted in the Charter Oath, uncertainty or lack of direction is one of the evil customs of the past. Yet science and capitalism also rendered (renders) Japan to the certainty of perpetual inferiority. Thus the problem was not only the uncertainty of direction, but also the certainty of inferiority. Japan was (is) located within one of de Certeau's scriptural tombs, that of the Orient; within the nineteenth-century, imperialistic world, it was a society revered for its antithesis to modernity, rather than as a dynamic society with its own autonomous history. In this sense it, too, faced many of the problems of colonized places, especially on the sociocultural level.[15]

But as in so many of modernity's contradictions, the very nature of Japan as past provided the venue for its movement out of that past. In the 1870s Japan, according to a developmental rendering of history, was still one of those "unexplored" lands that had suddenly been "opened" from "seclusion" (different metaphors for "mankind's exit from its self-incurred immaturity"). Japan became an opportunistic retreat for numerous Europeans and Americans who desired to observe its people and land and share their experiences with academic societies in Europe, such as the Royal Society. On the one hand, those accounts described Japan as a living past. Morse, for example, placed it within a nostalgic context: "To an 'active American' all this is a terrible waste of time—but charming, most definitely charming" (Rosenstone 1998, 125).[16]

But on the other hand, many of these same individuals operated within the nineteenth-century "planetary consciousness" described by Mary Louise Pratt in her marvelous book *Imperial Eyes*. Pratt describes the way that travel, science,

---

[15] I believe that this relegation of the past as if dead weighs heavily in today's penchant for interpreters of Japan to vacillate from Japanophiles to Japanophobes, describing either a good Japan (that is, dead—malleable to the wishes and interpretations of the West) or a bad Japan (that is, the ghost that haunts the modern West).

[16] For more on Morse's Japanophilia, see Ishikawa (1968, esp. 352). Morse's *Japan Day-by-Day* (1879) is filled with examples: his observation of Buddhism and healing can be found in 1:127.

and imperialism converged in the classification of objects throughout the world according to European categories of knowledge. She writes, "One by one the planet's life forms were to be drawn out of the tangled threads of their life surroundings and rewoven into European-based patterns of global unity and order" (1992, 31). While Pratt focuses on Linnaeas's project, travelers were also wandering the globe armed with science and history with which they sought to demystify the globe. Morse went to Japan to study brachiopods. Many others went to Ezo (present-day Hokkaido) and reported on the Ainu, where, like Morse, they revelled in the primitiveness, observing society as ethnographers speculating on Japan's protohistory.[17] Many were geologists who sought to demystify the Earth's geology by separating geophysical forms from the cultures that inhabited them and by placing this knowledge into a global geological history.[18]

Today we understand that imperialism is not unidirectional. While these travelers were attempting to integrate Japan into this planetary consciousness, the ambitions of Western explorers/travelers/scientists often converged with the desires of the Meiji government. The new government sought out those same scholars and explorers, experts who would foster the goal of *fukoku kyōhei*. Here, the goal of economic development coincided with the writing of history. For example, Benjamin Smith Lyman was one of the first Westerners to examine the geomorphology of the archipelago. His *Geological Survey of Hokkaido* (1877) maps the island and analyzes the mineral resources, especially coal, of what became the fourth major island of Japan. But this imperialistic endeavor to unlock the key to Japan also opened the way for Japanese to write a history; that is, to create a narrative of development that shows change beyond the category of primitive or Hegel's Descriptive. In his travels, Lyman also collected fossils, beginning the historicization of the archipelago. Others who arrived in Japan during the 1870s (many of whom were employed by the Japanese government) continued this synchronization of Japan into their modern world. The geological work of men like Morse, John Milne, and Heinrich Edmund Naumann released the past from Japan's classics by demonstrating a history prior to and separate from those accounts. In particular, Morse's "discovery" of the shell mounds of Ōmori, Naumann's mapping of the geological structure of the archipelago, and Milne's seismological studies gave the archipelago a history independent of any previous understanding of the past and comparable to that being written for the Earth in Europe. In other words, the synchronization of Japan in this case did not involve the placement of Japan into preexisting categories but was part of the reconceptualization of this history and movements of the Earth.[19]

---

[17] It seemed almost obligatory to visit the Ainu to explain the key to Japan's history. Isabella Bird (1984) [1880] devoted a considerable portion of her book to her discoveries in Ezo, while John Milne, a geologist who became one of the founders of modern seismology, made an early investigation in the north.

[18] For a description of geology and travel, see Leeds (1991, 198–204). For descriptions of American and European experts hired by the new state, see Beauchamp and Iriye (1990) and Jones (1980).

[19] For an account of the discovery of geological time in England, see Winchester (2001).

Today, it is hard for us even to conceive of how people understood their world without knowing the geological structure and history of the Earth. In Europe the idea that the Earth has a history that predated that of the scriptures emerged only in the eighteenth century. But with this knowledge, it became possible to conceive of a very different temporal understanding of the world and human relations (see, e.g., Toulmin and Goodfield 1965). The explication of the geology of the archipelago, too, was crucial in forcing a new temporal structure on Japan. It did two things: it showed that histories existed independent of what had been accepted as true, the accounts in the *Nihon shoki* and *Kojiki*; and second, it severed natural time from human time.

One of the most famous discoveries of the 1870s was Morse's excavation of the Ōmori shell mounds. Morse noticed the shell mounds on his first train ride from Yokohama to Tokyo in 1877 and began excavation within months. The principal publication of his findings was in the first memoir of the new Tokyo University (Morse 2539).[20] Morse pointed out that because mounds were usually created near water, the location of the Ōmori mounds about one-half mile inland suggests that the waters of Edo Bay had receded. In other words, it is evidence of geological change. More shocking was his conclusion that, based on the pottery, bone fragments, and stone tools, the people who left the refuse were a "savage" people who practiced cannibalism. He concluded, "It can be stated with absolute certainty that they are pre-Japanese; and there are as good reasons for believing them pre-Aino as early Aino" (266).

Morse has achieved status as the father of archaeology and anthropology in Japan. The significance of his discovery is that he was the first to place those stone implements, pottery shards, and human and animal bones into the temporal framework of modernity. Torii Ryūzō credits Morse for exposing a history of Japan that is not in the *Nihon shoki* and *Kojiki* (1967, 7–8). But as in the other discoveries that I write about in this book, Morse was not the first to see it. According to the *Hitachi fudoki* (713), such mounds are the refuse of giants who lived in the area, locals knew about shell mounds, and antiquarians had collections of artifacts from various sites. Torii writes that these sites were known by Tokugawa scholars such as Fujii Tadayoshi and Kariya Ekisai (1974, 128). These fragments were interpreted through the known history, that is, the *Kojiki* and *Nihon shoki*. Thus in the *Sandai jitsuroku*, because arrowheads were often found after thunderstorms, they were believed to have been deposited by rain and thunder (Bleed 1986, 58).

Moreover, Morse's discovery was possible only because of the modern transformation of which he was a part. To lay the track for the train from Yokohama

[20] This *Memoir* lists the year of publication as "2539 (1879)" in accordance to the recent changes in the reckoning of the calendar. The practice more common in the latter half of Meiji, such as Meiji 12, was not followed.

to Tokyo, crews had to cut through a shell mound, exposing it to a glimpse by those who could afford to ride the train. This itself was the changing dominance of a mechanized and efficient order over nature. Wolfgang Schivelbusch describes this transformation: "'Annihilation of time and space' was the *topos* which the early nineteenth century used to describe the new situation into which the railroad placed natural space after depriving it of its hitherto absolute powers" (1977, 10). In this case, the past—which had been an everyday space that people walked on and/or around—is only possible in the modern. The building of a railway facilitated a discovery that according to Torii made it "understood for the first time that there was also a stone age in Japan" (1967, 150). But even here, it is possible that this credit to Morse as the first is in error. At Ōmori, Morse reportedly ran into the young German geologist, Edmund Naumann, who some claim had already investigated the shell mounds (Yoshioka 1987, 40–43).

But it was Morse who not only publicized his discovery, but, more important, placed the archipelago within a Darwinian framework that raised a controversial issue—the possibility of humans hitherto unknown—that forced Japanese to question or defend their inherited knowledge.[21] One of Morse's former students, Ishikawa Chiyomatsu, recalls the impact of this discovery: "To us Japanese, who used to believe in the tradition of our ancestors [*sic*] coming down from heaven, the idea of the existence of the savages on our islands was quite a shock" (1967, 179). In other words, it was the possibility of a past that was prior to the beginning of time as it had been understood. Morse's public lectures were well attended, and it seems that many of the elite Japanese audience (attendees of the lectures, students, and avid readers of the *Tokyo nichi nichi* newspaper) were not bothered by a non-"Japanese"—even cannibalistic—origin, nor were they troubled by the idea of evolution. After one of several public and well-attended lectures on Darwin's evolution (his first was on October 6, 1877), Morse remarked with pleasure the positive acceptance he received from his Japanese audience. Miyake Setsurei (Yujirō) wrote:

> By far the greatest impression produced upon the thinking public of Japan was the advent of Professor E. S. Morse, who spared no pains to introduce the theories advanced by Darwin and Huxley. The Darwinian theory of man's descent from a monkey was in itself enough to surprise the Japanese students, and Professor Morse's eloquent discourses, accompanied by skillful figures on the black-board not only made a great impression on students, but also had a great influence on the public." (Wayman 1942, 249)

---

[21] Morse is generally acknowledged as the first to introduce the ideas of Charles Darwin to Japan. Morse's lectures on Darwin were translated by his student Ishikawa Chiyomatsu in 1881, and the *Descent of Man* was translated by Kōzu Senzaburō in 1881. The *Origin of Species* was not translated into Japanese until 1914, by Ōsugi Sakae. See Shimao (1981, 93–102).

Two groups—conservative Japanese and Protestant missionaries—did question his findings. Some conservative scholars and politicians criticized Morse and came to the defense of the classics. One reactionary bureaucrat wrote:

> Wait a minute, I looked at the excavation at Ōmori because of its novelty. Regardless of whether Morse's so-called cannibalistic practices existed or not, what were the relations between the Ōmori people and the ancestors of Japanese [i.e., gods of the age of the gods]? Morse says that the Ōmori people were earlier inhabitants without any connection to Japanese; but if so, why were such different people (*minzoku*) living in the Tokyo vicinity? This is unbearable. From the standpoint of one's strong faith in the *kokutai* (national body), this field called archeology is exceedingly dangerous (*yabai*). (Quoted in Tozawa 1977, 100)

Within a matrix of evolution or progress, Morse's discovery, which suggests a movement from primitive to more advanced, seems commonsensical. But these Japanese critics did not operate within the same temporal matrix; theirs was a space of experience, of which the most authoritative texts were the *Kojiki* and *Nihon shoki*. In this case, archaeology is dangerous because it brings a different time, a prehistory that is prior to that space, the founding of the country according to the age of the gods.

The general conservative reaction reflects these different temporalities: they criticized a reduction of Morse's argument from the idea that a pre-Ainu people were probably cannibalistic to Japan's ancestors were cannibalistic. Here, of course, it required a different temporality to accept that any people on the archipelago, created by the gods themselves, were anything but Japanese. In a conceptual world where a prehistoric time does not exist and cannot demarcate one type of society from another, the Ōmori discovery suggested that people in "Japan" were barbarians. These critics were still operating within the Chinese barbarian/civilized world order, rather than a progressive, primitive/civilization order.

The reaction of Matsumori Taneyasu is perhaps indicative of the difficulty that the new "deep time" presented. Matsumori wrote his critical reactions to Morse's shell mounds in 1878. But rather than a reaction or attempt at preservation, it shows a critical and careful engagement as well as the difficulty of moving from one temporal conception to another. Matsumori accepts the idea of human progress that divides human prehistory into the stone age, bronze age, and iron age. But then he seeks to understand this new time by locating his inherited knowledge in it. He criticizes Morse's hypothesis of a similarity between the pre-Ainu and peoples in North America. The idea that people at that time migrated is inconceivable; if sea routes were not open until Columbus discovered the New World, how could there be a connection between the pre-Ainu and North American Indians? He dismisses the idea of a land bridge as crazy (that is, the land is fixed). Instead, he argues that the similarity in the artifacts of the two peoples is because they are both at a primitive level with few resources. He then attempts to adjust the *Kojiki* and *Nihon shoki* to evolution. Matsumori locates the age of the gods as Japan's stone age. But because these sections refer to metal weapons such as the *ama no sakahoko* and the *kusunagi*, which were believed to be bronze and iron, he modifies this stone age to suggest that the commoners used stone while the gods (elite) used metal, and that many of the stone artifacts, such as the stone arrowheads and Tengu's rice paddles, were made by the gods before using bronze and iron (Katō 1977, 86–89). In this case, even though Matsumori accepts a developmental time, he does not give up his understanding of a "Japan," but tries to adapt the fixed world to a progressive one.

On the other hand, Morse did engage in a debate, but it was with other Americans—Protestant missionaries—and John Milne, who offered a different interpretation of Japan's origins. The most vehement criticism of Morse's lectures on Darwin came from the Protestant missionaries in Japan.[22] Henry Faulds attended (some would say hounded) Morse's lectures and tried to refute Morse's interpretation of evolutionary theory.[23] Another missionary lamented in the denominational newsletter *The Heathen Woman's Friend* in February 1879: "Prof. Morse is untiring in his efforts to sow scepticism. His peculiar socialistic views find a ready lodgements in the hearts of the Japanese and it has looked sometimes as though he were going to raze all that the missionaries are building" (quoted in Wayman 1942, 248). It seems that the demise of Christianity should not be blamed on a conservative, that is, national, reaction, but, just as evolution upset religion in the West, the introduction of science and evolution in Japan also upset Western theism.[24] For many Japanese students at that time, this debate questioned the unity between Christianity (especially Protestantism) and enlightenment. In this case, the Protestant missionaries were both defenders of an anachronistic past and the spiritual and ethical underlay of modernity (if one is to believe Weber and Bellah). In other words, Japanese who listened to evolution, which was just as unsettling to their inherited conception of the world, did not yet have enough of an understanding of their modernity to have a stake in a particular past. The Westerners were fighting over a difference of originary moments that was not yet at issue in Japanese society.

Morse's debate with Protestant missionaries replayed the battle taking place elsewhere. It indicates the centrality of the past to one's own understanding of modernity: the absolute necessity of a past for a horizon of some progress. But interestingly, a different critic, a fellow scientist, indicated another role of the

---

[22] For a discussion of this debate, see Ōta (1988, 41–67).

[23] In his travelogue, the only reference Faulds makes to his disagreements with Morse is the following oblique statement: "The Priests all seem to foresee the decay of Buddhism in Japan; and some of them also see pretty clearly that even now the battle amongst educated Japanese is between scientific agnosticism and Christianity" (1973, 104).

[24] This is especially evident in the report of Yoichi Honda, bishop of the Japanese Methodist Church: "Japanese Christians found the drift of the theory to be irresistible, and changed their logic, claiming theism to be consistent with evolution" (quoted in Wayman 1942, 248–49; see also Ōta 1988, 62–63).

newly separated past. John Milne challenged Morse's claim that a "pre-Aino" people created the Ōmori mounds; the implications were to push this discovery into a quest for the origins of Japanese themselves. Yoshioka Ikuo has argued that Morse's debates with other Western scholars are the origin of the question of race in modern Japan (1987, 12–13).

Milne was another hired foreign expert (*oyatoi*) who became professor of geology and mining at the Imperial College of Engineering in Tokyo in 1876. He is best remembered as one of the founding fathers of the modern field of seismology. One biographer writes, "It is not, I think, too much to claim that Milne lifted the science to an altogether different and higher plane" (Davison 1927, 177).[25] Especially before 1880, Milne, too, was interested in uncovering prehistoric Japan. Apparently he conducted his own excavations of shell mounds, burrowed into tumuli, and explored caves. He also worked with Morse, especially on visits to Hakodate and Otaru. In May 1880 he presented a paper to the Anthropological Institute on "The Stone Age of Japan" in which he outlined his disagreement with Morse.

Milne drew upon the work of Morse, his visits to the north, and also Japanese historical texts to offer a different interpretation. He argued that based on evidence of rectangular pits found on Nemuro and on Hokkaido at Hochishibetsu and Hamanaka, and their similarity to the houses of Aleuts and Kamchadales (also Kurilsky), the earliest inhabitants of Hokkaido were probably these Kamchadales or Aleuts. Given this evidence, Milne concluded that these people coexisted with the ancestors of the Ainu who migrated from Papua-New Guinea and first settled throughout the archipelago. The Ainu gradually moved north as another people migrated via the Korean peninsula and forced the Kamchadales to the north of Hokkaido. Here Milne turned to the accounts of the Ebisu in the ancient myths. But rather than basing his ideas on the myths like Matsumori, Milne used them to corroborate archaeological evidence. He also studied old maps and estimated that through the process of silting, the mounds at Ōmori were probably created between 1,500 and 3,000 years ago. In this case, he concluded that this evidence suggests that Ainu, not pre-Ainu, peoples left the shell mounds at Ōmori (Milne 1881).

This disagreement between Morse and Milne over the origins of Japanese was continued by professors Koganei Yoshikiyo and Tsuboi Shōgorō and has traveled through different manifestations up to the present.[26] The idea of a stone age or prehistory was part of a growing body of geological evidence, where "questions about the temporal sequence of those changes were inescapable"

[25] Because Milne did not enjoy sea voyages, he decided to go to Japan by traveling through Russia and China. He left London on August 3, 1875, and arrived in Shanghai on February 23, 1876. During his first night in Yokohama in March, he experienced his first, rather mild, earthquake.
[26] Koganei argued for the similarity of the Ainu and Jōmon and that the former were driven north by the ancestors of the present-day Japanese. Tsuboi argued that the ancestors of the present-day Japanese were the Korobokkuru, pygmies according to Ainu lore, today considered ancestors of Eskimos.

and snowballed into a new temporal framework. Other Japanese anthropologists, archaeologists, and paleontologists also began to excavate evidence of a prehistoric past. In the 1880s historians in Japan began to examine the *Kojiki* and *Nihon shoki*, exposing their inaccuracy or transforming them to the realms of literature and mythology. The idea of cannibalism disappeared (as did the dirty, unkempt, flea-ridden leader of Wa in the *Wei Zhi*), perhaps a casualty of the imperial history that would subsequently emerge.[27] But again we must remember the processual nature of this changing understanding. Morse's descriptions of transformation of the bay were supported by other scholars whose observations of Japan's geological structure suggested that nature has a history that is autonomous from human society. But just as early attempts to date the history of the Earth in Europe coincided with biblical history, even though both Morse and Milne calculated the silting of the bay as if nature, not humankind, was the cause, they dated the mounds around the mythical beginning of Japan.[28]

Any question of the possibility of maintaining a connection between the history of the archipelago and the ancient histories was removed by Edmund Naumann, whose careful surveys of the geomorphology of the archipelago and discovery of prehistoric elephants in Japan extended the past beyond an early presence of humans to a deep time. Naumann was another of the *oyatoi*, arriving in Japan in 1875 (one month shy of his twenty-first birthday) to teach at the Kaisei gakkō. Overall, he spent ten years in Japan, traveling throughout the archipelago and writing numerous papers, especially in German, that have established him as the founding figure of modern geology in Japan. During his early years in Japan he cooperated and competed with Milne, but by 1880 Milne's inquiries led him toward the investigation of earthquakes, while Naumann continued his geological mapping of the archipelago.

Naumann is best known for founding the Geological Survey of Japan in 1878, and it is this work that set the foundation for our modern geological knowledge of the geotectonics of Japan. To give an idea of its concurrence with geological activity elsewhere, the U.S. Geological Survey was established in 1879. In that year, Naumann began publishing his ideas on the origins of the Japanese archipelago, and it is largely his work that modern geologists have built upon, corrected, and modified.[29] Though he is not as famous (nor important) as Eduard Suess, as further evidence of the integration of Japan into this global geological map, Suess's important *Das Anlitz der Erde* discussed the geotectonics of Japan, primarily using the work of Naumann and his successor and former student, Harada Toyokichi (Yabe 1917, 75–104). Naumann's lasting contribution was the identification of a "rupture region" (Bruchregion), and after refining his

[27] For an attempt to revive this and other evidence of cannibalism, see Nishioka (1989, 19–20).

[28] For eighteenth-century efforts to date the Earth, see Toulmin and Goodfield (1965). Milne considered silting the primary force of change and dismissed land reclamation as inconsequential (1881, 413–20).

[29] His first essay was "Ueber Erdbeben und Vulcanausbrüche in Japan."

interpretations more in line with the seminal work by Suess on the Alps, he called this fissure that divides central Honshu from Shizuoka to Nagano the Fossa Magna. As he refined his understanding of the various mountain systems and geological features, Naumann speculated that the archipelago was formed from three foldings of the Earth's crust, in the pre-Paleozoic era, the late Paleozoic era, and the Miocene era, and that it is composed of two basic mountain systems, the southwest and northeast, each with an inner and outer zone. In other words, the archipelago formed over a long period in which the Earth's crust reformed to create the archipelago.

Second, in 1881 Naumann published the results of his investigation of fossils of prehistoric elephants in Japan. He did not excavate these fossils; they were in collections of Japanese antiquarians and unearthed by Westerners for more than a decade preceding this report. Also, elephants were known in Tokugawa society through Buddhist images, as well as the Korean embassies (Toby 1986, 415–56). Today, one of the elephants that Naumann studied and attributed to India, the *Elephas namadicus*, is known as the *palaeoloxodon naumanni*. This article further confirmed the archaeological and paleontological evidence reported by Morse by giving that prehistory greater precision. Naumann located these fossils in the late Pliocene era. But the main contribution of this essay was his connection of prehistoric creatures to geographic and geological transformation. He suggested that because the quantity of fossil evidence suggests that there were numerous such creatures, they came to the archipelago via a land bridge that at one time connected the islands to what is now the Korean peninsula to the south and the Kuriles and Sakhalin to the north. Finally, based on plant fossils, he argued that the climate of the archipelago during the late Pliocene era had been tropical (Yamashita 1992).

The synchronization of knowledge about Japan into the emerging science of the Earth, that is, into a universalistic framework where nature was separated from culture, ruptured previous knowledge that had made sense of the relation of the Earth to humans. In their quest to contribute to the rapidly changing geological knowledge of the Earth, these geologists brought Japan into the same kinds of morphological histories that comprised the discursive field of the West. Naumann not only provided empirical evidence of geological change—that the archipelago was not even an archipelago but an appendage of the continent—he also offered a chronology to the "stone age" that was not remotely connected to the *Kojiki* and *Nihon shoki*. It is a timeline of the archipelago—a prehistory: the Paleozoic, Cenozoic, Neolithic, etc.—that is completely autonomous from human activity.

ELEVATION OF TIME OVER SPACE

Interestingly, this reconstitution of space on the archipelago was completed almost without meaningful contribution from geography or its precursor in Japan, topography (*chishigaku*). This absence is not from a lack of concern. Quite the contrary, the first use of the word *chiri* (geography) in the new government occurred in 1869 when the Ministry of Civil Affairs reorganized itself into three units: geography, public works, and postal service (Ishida 1984, 29). Moreover, in the same year a Department of Topography (*chishika*) was established in parallel to the Department of History (*rekishika*). Other ministries, such as Education, Military, and Finance, also created geographical offices as early as 1870. In the initial period, even though the two departments were created in parallel, topography, possessing administrative and budgetary oversight, had preeminence over history (Miura 1930, 463). But this situation had completely reversed by the end of the century: the Department of History eventually emerged into the present-day Historiographical Institute, and its early members, such as Shigeno and Kume, raised a number of controversial issues on the relation of history and historical documents to the nation-state. The Department of Topography was subsumed by an earlier incarnation of this historiographical office and eliminated in 1893.

The most important individual in the development of topography in Meiji society was Tsukamoto Akitake (1833–85). Tsukamoto was a former bakufu retainer who became a professor at the Rikugun heigaku and in 1872 was appointed by the Dajōkan to lead the compilation of the *Kōkoku chishi* (imperial topography). Despite his background, he did not seek to restore the past; he was committed to unifying the nation-state and believed that information about the various places was crucial to that goal. Moreover, Tsukamoto was the petitioner for the reform of the calendar, certainly not an act of a conservative or traditionalist. The major publications of the Office of Topography were the *Nihon chishi teiyō* (2534), which was compiled as an updated geographical description for the Vienna world's fair,[30] and one volume (volume 3 on Awa) of a planned multivolume compendium, the *Dai nihon chishi*. Between 1904 and 1917, Yamazaki Naokata and Satō Denzō published all ten volumes.

From this early desire for knowledge about places, the limitations of such topographical knowledge to a modern world became increasingly apparent. Following the publication of the first three volumes of the *Nihon chishi teiyō*, the office was reorganized into the Office for the Compilation of Topographical Materials and was merged with the Office of Historiography (*shūshikyoku*). Until this office was terminated in 1893, its goal was to provide a more detailed topography, focusing on villages (*mura*) and counties (*gun*). The project sought to collect as much textual data as possible on all the villages and counties and also conduct field research. The information was organized spatially along the lines of previous topographies, such as the *fudoki* from the Nara period and the domainal topographies of the Tokugawa period. Much of the information was

---

[30] The first three volumes appeared in 2534 (1874), the year given on the title page. The following four volumes appeared by 1877.

based on texts that had been accepted as authoritative.[31] But the merger of this office with the Office of Historiography reflects the growing importance of time as a way to understand the past; when the offices were merged, the director came from the historiographical office. Indeed, when the office was abolished in 1877, it was over disagreements between the respective directors, Shigeno and Tsukamoto.[32]

This relatively low level of publication of the Office of Topography is reflective not of the marginality of geographical information, but of a changing valuation of space. The customary topographies were compilations to enable the local elite to know something about their lands. They were organized to highlight the locale and include information about the past, socioeconomic conditions, and production. This project generally followed this intellectual practice. For example, the draft on Ishikawa prefecture included a section on customs (*fuzoku*) of local people: "Being astute, they are obedient; however, they have an annoying habit of stealing time. They do not have a brave and adventurous character, and long ago had the system of four classes. Their customs are different, even the style of men's and women's hair" (Ishida 1984, 74). Even though, from our perspective, the descriptions bear more similarity to Tokugawa versions, the Meiji accounts did reflect changing knowledge structures, especially in the growing separation of culture from nature: entries were more descriptive and did not associate place with songs and poetry; data were also gathered from actual site visits; and they did try to include recent geological evidence. For example, the volume on Awa incorporates information on geological change—earthquakes, volcanoes, and sedimentation—that recognizes the historicity of the earth.

Thomas Richards (1993) describes this changing valuation about space during the nineteenth century as a penchant to know about the world, an obsession

[31] Some of the sources for a draft of the *Kōkoku chishi* for Ishikawa prefecture are *Hakusan sōgen kōki, Sannomiya kōki, Akamatsu saikōki, Kasukayama nikki, Heike monogatari, Taiheiki,* and the *Nihon sōkoku fudoki* (Ishida 1984, 55).

[32] The Department of Topography suffered through numerous organizational changes. After the Department of Geography was created in 10.1872 as part of the Seiin, in August 1874 it was combined with a similar office in the Ministry of Finance and merged into the Division of Geography (*chiriryō*) in the Home Ministry. One year later it was returned to the Seiin as the Office for the Compilation of Topographical Materials (Chishi henshū) and merged with the Office of Historiography (Shūshikyoku). This office was abolished in January 1877 and reorganized into the *Shūshikan* ten days later. In December 1877 Tsukamoto, the director of the section on topography, resigned in disagreement with Shigeno, and his office reappeared eighteen days later within the Ministry of Home Affairs. This arrangement lasted until 1890 when the Office of Topography was moved to the Ministry of Education, which housed it in the Imperial University. In 1891 it was merged into the Temporary Department of the Compilation of a Chronological History (Rinji hennenshi hensan kakari). This department was abolished in 1893 following the controversy surrounding Kume Kunitake, and when the Historiographical Institute (Shiryō hensanjo) opened in 1895, the section on topography was not continued (Ishida 1984, 43, 44, 60). Also see Mehl (1998a) for information on the various incarnations of the historiographical office.

with "the control of knowledge." The discovery of a past severed nature from culture and created the possibilities for the utilization of evidence differently. Virtually all topographical accounts of the Tokugawa period had been conducted by the domainal administrators to understand the social and economic conditions of their territory. Tsukamoto was an advocate for the use of topographical information for national, not local, purposes and sought to adapt their methods to the needs of the nation-state. Ishida writes: "There were many similar categories among [the village and county surveys] but they differed in the way they were recorded: to know the circumstances of all villages the village survey sought detail so that nothing would fall through the cracks; the district survey summarized minor matters of towns and cities and worked to bring out the general trends" (1984, 14). Even though Meiji topography drew on the *fudoki* and the domainal topographies of the Tokugawa period, unlike the earlier studies, which emphasized the peculiarities of each place, the new topography began to show the similarities. County studies now used the locale to describe and demonstrate the nation.

This changing valuation, however, where data became important for their relevance to temporal categories, the past and the prehistoric, and were shorn from their significance to place, the locales, was too much for a field of knowledge based on the peculiarities of place to survive. Ishida's account brings out the limitations; place-based compilations brought out the peculiarities and uniqueness. These compilations did not provide the generalizations, commonalities, and comparisons that would facilate interchangeability among regions. Nevertheless, one might argue that the decline of topography stems from the importance of its knowledge, increasingly severed from place. The two major types of information that had been its domain—statistics and history—gained autonomous status. Statistics, which was a category included in the initial compilations, gained increasing importance, but rather than enhancing the importance of topography, it gained autonomous status beginning in 1874. Various ministries also began collecting their own statistics.[33]

Accounts of the past, too, were separated from their specific locale and became data that made it possible to know the nation. The content that had filled the topographies became textual materials for the domain of history, statistical data about people and communities, and evidence for the workings of nature. This isolation of data is similar to the way that the objects within the Shōsōin gained in importance simply because they were old and historical evidence of imperial grandeur, and the way that archaeological and geological discoveries became objects and containers of inert things that could be measured and used to demonstrate the history of the archipelago. In the end, geography was seen as

[33] Statistics became sufficiently important that the Division of Statistics (Tokeiin) was organized in 1881; it was the predecessor to today's Statistics Bureau in the Prime Minister's Office (Ishida 1984, 19; see also Mizuchi 1994, 75–94).

an enhancement to historical study: topographical research was merged into the Temporary Department of the Compilation of a Chronological History (the predecessor to the Historiographical Institute) in 1891, and the initial lectures on geography at the Imperial University were taught in the history department by Ludwig Riess and Tsuboi Kumezō (1858–1936).[34]

When geography was institutionalized at the Imperial Universities (1907 at Kyoto and 1911 at Tokyo), it was with a historical emphasis in Kyoto or through geological sciences at Tokyo. In short, space was now studied through a temporal epistemology. When geography finally gained a professorship at the Imperial University of Tokyo in 1911, it was in the College of Science. The first professor, Kōtō Bunjirō, was a student of Naumann and specialized in geology, geomorphology, and seismology. Ironically, it is the field of study that contributed to the temporalization of the archipelago and separated culture from nature that becomes the foundation for the new study of geography at the Imperial University. In other words, spatial forms became primarily significant as containers for temporal categories; they became "conceptual spaces with a history."

In spite of this denigration of space as an object of study, we must remember that these fields were important in one very significant way: they began the reconfiguration of space from the parts to the nation. Japan was becoming the container that needed to be filled with content—a nation. This was a goal of Ninagawa in the *Jinshin* survey, as well as Tsukamoto in his compilation of topographical data. In his essays on the history of the discipline of geography, Ishida Ryūjirō laments that the singular focus on the nation as the principal political and geographical unit was one of the reasons that geography developed more slowly than other social scientific disciplines. Yet this criticism is also indicative of the success in beginning the transformation of the unit of analysis from the local to the nation. For example, the *Nihon chishi teiyō* also reflects this space of Japan as the principal unit, shifting topographical studies from the locale to the locale as a part of a whole. Historical information, the data that had given the local flavor and emphasized peculiarities of place, became important to show commonalities, especially those that helped unify the nation rather than points of differentiation. On the other hand, the writing of a prehistory of the archipelago confirmed the presence of a Japan that can be traced back beyond the Pliocene era.

In establishing the place of the nation as the principal unit, the idea of Japan was becoming a natural space. The discovery of a history of the archipelago actually strengthened the idea of a Japan as an always existing entity. Even though all discussions of the archipelago now had to recognize geological change, it became possible to talk of the archipelago, a "Japan," prior to settlement. The chronology now extended into the prehistoric era confirmed the idea of Japanese islands as if they had always existed as Japan. This prehistoric chronology

[34]Tsuboi graduated from the College of Science (Yoshida 1982, 192–205).

then continued into the historic, that is, the founding of the imperium by Jimmu and the calculation of years from that date. Publications from public institutions during the 1870s, such as the *Nihon chishi teiyō* and Morse's essay, use the publication date 2534 (1874) and 2539 (1879). In short, as the archipelago gained chronology and deep time, it became a natural place, shorn of its historicity.

This reorientation of space, or the "emptying of space," destabilized the categories and connections that had given meaning and content to places within the archipelago, now a unit. As the discovery of a prehistoric past severed the environment from culture, it exposed the limitations of the inherited knowledge forms in mediating what Blumenberg has called the absolutism of reality. We must remember that these myths existed, not because they were old or tied to some beginning, but because they "worked," that is, they alleviated anxiety in ways that connected to the humans. These stories stabilized their lives by "explaining" the unknown in ways that connected to their lives. But the discovery that the archipelago has an autonomous past separated nature from culture and destabilized these stories. In the next chapter I will turn to some of the agents, spirits and tales that had to be exorcised in this increasingly abstract world of rationality and science.

Chapter 2

"NOTHING IS THE WAY IT SHOULD BE"

> An enquiry into "time" . . . is a useful point of departure for
> the great spring-cleaning that is long overdue. there is always
> a need for it when an intellectual tradition providing the basic
> means of orientation within its societies has run its course for
> several centuries, as ours has from the (so-called) Renaissance
> to the present time.
>
> —Norbert Elias (1992)

THE GEOLOGICAL DISCOVERIES exposed a past separate from culture and destabilized those categories that had been used to allay fear and anxiety, that is, how
people were acquainted with what they could not control. But an awareness
of a natural history separate from human time and of some linear time, called
progress, does not ensure easy social adjustment to this discovery. Ninagawa's
preservationism showed some of this new awareness and interest in the past, but
it was limited by its reliance on the inherited knowledge that tied culture to
nature. More revolutionary change, "spring cleaning," was called for:

> Once the fact of geological change had been admitted, questions about the tempo-
> ral sequence of those changes were inescapable: what agencies were responsible,
> whether they were the same as those now acting, how long they had taken to pro-
> duce their visible effects. In their turn, these historical questions led to further re-
> search, and so to more discoveries, which rebounded once again on inherited ideas
> and assumptions. (Toulmin and Goodfield 1965, 142)

The cascade of uncertainty and the inquiry into virtually all "inherited ideas
and assumptions" is certainly applicable to Meiji society. Few questioned (I
have not seen any attempts to disprove this geological time) the idea that the climate and indeed contours of the land were considerably different in prehistoric
times. But to accept this temporality means that one must confront the very idea
that the environment and all inhabitants are the creation of the gods (or God).
The inherited ideas and assumptions that became suspect go back to the earliest extant accounts, the *Kojiki* and *Nihon shoki*. On one level, this problem is
not too much different from that of Ō no Yasumaro, the compiler of the *Kojiki*,
one of those foundational texts that had established the understanding of the
archipelago for more than a millenium. Yasumaro records his directive from
Emperor Temmu:

I hear that the *Teiki* and *Honji* handed down by the various houses have come to differ from the truth and that many falsehoods have been added to them. . . .

This is the framework of the state, the great foundation of the imperial influence.

Therefore, recording the *Teiki* and examining the *Kuji*, discarding the mistaken and establishing the true, I desire to hand them on to later generations. (Philippi 1967, 41)

Yasumaro's chronicles provided a temporality that was suitable for that world, one of spirits, gods, myths, and historical tales. Past was not separated from present; ghosts and spirits provided people with a way to deal with the prevalence of death and the mysterious (in a world without the certitude of science) and even suggested ways of acting to allay that fear. They were part of the conceptual system that helped to explain the uncertainty (though certainly not control it) and myriad unusual events that permeated the environment. Histories, on the other hand, alleviate the fear of disorder and chaos and also prescribe behavior to avoid such catastrophe. Just as Yasumaro's task can be likened to Elias's "great spring cleaning," the Meiji is another moment of discarding the mistaken and establishing the true. But it also involved a transformation of how people experienced objects and events, of "reality," no longer as wonder (myth) but as artifacts of the past.

The result will be the secular and antiseptic modern world we know today. Thomas Richards describes this transformation as "the role the science of form, or morphology, played in imagining a unitary natural world in which there would no longer be any room for monstrosity" (Richards 1993, 45). These "evils" or "monstrosities" take on numerous forms, but here I will discuss the two that were fundamental parts of societies on the archipelago: ghosts and histories. By discarding these "mistaken" ideas, the ghosts, spirits, heroes, and gods were calmed and turned into artifacts of the past; they became dead texts. This is a necessary condition to formulating a new truth in modern society.

SPACE OF EXPERIENCE: SHUTEN DŌJI

Today our division of human sensibilities into religion, folklore, mythology, psychology, and so forth is part of the fragmentation that emerged with the onset of *Neuzeit*. I have been struck in reading about medieval and nonmodern societies how inappropriate (or nonexistent) these categories are for discussing the ideas and constitution of each society. To get ahead of my story, these disciplines are the new categories that reinscribe meaning onto the abstract time of modern societies. What we today call mythology, folklore, and religion were key components of the knowledge system that enveloped people's lives in pre-Meiji societies. Ichirō Hori describes early life on the archipelago: "These unsystematized popular beliefs play various roles in the lives of the people, such as enabling decision of behavior or temporal resolution of daily anxiety. . . . the social meaning

of such superstitious or popular beliefs should be reexamined because they regulate the conduct of a great number of persons" (1968, 46).

A difficulty in writing about nonmodern forms of knowledge outside of modern categories, such as folklore, superstition, and belief, is the vastly different
world they occupied, one that I find rather difficult to conceptualize.[1] We must
remember that what we today call Japanese religions—Buddhism and Shinto—
were part of a different categorical system. These practices were not separated
from spirits, demons, and ghosts; they were intertwined and were part of an eschatological world, where life was organized as "spaces of experience."[2] In pre-
Meiji societies, ghosts and magic were identified and recognized through
names that acquainted people with the inexplicable, the relation between humans and nature in both peasant and aristocratic societies. They served as scape-
goats to blame misfortune and as supernatural agents to attribute good fortune.
Many ghosts were tied to agriculture, where the holidays of the lunar calendar
marked the rich heritage of rituals placating the spirits connected to the growing
season (Hori 1968, 21). Once recognized, they could be pacified through rituals and prayers. Appeals to the particular bodhisattva and kami were constantly
made to ward off misfortune brought on by mischievous spirits, demons, and
ghosts. Blumenberg points out that the significance of myth (like the *Kojiki*) is
in its naming function; it acquaints people with objects and phenomena. He
writes: "So the earliest and not the least reliable form of familiarity with the
world is to find names for what is undefined. Only then and on the strength of
that can a story be told about it." Naming offers familiarity, but more important,
it orients people in their interactions. It does not extend to certainty and predictability, but as in the *Kojiki* it does have the potential to determine truth
(1985, 35).

The connection between mystical, naming, and trust also pervades what had
been "historical reality" up to the Meiji era. Though this might reflect my my-
opia as a historian of the modern world, I have been struck by the different
boundaries that demarcated human existence. First, unusual weather and natural disasters were usually discussed in combination with some ghost or spirit.
Second, there is a similarity in these stories between humans, ghosts, and spirits.
Of course, this does not signify a corporeality, but that the conceptual sphere of
ghosts and spirits contained a humanlike quality; they had the same qualities
and failings as humans. Ghosts became humans, humans became ghosts. The
past coexisted with the present; indeed, there was no separation. Moreover, they
were unpredictable; it was unclear when or under what circumstances they
would appear, help, or hurt people. People did not necessarily "believe" that
they existed; instead, the named phenomena acquainted them with a "reality"
for which they had no alternative explanation. This was an other world, one in

---

[1] For a fascinating and provocative inquiry into belief, see Asad (1993).
[2] See, for example, Hearn (1971); and Lowell (1984). For images of ghosts, see Addiss (1985).

which the idea of the human interacted with the spirits and where past lived on in the present. Naming provided a framework to control these worlds of very, very different material conditions that existed. In his meditation on the dying, Norbert Elias writes that "life in medieval feudal states was . . . passionate, violent, and therefore uncertain, brief and wild" (1985, 13). Even though he is describing Europe, this passage seems relevant to pre-Meiji communities on the archipelago. Misfortune was probably more the norm than the exception. Death was prevalent, and peasants' livelihood, even assuming sufficient land to sustain a family, was tied to climate and natural disaster.

The story of Shuten dōji is an example of such a different epistemology of the relation between humans as well as between humans and nature. It certainly does not suggest an autonomous ontogenic being. The name translates as sake-drinking child. Shuten dōji and his compatriots are "children," but their role is not that of the "child," but of a hidden world from which inexplicable events emanate. Shuten dōji was a powerful ghost who lived on Mt. Ōe (ghosts and spirits usually dwelled in the mountains in pre-Meiji Japan) near Kyoto and terrorized the region during the reign of Emperor Ichijō (986–1011).[3] This popular story has been the subject of nō, kabuki, bunraku, picture scrolls, otogizōshi, and more recently children's books.[4]

Although the beginning varies, I will start in 989 with a tornado that hit Kyoto. Soon thereafter people—male and female, rich and poor, near and far—began disappearing. People in the capital prayed for a return to peace. Fujiwara no Michinaga, who lost his son, consulted the most powerful diviner, Abe no Seimei. Abe discerned the cause: the demon who lives on Mt. Ōe to the northwest. He prescribed prayer to the gods and deities (shinbutsu), and Michinaga summoned Minamoto no Raikō to quell the demons. During the six months that Raikō prayed to the gods at Sumiyoshi, Kumano, and Hachiman shrines, he had a dream that divulged a strategy to subdue the demons.

After embarking, Raikō divulged his dream and a plan of action to his companions Fujiwara no Yasumasa and the shitennō (Watanabe no Gengotsuna, Sakata no Kintoki, Urabe no Suetake, and Usui no Sadamitsu). They would proceed alone, disguised as lost yamabushi (mountain ascetics)[5] to trick the demons into letting them stay the night. On the way, they met three old men who helped guide them up the mountain and also gave them a special sake that

[3] Komatsu Kazuhiko writes that Shuten dōji was the most powerful ghost, an interesting comment. Scholars debate the precise dates of his appearance. According to one story, Shuten dōji appeared in Kyoto around 987–88 and moved to Ōeyama on 9/16/990. According to another story, Shuten dōji and his buddies terrorized the capital and surrounding villages between 990 and 994. See also Satake (1977). Ōeyama no shuten dōji is a new version; it is an attempt to prolong the life of the story, taking advantage of the popularity of folklore and ghost stories.

[4] My summary follows Komatsu, who builds his story from the oldest written account, the Shuten dōji emaki from the Itsuo Bijutsukan.

[5] These priests were said to possess magical powers against evil beings.

"when consumed, gives humans the strength of a hundred and paralyzes demons" (*Ōeyama no shuten doji*, 15). Then, deeper in the mountain, they met an old woman washing the blood-stained clothes of maidens whom the demons had consumed; she provided information about the fortress. She, too, was originally kidnapped by Shuten dōji to be eaten, but because her bones were large and muscles hard, she was ordered to wash clothes instead. She had been there for two hundred years.

When they first saw Shuten dōji, he appeared as a child (*dōji*) with considerable wisdom. He was taken in by their ruse to be *yamabushi* and invited them to a banquet. There, the samurai gave the demons the magical sake, waited for it to take effect, put on their armor, and attacked. During the conquest, Shuten dōji changed form, from childlike to a huge demon with red body and head, black left leg and white right leg, green left arm and yellow right arm, fifteen eyes, and five horns. The samurai succeeded in decapitating Shuten dōji, but his head flew up, twirled around, screaming, and landed on Raikō's helmet. The victorious samurai returned to Kyoto in a triumphant procession led by the decapitated head mounted on a platform and followed by the freed maidens.

This story, unbelievable as it is, is indicative of an epistemology quite alien to us today. I do not argue that all people necessarily believed that Shuten dōji existed, but the fact that the story of Shuten dōji has been adapted to so many media, and that it has continued through to today, indicates that it offers some significance. It has the durability of many myths, both for its constancy and for its mutability to different forms and locales.[6] Part of its significance is to make the inexplicable from a hidden world visible. When we view this myth for its orienting function, rather than whether it fits our categories of knowledge, it corresponds to characteristics we know about early societies. For example, Shuten dōji's abode in the mountains is typical of early societies on the archipelago where mountains bore some sacred or spiritual value. Mountains were often the site for the soul of the dead and angry spirits. Some active, volcanic mountains, such as Asama and Fuji, bore sacred value for both their destructive and life-giving powers (Hori 1968, 141–79; Earhart 1989, 205–26). Second, Kyoto at the end of the tenth century was in decline. The western half of the city was in ruins and virtually uninhabited. Official buildings were often poorly maintained, and fire and epidemic frequently plagued the city (Sansom 1958, 195–96). Third, ritual, prayer, and divination were integral parts of society.

The story of Shuten dōji indicates a quite different conceptualization of difference, of otherness. He is not some fixed boundary, an "Other" to the human "Same." He exists in both worlds, easily entering Kyoto to kidnap his victims and returning to his mountain palace. While Shuten dōji is monstrous, the agency of this story is in the human and humanlike, which makes it meaningful to a

---

[6] The most recent variation of which I am aware is the *anime* series by the name Shuten dōji, but rendered now as Starhand Kid.

space of experience. Time is not the principal marker. In this world, past and present are not clearly demarcated; Shuten dōji, a ghost of the dead (as a child), is haunting the present (as a ghost); he is over two hundred years old, yet still a child; and the woman washing clothes has been there for over two hundred years. This alter provides agency for the unknown: "horror and shuddering, sudden fright and the frantic insanity of dread, all receive their form in the demon" (quoted in Diamond 1996, 63). Death was prevalent, but it was less a fear of death as today than a belief that the dead became spirits. Hori states that "people were afraid of spirits of the dead, who preyed upon them. All social and personal crises . . . were believed to be the result of the vengeance of angry spirits of the dead" (1968, 72).

Moreover, Shuten dōji suggests a different understanding of the child and the human being. Childhood in early Meiji Japan bore more similarity to Wolfgang Edelstein's description of the child in premodern rural Europe than to modern Japan: "the bond of meaning and mutual responsibility [is] in a world of work that does not know childhood as an age of play but, rather, an age of transient functional imperfection" (1983, 59). Isabella Bird's description in 1878 of Japanese children as "little men and women rather than children" indicates a similar world of transient functional imperfection (1974, 80). Children did not exist as future citizens, but as members of their locale. Prior to the Meiji period, childhood was not a unifying category that rendered children as some empty vessel, a metaphor for some romantic period, or an early stage of human development. Children were considered godlike and not yet subject to the rules of human society. Seven, as reflected in a proverb that children are "among the gods until seven," was a watershed year, marked by recognition paid to the gods. This observance was conducted in the home.[7]

This understanding of children as godlike and human is tied to the simultaneity of past and present. Death was ever present. Infant mortality was high, and life expectancy throughout classes was low. A reasonable estimate is that about half of children born reached their fifth year. This is similar to Europe, where historian Keith McManners (1981) estimates that between 40 and 65 percent (depending on region) reached their tenth year.[8] Moreover, infants (and people) with unusual or nonhumanlike attributes were often marginalized from society. Shuten dōji is said to have been a child genius and thus was expelled from the human world. Here, like other spirit mediums, some mental or physiological difference is evidence of spirit possession, not of variation of the human body.

---

[7] Children were generally naked, kept warm within the clothes of the caregiver until the age of three (Kuroda 1989, 89–94). Although not rigidly codified, samurai marked changes at the third year by no longer shaving children's hair; at five, boys received a *hakama*, the traditional skirtlike pants; and at seven, girls began wearing the *obi* (the girdlelike sash).

[8] For studies that discuss mortality rates in Japan, see Hanley and Yamamura (1977, 243–44); Sasaki (1985); and Morris and Smith (1985).

Finally, this story also explains unusual and abnormal happenings. According to a chronological listing of earthquakes recorded throughout Japanese history, in 989, the third year of Eien, a comet appeared, natural disaster struck (*tenpen*), and an earthquake shook the capital. Not all versions of this tale begin in 989, but all do start with various natural disasters that befell upon Kyoto. In this way, Shuten dōji indicates the conceptual markers of that society, where unusual events were attributed to demons who deceived the unwary and could be pacified through the wisdom of the gods and deities. Interestingly, even though the demons could not be controlled at that time, time could start anew; on the eighth day of the eighth month a new era, Eiso, was declared, purifying the present of the uncertainty wrought by those calamities that had stricken Eien.[9]

NATURE AS A MACHINE

These worlds that Shuten dōji exemplify were completely transformed by the discovery of pasts. Shuten dōji was a story that "named" inexplicable phenomena, including natural disasters. The cosmos was not a vast, open, always silent space, but a world in which all things possessed a spirit that was capable of being acted upon and acting upon mankind. The cosmos was active, and the "past" was alive and active in the present; demons, spirits, and mischievous creatures were the agents of unusual and otherwise inexplicable calamity or fortune.[10] Mountains usually possessed some kind of sacred or spiritual value. The dead were believed to reside there, as did mountain ascetics, the itinerant Buddhist priests who served as mediators between the known and spiritual worlds.

The separation of nature from culture destabilized such inherited understandings that had organized society and raised the possibility that the texts and knowledge that had been accepted as natural or originary are cultural, that is, created. The transformation that emerged did not eradicate the "evil past" but instead relocated parts (that is, gave them new meaning) along an emerging understanding of developmental or progressive time. But interestingly, the historicization of society emerged from science, not from the field of knowledge we now call history. In particular, the geological sciences, and later psychology, were crucial to understanding those "laws and mechanisms" that are both "complex and independent" from nature.

---

[9] This interaction of natural disaster and time recalls Michel Serres's reminder that the French word *le temps* means time and weather. Serres argues that time is not linear, but an "extraordinarily complex mixture" with "stopping points, ruptures, deep wells, chimneys of thunderous acceleration, rendings, gaps" (1995, 57).

[10] The ideographs for *jishin* (earthquake) are read as *naifuru* in old texts. Kigu Yasuhiko suggest two possible etymologies: (1) the source (*nai*) of rumbling; or (2) in popular society, the place where fish (*na*) shake (1937, 1).

Up through the nineteenth century, geological events such as earthquakes were blamed on mischievous spirits: in the ancient and early modern periods, they were often attributed to a giant earth spider, and soon after the Ansei earthquake, which devastated Edo on the second day of the tenth month of 1855, woodblock prints of catfish (*namazu-e*) appeared for the first time, clearly attributing the destruction to a giant catfish.[11] The idea of catfish is consistent with the use of the fantastic—ghosts and supernatural animals—to explain abnormal happenings. According to lore, the catfish was kept under control by the Kashima deity, who used a sword and the pivot stone (*kaname-ishi*). But the catfish was also a bearer of gold and silver. Thus the catfish was both destroyer and restorer, one who brought misfortune and fortune. Indeed, some of the *namazu-e* connect the catfish with *yonaoshi*, the millenarian idea of world renewal on the rise at the end of the Tokugawa period. The text of one print declares, "Taking advantage of the absence of the gods, the good-for-nothing catfish played his pranks and then remedied the subsequent destruction; world renewal, world renewal, reconstruction" (Ouwehand 1964, 16). The pervasiveness of this idea of *yonaoshi* is evident in the 1891 Gifu earthquake, where seismologist John Milne recorded: "At one place they shouted '*jishin! jishin!*'—'Earthquake! Earthquake!'—and at another '*yonaori! yonaori!*'—implying that something has disturbed the universe (*yo* universe, *naori* to be repaired)" (Milne and Burton 1894, plate 11).

The geological research of men like Milne and Naumann was instrumental in demystifying this amalgamation of the human, natural, and spiritual worlds by bringing in the abstract arena of science. These scientists were hired by the new government to teach modern ideas and industry to the new nation-state. Both were also participants in the worldwide quest of late-nineteenth-century geology to know the origin of mountains and the corollaries, volcanoes and earthquakes, and both made important contributions to an understanding of these forces in Japan as well as in their respective fields (see, e.g., Oreskes 1999, 10). The accounts of Milne's and Naumann's expeditions clearly juxtapose the ideas of the locales as superstitious in comparison to their science. In other words, geology turns inherited forms of knowledge into textual forms; practices to ward off disaster became superstitions, a time-concept that relegated ghosts and wonder to a "scriptural tomb."

In 1877 Milne and Naumann investigated a volcanic eruption on the island of Oshima outside of Tokyo Bay, though they wrote reports separately. Both reports

---

[11] One samurai recalled the destruction: "As I emerged from the gate, I had an extensive view of the city, and saw flames burning forth far and near in every quarter. When I reached the foot of the hill on which the Palace stood, I found the streets utterly impassable. The roofs of the houses on both sides had fallen into them, and from beneath the debris the cries of men, women, and children were heard on all sides calling for others to come to their rescue" (Hattori 1878, 268–69). One estimate of casualties in this earthquake exceeded 200,000 killed (Ouwehand 1964, 3), but Hattori believes that to be grossly exaggerated (269–70).

on the geological structure of active volcanoes are rather prosaic, that is, scientific and objective. As part of the science of volcanoes, these reports have little scientific value today, but they are of value both for an understanding of history of geology and for my purpose, the relation between geological discoveries and the transformation of society. Milne's contrast between himself, the scientist, and the natives suggests the transformation of systems of understanding:

> Coming, as we did, so suddenly upon the precipice-like edge of a huge black cauldron, roaring, shaking the ground, and ejecting a dense column of red-hot stones and ashes, the wild and dismal aspect of which was heightened by dark clouds, driving rain, and a heavy mist, produced at first a feeling of timidity, which was so strongly shown by our six so-called guides that it was with difficulty they were prevented from taking to precipitate flight. (1877, 197)[12]

The guides were islanders whom Milne and his party had hired to lead them to the summit. Milne writes that none of the locals had been to the crater, despite living only four miles away, and they feared going to the summit.[13] The picture of the locals is of ignorant people; this trope of timidity and superstition is common in travel and exploration writings of the time. But despite Milne's celebratory description, he also recognizes the very different conceptual worlds; for the locals, the mountain is a sacred part of their world and lives, while for the Westerners, it is an object to observe and describe. At the end of the article he writes that the locals had been to the summit: "From the inhabitants we learnt that the mountain is regarded as being holy, and that at certain seasons they make solitary pilgrimages to its summit. We, however, had been the first to see the eruption" (199).

The volcano has no spiritual power over Milne; it is an object to be observed. His "seeing" meant actually looking into the crater:

> The great interest in this eruption lay in the fact that we were able, on account of our position, to look down into the crater. In the intervals between the ejections the interior could be well seen, and it was observable that the sides had a slope of nearly the same inclination as the exterior. . . . At each explosion [molten lava] rose in waves, and swayed about heavily like a huge basin of mercury. . . . The explosions, which I have referred to several times as resembling outbursts of steam, might be compared to the escape of steam from a slowly-working non-condensing steam engine greatly magnified. (197)

In Milne's description, the eruption is like a machine, a "slowly-working non-condensing steam engine." His descriptions are filled with various forms of mat-

---

[12] For Milne's discovery in context with seismology, see Herbert-Gustar and Nott (1980).
[13] Milne attributes this fear to ignorance of the path up the mountain, "After struggling along for nearly two hours, we found that the men we had engaged as guides did not know the road and were leading us round the island rather than up towards the crater" (195).

ter—ash, rain, lapilli, etc.—that had to be activated by energy—heat. This is not accurate by today's understanding; his discovery followed existing geological knowledge, thereby authenticating his findings. Thus the prevalence of steam reinforced contemporary scientific views that water, turned into steam and trapped underground, was the principal cause of volcanoes. This theory was also reported by Tsuda Mamichi in 1874. Tsuda, who was one of the first Japanese to receive an education in Europe (Netherlands), wrote an essay on earthquakes in the *Meiroku zasshi*, the premier journal expounding enlightenment, in which he stated that "Westerners compare volcanoes to the escape valves of boilers" (in Braisted 1976, 220).[14]

One year later, Milne built upon his observation at Oshima as well as throughout Japan to speculate on the formation of volcanic mountains. "I think we are justified in regarding mountains, similar to those about which I am now writing [conical ones like Mt. Fuji, Kumagatake, Oshima, and Vesuvius], as having a form mainly due to the simple piling up of material, and not as cones which have been subsequently modified by a number of secondary causes" (1878, 343). In other words, mountains too are but matter created by energy; they have not always existed (that is, were not created by the gods) but have emerged over time.

In 1880 in Tokyo, Milne shifted his attention to earthquakes, and it is for this work that he is most famous. Shortly after experiencing a tremor, he began to systematically collect information on the effects of earthquakes, trying to determine their direction and source. As a part of this effort he organized the Seismological Society of Japan, which held its first meeting on April 26. This work quickly evolved—with the support of the government—into instruments that measure tremors, and with the help of two professors of engineering, James Alfred Ewing and Thomas Gray, he developed a seismograph, which became known as the Gray-Milne seismograph. Milne eventually had over a thousand centers in Japan sending information about tremors in the local region. He also had a plan to equip the telegraph offices on the Musashi plain with seismographs so that he could precisely measure the time, location, and direction of the tremors (Herbert-Gustar and Nott 1980, 78). But we must not transpose our understanding to Milne. Milne's description of the volcanoes as well as the measurement of earthquakes and tremors accelerated the demystification and objectification of the Earth, but measurement and more knowledge did not eliminate catfish, but trivialized such "old" beliefs as evidence of "primitiveness" and drowned those stories in a mountain of data. As important as Milne's work was toward advancing the understanding of earthquakes, it was still highly speculative; in his book *Earthquake*, he still speculated that a buildup of steam

---

[14] Tsuda's purpose too was to use this knowledge to expose the fantastic nature of popular understanding of earthquakes in Meiji Japan.

was a principal cause, as was the "general process of mountain formation" (1886, 277–96).

We also should be careful not to extend Milne's trope of superstition and timidity to all of what would become Japanese culture. In his studies, Milne pointed out the commonality of attributing earthquakes to supernatural beings: "Throughout all history we find speculations as to the cause of these terrible disturbances. Almost every nation, from the Kamchadales to the Patagonians, has its myth explaining the origin of Earthquakes, many of them attributing these movements to the unruly behaviour of some monster or god imprisoned beneath the earth" (Milne and Burton 1894, 2; Milne 1886, 7). On this level, those parts of the population that believed in the sacredness of volcanoes might fit this category of "primitive" by standards of enlightenment.[15] But it is important to remember that many educated Japanese (as in the case of the educated in Europe), such as Tsuda, sought more rational reasons.

This discovery of a natural history involved more than the synchronization of the archipelago into a global knowledge system, what would soon become known as "world time" (Dohrn-van Rossum 1996, 348–50). It also began the emptying of the spaces of experience.[16] The work of these earth scientists is in some ways like the masses tearing down the edifices of power, the temples and Buddhist icons. They were releasing themselves from those traditions that had enveloped and restricted them. Carolyn Merchant's description of the mechanization of nature is apt: "The removal of animistic, organic assumptions about the cosmos constituted the death of nature—the most far-reaching effect of the Scientific Revolution. Because nature was now viewed as a system of dead, inert particles moved by external, rather than inherent forces, the mechanical framework itself could legitimate the manipulation of nature" (1980, 193).

At this point, the separation of nature from culture leads to two different types of knowledge forms.[17] On the one hand, the inert particles become the matter of science, to be exploited (that is, controlled) by man. We must remember that these earth scientists were hired by the new government to teach at the new universities, to survey the land, and to identify natural resources. They were part of a broader endeavor to understand and utilize a land that had been primarily organized around local knowledge. The rapid development of copper mining at

[15] Even Kant wrote skeptically on the human potential to control earthquakes: "From the Prometheus of modern times, Mr. Franklin, who wanted to disarm the thunder, to the person who wants to extinguish the fire in Vulcan's workshop, all such efforts are evidence of man's daring, which is joined to a capacity that is very small in proportion to it, and finally lead him to the humbling recollection—with which he would have done well to begin—that he is, after all, never anything more than a man" (quoted in Blumenberg 1985, 569).

[16] See also David Harvey's discussion of situated space, where he discusses Leibniz, whose ideas embed a conception of space and time that was relational, that is, that both existed only "from the substances and processes they contained" (1996, 250–61, quote from 251).

[17] For a more complete account of the idea of nature in Meiji Japan see Thomas (2001).

Ashio, as well as the tragic pollution, was an outcome of this new attitude.[18] Now, natural occurrences were studied independent of the local communities and the knowledge that had connected the two. Mountains were severed from the local landscape and the spirits that resided there, and the sacredness of mountains, such as Oshima was simply ignored. Even though causes were still unknown, everything was to be observed, measured, and catalogued into geological and paleontological categories. In short, the archipelago was being emptied of the ideas that had given meaning to the spaces of experience of communities there.

On the other hand, the stories that had accounted for natural phenomena were increasingly seen as fictions of the primitive or immature human mind. Eventually, these stories would become preserved and categorized as historical evidence of the blank space of a Japan. But for now, it is perhaps fitting that on June 14, 1878, the *Tokyo eiri shinbun* reported that an Englishman living in Kobe shot a giant catfish, over fifteen feet long. The catfish was reportedly far from the *kaname ishi* of Kashima. Despite being wounded, it escaped the Englishman, but it was discovered two days later near Himeji by three fishermen from Ishizu village in Senshū. According to the paper, they attempted to take the catfish to the local natural history exhibition (*hakurankai*) (Yumoto 1999, 121–22).

(An)Other View: Durability of the Imprinted Form

As geologists were surveying the archipelago, and as other Europeans and Americans were helping the new state establish a new infrastructure, the locals, too, observing these strangers, were exposed to examples of civilization. Moreover, the 1870s was a decade in which the new government completely changed the political and economic contours of their lives. In addition to the calendrical reforms, the Dajōkan ordered a new household registration survey; consolidated the approximately 270 domains into 72 prefectures (*ken*) and 3 urban administrative districts (*fu*), which included changes in local authorities; imposed compulsory elementary education; transformed the taxation system; and began conscripting young men (usually peasants) for the new military.[19] But exposure to enlightenment and its purveyors often confirmed the validity of the inherited knowledge.

The power of this imprinted form is obvious to us as we look back upon peoples who failed to change and to become more like us. Local sightings of *ijin* (strangers) confirmed for them the presence of demons who bring misfortune, but to us, it is proof of their ignorance. In early Meiji society the idea of foreigner

[18] For a discussion of the Ashio pollution incident, see Notehelfer (1975) and Strong (1977).
[19] In 1889 the number of prefectures was reduced to 42.

did not necessarily signify a non-Japanese. Instead, it was used for people or things that were from outside the community. As Kawamura Kunimitsu (1990) points out, the word *ijin* could be used to categorize people of another community, itinerants, ghosts, demons, animals with supernatural powers, as well as foreigners. Demons, like Shuten dōji, and catfish were identifiable forms that could account for agency—that is, who caused such a disaster—in a nonscientific world.

It is less obvious to us when our own imprinted form constricts our understanding of history. Despite historians' efforts to downplay the Meiji *Ishin* as a political change led by a small band of samurai and as a transition relatively free from violence, the decades before and after the *Ishin* witnessed considerable unrest.[20] Such arguments that emphasize samurai and ignore or trivialize quite violent popular outbursts suggest ways that historians have protected what Blumenberg (1985) calls "the unrecognized preestablished patterns."[21] To give but one example, the Takeichi riot, which broke out on the eighth month of 1871 in Hiroshima, lasted for over two months; approximately twenty-five people were killed and over two hundred homes, especially those of village headmen, were destroyed. Such disturbances did not necessarily support nor oppose the new government. They are better seen as the anxiety of people toward new, "acute experiences." People were trying to make sense of their changing situated space, to which both the old and new governments were related. These riots indicate both the confluence of different conceptual systems and the initial stages of the transformation of social boundaries, from those situated spaces of local communities to the abstract space of a nation. In short, the Meiji *Ishin* was much more than a political change; it also encompassed the very concept of society and culture.

This connection between such acute experiences and the imprinted form is evident in a riot in Kōchi on *ōmisoka*, the last day of 1871. Earlier in the year, a mountain ascetic spread a rumor of a divine message that connected political change with the idea of *ijin* and the foreigner. There were four parts to the message: (1) the abolition of the positions of village headmen and elders and their replacement by district magistrates indicated favoritism toward strangers (*ijin*); (2) Japanese were being sold as slaves or prostitutes to the hairy foreigners (*ketō-jin*), and this trade was fostered by corrupt officials who used the household survey and received commissions for their deeds; (3) the recall of the old leaders to

---

[20] See, for example, Umegaki (1986). For an argument for the rather broad base of unrest that surrounded the change, see Wilson (1992). Studies that focus on local change suggest much more discontent and protest than those that take a Japan as the unit of analysis. See Kelly (1985), Baxter (1994), and Bowen (1980).

[21] Blumenberg writes: "It ties acute experiences and important current events into the context of long familiarity and creates prefiguration, but also a decrease in the expectation of freedom, a decrease in what is conceded to candor and ultimate self-knowledge, since these come under the protection of the unrecognized preestablished patterns" (1985, 95).

the capital was a result of their opposition to this injustice; and (4) in their brutal lands, the ugly barbarians (*shūi*) throw bodies into fires, liquefy the fat, and drink it (Satake 1977, 209–12). As in the story of Shuten dōji, these rumors are rather incredulous to us today. Yet they do fit the orienting function that connects the new and unknown to prefigured knowledge. Three of these items were directly connected to administrative changes that fostered the increasing penetration of the central government into the locales: the transfer of administration from village headmen to district magistrates; the abolition of domains and the reorganization of locales into prefectures, with the new governors being appointed by the central government; and a household survey, probably the most immediately threatening.[22] The fourth item was confirmed by various sightings that provided "empirical" verification.

One of the interesting aspects of international encounters that we too often forget is that "understanding" of others emerges through the inherited knowledge of the viewer.[23] This was certainly true for the archipelago during the 1870s; for as Americans and Europeans were traveling throughout the territory describing the people and land through temporal categories, such as primitive, quaint, charming, and simple, local inhabitants often viewed these outsiders through their understanding of strangers. In other words, the principal boundary was community and *ijin*, not nation and foreigner. In short, the distinctions of the modern world, which eradicates the nonrational, depends on a clear separation of the past (dead) from the present, and demarcates foreigners as the principal outsiders, were not operating at this time.

In the early 1870s, numerous "eyewitness" reports circulated throughout the archipelago of strange beings (*ketōjin*) who drank a deep red liquid that looked like blood and ate fat (meat with fat). These were more than rumors: Kawamura has connected geological surveys by Westerners with disturbances in Okayama and Tottori that broke out after their visit (1990, 19–21). In other words, Westerners were not examples of new civilized ideas and processes, but verified the idea of *ijin*. In addition, institutions of the new regime often verified inherited knowledge; a new hospital built near Kōchi city was equipped with beds (made with iron grids) that locals rendered as grills for the extraction of fat from the sick (Satake 1977, 211–12). The rumors of outsiders coming in and "stealing fat" were prevalent around 1871 and 1872; they were connected to fears that young women would be sold or abducted. (This is not a too far-fetched way of thinking about the human as a commodity, now labor, nor an interpretation of the recruiters seeking factory workers.) In contrast, the announcement of conscription in 1873 used the word "blood tax." Subsequent rumors and disturbances sought

---

[22] This household survey, which was the first attempt of the new government in the seventh month of 1870 to gain a more accurate picture of population and production, collected information on topography, households and local products (Mizuchi 1994, 75–94).

[23] For a fine study that lays out the dialectics of intercultural understanding, see Howland (1996).

to prevent the abduction of men. The blood-tax riots erupted in 1873 in Okayama and Kagawa prefectures in the year following the implementation of the draft (11/1872).

We might dismiss these accounts as superstition of the ignorant and vulgar (which is indeed how they were handled by the authorities),[24] but we must remember that such accounts of eyewitnesses were placed within the knowledge structure of the time, thereby verifying the rumors. One such category was the connection of an appearance of a stranger with life-taking phenomena, blood-sucking, removal of body fat, child abduction, or kidnapping. The rumors that set off these riots bear a resemblance to the story of Shuten dōji (abduction and the prevalence of blood), and more closely to lore that tied Buddhist mystical powers to the pacification of demons that pervaded Japan. For example, many of the rumors seem to follow the general contours of the story, "How the Great Teacher Jikaku Went to Tie-Dyeing Castle," in the *Uji shūi monogatari*.[25] It is a story about Jikaku's journey to a far-away land where innocents were befriended, tricked, trussed up, and their blood drained. In the more popular form of these stories about fat stealing, a common theme was the need for vigilance and a caution to the lazy who are the easy prey of those demons who steal fat (or blood). Since the longevity of myth is in its utility, not in any timeless characteristic, these myths explained the Americans and Europeans who drank wine, ate meat, and lived using strange implements and cautioned locals about conscription and labor, the beginnings of the commodified citizen/laborer. On the one hand, these myths acquainted locales with the unfamiliar by giving these encounters a "life-stabilizing quality" (Blumenberg 1985, 127). They do not provide all the answers but suffice to offer a possible mode of action that enables individuals to act to ward off misfortune. In the case of Shuten dōji, the power of Shinto mysticism over demons (outsiders), that is, prayer and adherence to ritual, might protect people. On the other hand, these myths also helped to solidify the community. They usually end with some ethical lesson: efficacy of following the ethical deeds of the heroes and/or the reform of the wayward, and the reinforcement of community boundaries (Satake 1977, 233). In the case of 1870s Japan, it was a way of warning people that misfortune might strike those who come into contact with the foreigners.

The conflation of foreigner with *ijin* does not mean that there was no conception of the foreign. Kawamura discusses the expedition to Taiwan (1872) as the beginning of a reformulation of the stranger. A separation between Taiwanese and Japanese did exist, but it was within a conceptual structure of barbarian (*yaban*) vs. civilized (*bunmei*), not the evil past (*kyūhei*) or primitive vs.

---

[24] The *Tokyo nichi nichi*, in reporting on many of these outbreaks, called them acts of ignorance (Satake 1977, 223).

[25] For this story, see Mills (1970, 390–93). According to Satake, Ihara Saikaku's *Honchō nijū fukō* also draws upon this tale.

enlightenment (*bunmeikaika*) (1990, 35). My point is that there were many modes of marking difference at this time, but one was not the temporal hierarchy that is common today. This places the reaction against Morse in greater context. The idea of cannibal was analogous to barbarian, and certainly by end of the 1870s Japan could not be at that opposite pole of civilized, on the same level as cannibals. Even though the idea of progress has not eliminated this issue of inferiority for Japanese, the resolution to this uncertainty was to give this inherited knowledge new meanings. Just as the separation of nature from culture turned nature into inert objects, it was necessary to eradicate the spirits, wonders, and mythical from the human world.

"Secrets of the Human World": Meiji Ghosts

In studies of modernization/Westernization of non-Western nation-states, most accounts follow some variation of opening, early infatuation and adaptation, conservative reaction, and finally, either the impartial institutionalization of liberal capitalism or the turn against it.[26] But rather than seeing the 1880s as a moment of conservative and nativist reaction, I prefer to characterize this decade as one of skepticism and formulation. Like Yasumaro, these intellectuals sought to "discard the mistaken and establish the true." Many were astute enough, however, to learn that both the inherited forms of knowledge that had organized society and Western forms of knowledge, especially the unreflected idealism of its promoters, are suspect.

The cascade of inquiry soon reached those ideas that had been foundational to societies on the archipelago. As early as 1878, Naka Michiyo had questioned the veracity of the accounts of early emperors and empresses in the *Kojiki* and *Nihon shoki* prior to Ingyō (412–53) (1991, 301). He proposed a revised chronology in 1888 and again in 1897. In 1882 Inoue Enryō suggested that Yao and Shun were mere idols of Confucianism created by later scholars, and in the following year he questioned whether Toyotomi Hideyoshi, prior to his attempted conquest of the Korean peninsula, really went to Itsukushima, threw a hundred coins, and prayed.[27] During the 1880s, numerous historical figures, "real" for centuries, were either debunked or lowered from their lofty status. And, in 1885, Mitsukuri Genpachi, an early historian of the West trained in zoology, wrote an essay introducing England's Psychical Society to question prevalence of divination, oracles, ghosts, fox possession, and so forth.

[26] An interesting critique of this process is Escobar (1995). Totman has provided a novel periodization of Japanese history in his *A History of Japan* (2000). For late-nineteenth-century Japan, see Gluck (1985).

[27] Enryō (1858–1919) was among the intellectual elite: he studied philosophy at Tokyo Imperial University, was a proponent of modern Buddhism, became famous for his ghost studies, *yōkaigaku*, was one of the first to write on psychology, and founded Tetsugakkan.

But even among the most skeptical and conservative, clearly the desire was to transform society into a modern place. We must remember that at this time, independent laws of modern society were still in process of articulation in the West as well as Japan. The transformation to the modern embeds a potentially contradictory process, the denigration of the immediate past and the necessity of a past, both to constitute the idea of a nation and to narrate a story of development or progress. Naka explains his exposure of the fictiveness of the earliest emperors and empresses as a "return to reality." He writes: "Overall, such doubtful points are dark clouds that obscure the facts of ancient history. For this reason, I cannot avoid suspicion of even the geneaology, deeds, and ethics recorded in the *Kojiki* and *Nihon shoki*. . . . The reason I do not accept the chronology in the *Kojiki* before Emperor Ingyō is to believe in the *Kojiki* and *Nihon shoki*" (1897, 1229–30). Intellectuals, leaders, and the masses had to determine which past (or inherited knowledges) needed to be eliminated and which was most apposite.

This was not a task of mere replacement. As the rumors of *ijin* and the subsequent protests suggest, exposure to enlightenment can reinforce the inherited forms rather than lead to their transformation. Even though the problem began as the application of science to society to effect that spring cleaning, work soon evolved into discerning which pasts should be retained and which could or should be forgotten. One effort to deal with this heterogeneity was through the field of knowledge that began as psychology and is today known as folklore. In 1886 Inoue Enryō, a student at Tokyo Imperial University, organized the Fushigi kenkyūkai (Mystery Research Society) and between 1893 and 1894 published the results of his surveys and research in his *Yōkaigaku kōgi* (Studies in Wonderology).[28] In the introduction to the eight-volume series, he writes:

> How is it that no one asks those who, amid the wonders of heaven and earth, shine a light on mysterious thinking and know the life of those humans? If so, those who see the majesty of all things in their life actually have the light of an enlightened mind; thus those who foster this light are the fuel (oil) of all learning. For this reason, academia is gradually advancing, the enlightened mind is gradually shining and getting brighter, and nature is more and more beautiful. How can those of us who are already enlightened shirk the learning of academia? For this reason last year I organized research on ghosts. (1979, 1:1)

Inoue's invocation of those independent laws is possible only because of an inert nature that no longer contains the mysterious and is separated from the "enlightened" mind. His invocation of the metaphor of oil to fuel enlightenment

---

[28] The members of this research group became central figures in the development of academia and science in Japan: Miyake Yūjirō (Setsurei), Tanaka Kanaikichi(tate) (physics), Mizukuri Genpachi (Western history), Yoshitake Reinoshin (chemistry), Hirai Masagoro (anthropology), Fukke Umetaro (agriculture and forestry), Tanahashi Ichirō (Chinese classics), and Tsubouchi Shōyō (literature). For a fine account of this transmutation of ghosts, see Figal (1999).

suggests the relation of this exorcism to the operation of a mechanical, productive society.

The purpose of this organization followed the lead of Mizukuri: to use various scientific disciplines to dispel the many practices, rituals, and beliefs that fit the category of mysterious things. In his introduction Inoue writes:

> We should point out that if we can extend the railroad of all learning and shine the light of knowledge onto the ignorant, for the first time we can completely succeed in the great enterprise of Meiji. Then, to achieve this goal, we must apply all learning, in other words, an inquiry into *yōkaigaku*. If the minds of nationals (*kokumin*) are opened to this new, enlightened realm [lit. "heaven and earth"] it is not an exaggeration to say that this great deed will not at all defer to the building of railroads and telegraphs. (1:2)

The language here is interesting; he mixes metaphors of mechanization and enlightenment with the condescending language of the Edo elite toward the *gumin* (foolish masses). But also, there is an awareness that the transformation of knowledge and practices has the same kind of materiality as railroads and telegraphs. A necessary step that follows this recognition is the need to transform the ways people think, that is, to turn *gumin* into *kokumin* (nationals). To carry out this research, Inoue turned to the nascent fields of psychology and ethnography. During this period, he walked throughout Japan searching for stories of strange and inexplicable phenomena (*fushigi*), visiting over 250 places in 48 prefectures. Through such travels, he became known throughout Japan as the professor of ghosts (*yōkai hakase*).

In 1894 and 1895 Inoue published two books targeted at a broad audience, *Kiokujutsu kōgi* (On Techniques of Memory) and *Shitsunenjutsu kōgi* (On Techniques of Forgetting), which combined his work on ghosts and psychology.[29] He writes: "Just as one must weed after sowing seeds, after one plants the seeds of new knowledge, one must remove myriad, useless ideas from the mind. The removal of such useless ideas is through techniques of forgetting" (1992, 356). Inoue was addressing the multiple temporalities of society, alluded to above, that "even though civilization and enlightenment advanced in structure (*seidō*) and form, they did not penetrate to the practices and superstitions at the base of commoner life" (Haryū 1987, 412). No doubt, he was disturbed by the riots and protests that claimed fat stealing and blood drinking by outsiders. But he seemed to understand that accusations of ignorance and appeals to civilization did not alter, indeed often verified, inherited knowledge. For Inoue, ghost studies was a way to address this heterogeneity directly. Psychology provided an alternate understanding of the mental processes that resolved the absolutism of reality, while ghost studies provided the case studies that demonstrated the

---

[29] In 1917 these were combined into *Shinkiokujutsu* (New Techniques of Memory). The "new" was intended to signify the elevation of forgetting.

power of science. Moreover, his frequent public lectures, the application of knowledge to everyday issues, and the formation of the Tetsugakkan (now Tōyō University) were all part of his effort to synchronize the rift between the masses and new political structure.

Inoue's interpretation depends upon the discursive separation between humans and nature. While he considers humans a part of the natural world, he also distances the human from the natural, "The human world is between the natural and the mysterious worlds" (1902, 97). Building on the ideas of Darwin and Spencer, he argues that at one time humans and animals shared the same ancestry, but through natural selection they have generally developed quite differently (1979, 2:248–52). But what separates them is that humans have the ability to understand more than their immediate surroundings, to discern those invisible principles in nature and the mysterious worlds. No longer is nature integral to their lives; it is now separate. Humans divide a single universe into a dualistic structure of matter and spirit. The mediating organ is the human mind.

One of the more forgotten aspects of Inoue's career is his work as a pioneer in psychology. One possible reason for this is that his psychology focused on the interaction between individuals and their sociocultural environment, recognizing the reflexivity that is involved. It is a psychology that emanated more from philosophy, probably Nishi Amane's translation of Joseph Haven's *Mental Philosophy* and Inoue Tetsujirō's translation of Alexander Bain. It is also a psychology more similar to what is called a sociocultural approach to psychology today than to the experimental psychology that entered Japan with the return in 1889 of Motora Yūjirō (1858–1912) from his study with G. Stanley Hall and of Matsumoto Matataro (1865–1943) from his work with Wilhelm Wundt.

Inoue Enryō's work is part of the transformation of the world into one that prioritizes abstract concepts as the governing criteria over experience. In his 1887 introduction to psychology, *Shinri tekiyō*, he divides the operation of the mind into three general categories: sensate, knowledge, and will (the blurring of philosophy and ethics with psychology was common at this time). The first two, he argues, operate in reaction to external stimuli, while the latter depends upon internal processes. Development occurs from simple sensate experience to the complex processes by which people discriminate among and recall experiences. Intellect, that which distinguishes humans from animals and adults from children, is the progression of internalization from the sensate to the conceptual.[30] Even though we apprehend objects through our senses, we sense things because of their connection to ideas we already possess. In other words, the application of a developmental framework elevates language (science) over the senses. This conceptual framework, then, gives him the possibility of exorcising people's fears and anxiety that are tied to the mysterious: emotion, he argues, is a process of place (*tokoro*), while intellect is one of ability (*nō*) (1991, 9:48).

---

[30] Inoue orders this development as follows: sensate (*kankaku*), perception (*chikaku*), recapitulation (*saisō*), new conception (*kōsō*), general idea (*gainen*), definition (*dantei*), and reasoning (*suiri*).

For Inoue, most ghosts can be readily explained because they are tied to emotion (place) rather than intellect, or attributable to an imperfect understanding of external phenomena. That is, people attribute to ghosts unusual or abnormal happenings (*ijō hentai*); but these ghosts become causal agents because people have a poor understanding of matter, that is, science. Ghosts, he argues, are mental images (*shinzō*) (using Blumenberg, I have called this myth) that explain the interaction between society and nature: "Ghosts from one's mental image, even though a type of provisional ghost that belongs to the natural world, connect our mind (*kokoro*) to the external world (*gaikai*), and organize the human world" (1902, 97–98). Thus, depending on the level of knowledge, people have created images that play an important role in making sense of the inexplicable. Ghosts filled varied and unpredictable roles; they were truly alter, the external and internal that constantly shifts back and forth. But it is because of the uncertainty of this alterity that it is necessary to silence ghosts in modern society.

Inoue's understanding makes sense to us because human apprehension of the external world (now nature) is placed in a developmental framework rather than an eschatological one. This is a key juncture: he is establishing the possibility for a horizon of expectations. On a phylogenetic level, in discussing the level of human knowledge, Inoue uses the word *shinpo* (progress). He writes: "What we do not know does not signify the strange and unknown. It means that when we experience the strange and unknown, even though we do not know it today we will know [it] in the future" (quoted in Miyata 1990, 50). In other words, most ghosts and mysterious happenings are strange only because people's knowledge of the universe has not progressed enough to understand the causes (1902, 89–90). For example, spirit possession was blamed for illness, abnormalities, or delusions before current advances demonstrated the externality of disease, and ghosts were blamed for eclipses in the ancient period because of an ignorance of astronomy (Onda 1991, 416).

To analyze the mysterious, Enryō first divides ghosts into two basic categories, actual (*jitsu*) and false (*kyō*).[31] (At this point it is worth remembering that the category of ghost encompasses a wide range of phenomena: ghosts, demons, fox possession, divination, wonders, etc.) False ghosts are rather easily dealt with; Enryō sees them as human creations, either mistaken perceptions or willful deception. The much larger category of actual requires science to further determine true from provisional ghosts within the category. Provisional ghosts exist in the natural world; they are both material and imaginary. For example, material ghosts result from an uninformed understanding of the sciences and can be better understood through botany, zoology, human physiology, chemistry, physics, geography, and astronomy. Imaginary ghosts are created through some transformation of human will, knowledge, emotion, or memory and are best explained

---

[31] I realize that in English these categories are either nonsensical or oxymoronic. Yet Inoue readily affixed characters such as *jitsu* (real), *shin* (true), *kyō* (false), and *go* (mistaken).

using psychology or philosophy; *kamioroshi*, divination, prophecy, as well as dreams can be exposed through studies of memory and mnemonics. He concludes: "Thus when one researches false ghosts, one can know the secrets of the human world (*ningenkai no kimitsu*); when one researches provisional ghosts, one investigates the secrets of the natural world; and when one researches the real ghosts, one can surmise the mysterious world" (1902, 97). By exposing the unknown, psychology establishes a new basis to resolve the absolutism of reality.

Inoue believed that the recategorization of ghosts would change the common understanding of "reality" among the masses. He states: "Even among provisional ghosts, because all images of the external world appear in our minds, with changes in our mind, the external world necessarily also changes" (1902, 98). In other words, changes in knowledge alter human understanding of the external world. In his rendering, "reality" shifts from the immediate, sensory, and emotional to abstract categories of knowledge that one knows but does not necessarily learn from one's senses. With the exception of the first volume, which introduces his idea of ghost studies, Inoue organizes the subsequent volumes according to scientific categories that provide rational explanations for what had been attributed to the mysterious. The organizing theme of the subsequent volumes are physical sciences (*rigaku*), medicine, philosophy, psychology, religion, education, and miscellaneous. Moreover, rather than recounting stories, Inoue discusses the attribution that people offer to specific phenomena and then offers an alternate reality, explainable through science.

That alternate reality is increasingly organized into general categories that can be discussed through scientific categories. Each section follows a general pattern: Inoue mentions some of the common beliefs, of fire wells to the west, and of stories that connect these places to the gods and spirits. But since he is interested in explaining the "real" cause, he then gives a scientific explanation. Yet these categories are not all familiar to us today, but reflect the changing understanding of the world. For example, he separates earthquakes from volcanoes, instead connecting volcanoes with hot springs (1979, 2:66–70).[32]

The section on earthquakes is similar. He acknowledges that earthquakes are among the most feared of phenomena in popular belief, but he calls many popular explanations hilarious. In addition to mentioning catfish and spiders, he includes passages from old texts, such as the *Jishin kō* and *Kaii bendan* (Stories of the Mysterious) by the astronomer Yoshikawa Joken (1648–1724), which attribute earthquakes to the loss of yang and the dominance of yin. But while he dismisses these beliefs, he also sees them as proto-scientific reasoning through which people attempted to explain the absolutism of reality:

---

[32] In the 1890s scientists were beginning to understand some of the forces that cause volcanoes and earthquakes, but they still did not know about plate tectonics. Instead, contemporary scientific understanding argued that the earth's inner core heats water, which seeps into the earth, and the resulting buildup of steam, depending on vents and outlets, creates hot springs or erupts violently.

That people imagined that a kind of animal lived under the earth and had the power to cause the ground to shake seems to be the delusions of ignorant who do not understand the logic of cause and effect. But one cannot doubt that this is the product of imagination using a logic of cause and effect and one should say that today's science (*rigaku*) is born from such reasoning. First, the imagination that the shaking is probably caused from below is a form of scientific reasoning; then hypothesizing on what could possibly cause that movement, returning to an animal is, in part, clearly a scientific deduction. (1979, 2:79)

Inoue ends by listing the four most probable causes of earthquakes based on current scientific knowledge in physics (*butsurigaku*) and topography (*chishigaku*): (1) slippage along a fault; (2) sinking, caused by the erosion of material from a mineral spring; (3) volcanic explosions; and (4) ruptures to the earth's surface created by the buildup and expansion of steam. He says that the first and last are the most common on the archipelago (1979, 2:76–77). Here Inoue is more interested in explaining why the ground shakes so that he can disprove earlier stories than in explaining the cause of earthquakes.

These categories serve as the containers for his collection of stories gathered on his travels. Here, science becomes the tool to denature the inherited knowledge of spirits and ghosts that had been connected to earthquakes and volcanoes. Catfish, earth spiders, and mountain gods and spirits now become denatured documents, anachronistic and superstitious beliefs from the past. Foxes, badgers, goblins, and so forth, now explained through animal physiology, also suffered this transformation to texts. But they are not eliminated. Like an exorcism, they are relocated to the past, now an earlier state of some unknowing condition, but one that fits into an "a priori totality" of progress. As part of his descriptions of earlier interpretations, both catfish and yin/yang, Inoue compares them to the thinking of a child. He cites a popular song—"Even if the ground shakes the *kaname ishi* will not disappear as long as the god of Kashima is there"[33]—as proof of this childlike thinking.

Inoue points out that this low level of understanding is not, however, unique to Japan. It is a universal category of development that all societies have passed through. As examples, he cites Anaxagoras, the English William Stukeley and Joseph Priestley, as well as the popular beliefs in Europe similar to the catfish and earth spider. The likening of catfish to popular beliefs in Europe is a powerful argument that helps authorize the transformation of beliefs into the rational system of modernity. This categorization of inherited knowledge as prior to the present along a linear, progressive time eliminates the alterity of ghosts and wonders in favor of an otherness as the past, in other words, as dead objects (thus predictable). Provisional ghosts are severed from the present and located as part of the past, now as superstitions that emerged because of insufficient knowledge of the universe, that is, science. For Inoue, stories of ghosts are a

[33] "Yurugu to mo yomoya nukeji na kaname ishi kashima no kami no aran kagiri wa" (1979, 2:71).

window into inherited knowledge and practices, but they are also a window to
those anachronistic beliefs too closely connected to emotions and place that
must be eliminated for society to advance. As the superstitious or primitive earlier state, this past, separated from the present, reinforces both the advanced
(enlightened) nature of the present and the continuity of a new space, the
nation—Japan.

In his "Yōkai dangi," Yanagita Kunio, the founder of Japanese folklore studies
(*minzokugaku*), accused Inoue of attempting to destroy ghosts, thereby eradicat-
ing folk beliefs. To an extent, this is true: he used ghost studies as a way to identify these stories as superstition and as anachronistic beliefs. But it would be
more accurate to say that Inoue is freeing culture of the same kinds of mediations that had ensured its integration with nature. This was now possible because
of the geological work that had begun the separation of nature and culture. By
placing these stories into scientific categories, Inoue is able to explain why particular stories must be relegated to that anachronistic past of modernity that has
been superseded by scientific explanations. In a sense, the reconstitution of
these stories into texts was an act of preservation, but in that act, Enryō killed
them in a different way by categorizing them and fixing them as discrete objects
from the past. In other words, they were dead because they happened and are no
longer relevant to the present. Yanagita would revive these stories (as well as
collect much more) and turn them into folklore. But even though Yanagita saw
these as part of his present, folklore in the twentieth century had already become
a temporal category that celebrates its contents because they are the primordial
moment prior to historical time, in other words, a mythic category that gives
"permanence" to the nation-state.

STORIES, TALES, HISTORY

It is rather easy for us to understand the relation between modern time and
wonders, that is, the exorcism of ghosts, spirits, and the strange from society, and
their replacement with science. Wonders that served as the mediating knowledge that alleviated the absolutism of reality in nonmodern epistemologies have
been replaced by science in the transformation to modernity. A similar transformation occurs among histories. Just as the separation of nature from culture required a transformation of how one thinks of human beings, it also forced a
reconceptualization of how that past constitutes society.

One of the interesting aspects of this transformation of temporality in Japan is
the relative absence of history as a discrete field of knowledge. History as we
know it today was not established until 1887 with the founding of the history department (*shigakka*) in the newly reorganized College of Letters at the Imperial
University at Tokyo. Ludwig Riess, a German historian and distant student of
Leopold von Ranke, was hired to help direct the new field. In 1889 he also

helped to found the Japanese Historical Association (Shigakkai). In short, the transition to History beyond histories did not occur until the late 1880s.[34] Those histories that had served as the authoritative accounts were mythic chronologies, such as the Six Histories (*Nihon shoki, Zoku nihon ki, Nihon goki, Zoku nihon goki, Nihon buntoku tennō jitsuroku,* and *Nihon sandai jitsuroku*); the *Kojiki*; and tales of the great exploits of heroic figures, such as the *Heike monogatari* and the *Taiheiki.* These authoritative accounts, too, were now questioned, a result of that rebound mentioned by Toulmin and Goodfield (1965).

As the reform of the calendar suggests, the new government was very concerned with the past as a means to legitimate its rule. In 1869 an imperial rescript was issued that began: "Historiography is a for ever immortal state ritual and a wonderful act of our ancestors" (quoted in Mehl 1998a, 1). This passage suggests that early concern for accounts connecting the new government to earlier moments was still operating within an inherited temporality. In that year, the Dajōkan opened the first of a series of offices of historiography to compile a history along the lines of the Six Histories, which were written during the Nara and Heian periods when the court did possess power and authority. The purpose of this new history was to reestablish the prestige of the Imperial Household.[35] In 1881 the office was directed to compile a chronology of Japan from the fourteenth century. This moment was key to the authority of the new government. It grounded the legitimacy of its acts as a restoration of imperial power (hence the Meiji Restoration), the fruition of the most recent attempt, the Kenmu Restoration (Go-Daigo's efforts to restore imperial power in the fourteenth century). Accounts of events surrounding this antecedent were commonly available in texts like the *Taiheiki, Nihon gaishi,* and *Dai nihonshi,* as well as in private libraries throughout the archipelago.

As the quote from Richards at the beginning of this chapter suggests, science altered the criteria for remembering data from the past. Not surprisingly, the activity of the members of the Office of Historiography and the Office of Topography raised questions about the first histories, like the *Kojiki* and *Nihon shoki,* and what had been accepted as authoritative accounts of the fourteenth century, like the *Taiheiki* and the *Heike monogatari.*[36] The very work of compilation depended now on a different understanding of data. The topographical studies severed from their locus, discussed in the previous chapter, now became evidence

[34] This is an adaption of Droysen's "beyond histories there is History." Quoted in Koselleck (1985, 28).
[35] For an account of these different offices, see Mehl (1998a). There had been few official histories written since these documents. All served as accounts tied to the new government; for example, the *Tōgan,* written during the Kamakura period, the *Zoku honchō tsugan* (1670), which covered the period from Daigo to Goyōzei, and the *Dai nihonshi* of Mito domain.
[36] War tales like the *Taiheiki* are filled with the supernatural, gods, dreams, and omens. Prayer to the kami and bodhisattva was an important way to ward off misfortune. But above all, these were accounts of exemplary men. For example, Kusunoki Masashige, who became a central actor in the debates over history, is introduced through a dream by Emperor Go-Daigo (McCullough 1959).

to corroborate or disprove events organized chronologically. Time allowed the reorganization of data across regions; this expanded archive made possible cross referencing and corroboration that could bring out inaccuracies as well as, in theory, write a richer, fuller history of the whole of Japan. But unlike Yasumaro's project, it became increasingly clear that, like ghosts, the inherited knowledge about the past could not be simply updated and transplanted onto the new political system.

The two historians who placed themselves at the center of this problematic were Kume Kunitake and Shigeno Yasutsugu. We must remember that their background did not predispose them to prepare a history that would be considered antination. Both were trained as Confucian scholars and worked assiduously to formulate and compile a history that would be useful to the state. Shigeno was from Satsuma, while Kume was the historian on the Iwakura mission of 1871–73. They became the two most significant historians in the various offices that preceded the Historiographical Institute and were the first professors of Japanese history at Tokyo Imperial University. But we must not begin an account of this transmutation of the past from their reputations. Three lectures presented by Shigeno in December 1879, February 1884, and December 1886 show his learning curve: he shifted from initial efforts to write a narrative of the past meaningful to the new government and society to a realization that a full reevaluation of the past was required.[37]

In his first essay, Shigeno describes the limitations of extant methods that were based on Chinese historical methods. He argues that there were three principal modes of writing: chronology, biography, and accounts of specific events. Japanese histories follow too closely along these lines; for example, he says that the *Nihon shoki* is chronological while the later histories (like the *Nihon goki* and *Zoku nihon goki*) recount activities of the throne. Their strengths, though, are the attention to status and order (*meibun*) and careful textual reading (1991a, 215–17). Importantly, Shigeno no longer accepts the inherited accounts as given. For example, while he complains that the *Dai nihonshi* is merely a compilation of war stories, he faults it because of its point of view. This, he suggests, is evidence that a common distinction that Japanese histories are public and Western histories private is a false distinction.[38] All histories, he says, have a particular point of view.

Shigeno points out that a second problem is that Japanese histories do not describe the political and economic structures—the development of the political system and the changing finances. As an example of a model history, he turns to Augustus H. Mounsey's *The Satsuma Rebellion*, which goes well beyond the

[37] These essays are "Kokushi hensan no hōhō o ronzu," "Sejō rufu no shiden oku jijutsu o ayamaru," and "Shi no hanashi." They are available in Tanaka and Miyachi (1991, 213–21, 339–55).

[38] This discussion refers to a distinction made by Kume about a relative absence of private histories in the archipelago, which is discussed in chapter 3.

immediate actors to discuss the fall of the bakufu, railroads, the 1870 incident, and ends with the assassination of Ōkubo Toshimichi in 1878. In this sense, Shigeno is trying to broaden the realm of a proper history: it requires a new subject, that of the nation, rather than the court or any lord. Shigeno was not alone in this desire. In 1877 and 1879 the Ministry of Education published *Kokushian*, a history of Japan, by Kimura Masakoto. Kimura writes in the introduction, "This book is a history of Japan, not a record of the Throne. For this reason, despite the great deeds of the emperors, they are not recorded unless they are connected to the interests of the whole country" (1991a, 220).

At this early stage in the compilation, Shigeno is optimistic that new methods will suffice; he calls for historians to turn to the West and adapt some of its methods. In an afterword, Katō Hiroyuki praises Shigeno and also calls on historians to learn from men such as Francois Guizot, Henry Thomas Buckle, John William Draper, Gustave Klemm, Otto Henne Am Rhyn, Georg Friedrich Kolb, and Friedrich von Hellwald. Kato concludes, "This form of history is very different than the usual; trivial matters are completely eliminated; in particular, they inquire into the cause of progress and enlightenment and describe those results. We should truly call this the essence of historical compilation" (in Shigeno 1991a, 221). Of course, it is possible to argue that this was Katō's Western moment, before he turned back to tradition. But already, he had advocated the teaching of Japanese and Chinese literature in the new College of Letters, and he probably agreed with Shigeno that Rai Sanyo's *Nihon gaishi* is an example of an indigenous history that does discuss a Japan.[39]

But by his 1884 essay, Shigeno recognizes the problems created by the new archive. He attributes the errors in the hitherto authoritative accounts to faulty data, which he says can be exposed using the information collected from throughout the land. In this work, he focuses mostly on events that led up to the Tokugawa period, surrounding Oda Nobunaga, Toyotomi Hideyoshi, and Tokugawa Ieyasu. Such a critique of Tokugawa historians fit the political needs of denigrating the immediate past, but by 1886, Shigeno argues that the historical tales and many other accounts that the state had hoped to use are fraught with inaccuracies and often based on legends and myths. Again, he is not alone, for in an 1885 memo defending the work of the historiographical office, Kume writes that its significance is in "correcting mistakes and eliminating falsehoods; the reliability of those histories are no more than 20—30 percent" (1991a, 229). While Shigeno's lecture began as a critique of the *Dai nihonshi*, he too turns to the unreliability of the *Taiheiki*, which, he claims, provides 70 to 80 percent of the information about the dispute over the northern and southern courts used in the *Dai nihonshi*. (To accept the legitimacy of the northern court is to call into question the narrative that the imperial court has ruled continuously since Jimmu.)

---

[39] Sanyo's *Nihon gaishi* was the text selected for the first Japanese history class taught at the First Normal School.

Shigeno's method is to corroborate events in the *Taiheiki,* looking for verification in other texts. He compares events and tales with newly collected texts,
such as the *Baishōron* (ca 1349) and the *Masu kagami* (ca 1376), which he argues are more accurate but were ignored because they are more sympathetic to
the northern court. For example, he cites Kusunoki Masashige's battle at Ten-
nōji, which, according to the *Taiheiki,* occurred on 5.1332. But then he cites the
Kusunoki kassen chūmon, discovered in the collection of the Maeda family of
Kaga domain, which records the battle as taking place on 1.1333 (1991c, 350).
There are many examples of the fruits of the growing archive. Shigeno is working at a level of detail and careful sleuthing that is one of the hallmarks of
archival research. But the texts have changed; he is now using a new understanding of time—temporal precision—to verify the utility and veracity of formerly authoritative accounts. This compilation of texts and the development of
a historical, dead, time makes possible the reconfiguration of information—now
data—into some form that adheres to standards of accuracy.

This transmutation of the war tales into inert data is evident in Shigeno's evaluation of their utility. When he asks why the *Taiheiki* has gained such an authoritative status, he says that the stories appealed to people, were a common
genre of the time, and gradually became accepted as true. He describes this
genre: "The genre of stories and war tales aroused the senses of people and are
easy to remember even for women and children; the stories aid the weak and re-
sist the strong, have pity for the defeated and despise the victorious. The authors
paid attention to common human feelings and distorted events by embellishing
and fabricating facts" (1991c, 350). In other words, the events themselves are
unreliable because the records are temporally imprecise, but they give a sense of
the feelings (*ninjō*) and conditions of the time. For this, he says, they are superb
data (1991c, 353). But where Shigeno was satisfied to keep the tales as a record
of feelings and conditions of the past, his colleague Kume goes even further, arguing that such tales as the *Taiheiki* are not history: "We should understand that
there is no academic value of the tales. When we know that its [account of] politics and affairs of state are lies, when talking about this war, too, we know that
the critical places of the military battles are also lies" (1991a, 226).[40]

Kume and Shigeno did not feel beholden to the simultaneity of past and
present. Their access to the regional texts collected through the compilation of
historical and topographical material, now separated from their locales and
centralized in a repository in Tokyo, gave them the data to write with the au-

---

[40] Kume's methods were similar to Shigeno's. For example, he cites the incredible story of the priest
Shunkan, the advisor to Fujiwara Narichika, who was exiled (originally with Taira Yasuyori and Fujiwara Naritsune, who were ordered back) and lived alone on Kikai ga shima (lit. "Island of the
Devil's World"). Kume expressed doubt that, based on a comparison of old texts from Satsuma and
the *Tōgan,* an exile was to this island. He also suggests that from a poem (*waka*) with a passage about
Yasuyori being sent to an island (Satsuma ga taoki), it became reality and was later embellished as
an oral tale (1991a, 223).

thority of the dispassionate eye. Kume writes, "The passages of the *Heike mono-gatari*, being the imagination of those in the capital, are nothing more than being forced to listen to a child" (1991a, 223).[41] Shigeno published numerous articles questioning the veracity of inherited knowledge. For his research that claimed that Kojima Takanori, loyal retainer to Go-Daigo in the *Taiheiki*, did not exist, and essays that point out the inaccuracy of events attributed to Kusunoki Masashige, Shigeno earned the derisive title *massatsu hakase*, (professor obliterator). Kume, too, was relentless. He questioned whether the *Taiheiki*, until then the authoritative account of the events surrounding the Kenmu Restoration, contained any historical utility. His evaluation of the narratives and chronologies written after the Six Histories was as follows: the *Azuma kagami* is the most accurate; over half of the tales (*Genpei seisuiki, Heike monogatari, and Taiheiki*) contain mistakes and falsehoods; the *Zoku honchō tsugan* is incomplete; and the *Dai nihonshi* is a compendium of war tales. He gained infamy for his 1892 essay "Kamiyo wa shinsai no kozoku nari," in which he pointed out that the section on the age of the gods in the earliest extant chronicles, the *Kojiki* and *Nihon shoki*, is made up from legends created by the early clans. In these examples, Shigeno and Kume devalue the content of these stories in a way similar to that in which Inoue exorcised ghosts, by placing them in some primitive category of cognition. But whereas the exorcism of ghosts facilitated the modernizing agenda of the state, opening up the possibility for the transformation of inhabitants into citizens, the debunking of the great tales destabilizes the legitimizing institution of the state, the imperial system that was based on those very tales.

Rather than using a modern/tradition or West/indigenous explanatory dualism, these historians are grappling with the changing utility of information from the past. Just as it was necessary to exorcise ghosts, some of the inherited knowledge of society needed to be forgotten. The discovery of the past did raise questions about such accounts, which we categorize today as literature, folklore, myth, and chronicles. But those forms are part of a history without time as we understand it today. Texts about the past, like the Confucian classics, the *Kojiki* and *Nihon shoki*, and the war tales, were significant because of the simultaneity of their ideals with those of the contemporary. This form of history is akin to *historia magistrae vitae*, that is, history as an example for the conduct of life.[42] This does not mean that change did not occur, but the texts that remained authoritative did so because of their meaningfulness and transferability. But such transferability and the exemplary nature of these accounts are counter to a modern time that demands accuracy, regularity, and replicability (that is, verification).

---

[41] For a detailed account of the the changing interpretation of the *Heike monogatari*, see Bialock (1999, 151–78). Interestingly, but not surprisingly, Bialock focuses on interpretations from the national literature chronology and omits a discussion of Shigeno and Kume in the transformation of this text.

[42] For a discussion on *historia magistrae vitae*, see Koselleck (1985, esp. 21–38).

The history of Kume and Shigeno begins the movement of historical study closer to *Geschichte* (*rekishi*), or History. Both fall within the epistemological shift in which time is being elevated over space, altering the meaning of particular pasts. The time that they are bringing to accounts of the past is a precise time where all events must be verifiable and datable. Information is no longer "significant," but relevant because it is datable according to some chronology. By reconfirming information that had been restricted to particular regions, Shigeno and Kume altered the value of that space and event, that is, the notion of "significant" changes from one of relations to that of empirical certainty. Possessing texts that had been limited to locales, they now found it possible to examine the accuracy of accepted truths and emplot them along a timeline of development.

Denigration of Experience

While such debunking of tales and forgetting of superstitions seems commonsensical to us, and I certainly would not advocate a return to some prescientific belief system, this is part of the disconnection that modernity imposes on humans. This displacement is in the transformation of the meaning of inherited knowledge, ghosts, myths, and tales, from site-specific explanations of human relevance in one's environment to temporal (past) and conceptual (scientific) categories that connect heterogeneous people to a center. At this point, Francis Bacon's transformation of the notion of experience is particularly relevant:

> There remains by mere experience, which when it offers itself is called chance; when it is sought after, experiment. But this kind of experience is nothing but a loose faggot, and mere groping in the dark, as men at night try all means of discovering the right road, whilst it would be better and more prudent either to wait for day or procure a light and then proceed. On the contrary the real order of experience begins by setting up a light, and then shows the road by it, commencing with a regulated and digested, not a misplaced and vague course of experiment. (Quoted in Agamben 1993, 17)

To place the ghosts and historical tales within Bacon's understanding, they are but evidence of darkness and chance. What had constituted experience and common sense is now evidence of a lack of understanding and reason, immaturity, or childhood. In the latter chapters I will address Bacon's new notion of experience as regulated and digested.

Like Yasumaro's quest to discard the mistaken and establish the true in the *Kojiki*, these Meiji intellectuals began the process of resituating the boundaries of human society. At this point, even though they sought greater unity of a Japan, the strength of their work was to weaken the ties that connected people to their locale rather than to strengthen the nation. If we accept one definition of culture as "the way of life of a particular people living together in one place," then there were still many cultures, but the idea of living together in a particular place had begun to emerge (Eagleton 2000, 112). In a section on outsiders (*ijin*), Inoue Enryō attributes the stories about these ghosts to various misapprehensions of the unfamiliar. First, when people venture deep into areas (especially mountains) and encounter an animal not normally seen, they report it as a beast or demon. Second, when people encounter an unfamiliar kind of person from a "different tribe," they give it the name mountain man or mountain woman. He says that these tales probably began long ago when the Ainu (*emishi*) lived on Honshu or when people from Southeast Asia probably drifted to Shikoku and Kyushu, but they continue when people venture into remote areas and encounter recluses or uncommon animals. Third, the encounter with an old, grey-haired person, especially in the mountains, often led people to react that they had seen a wizard (*sennin*). And fourth, a ghost "seen," especially in the mountains, is usually a hallucination. Here, he cites the snow woman as an example (1979, 2:261–65). Many of these explanations recall the accounts of blood-drinking and fat-stealing foreigners. But by emplotting such accounts as backward or childlike, Inoue accomplishes two things: one is to denigrate the way of life that had existed on the archipelago. The experience of people now becomes evidence of "groping in the dark."

Second, this unfolding of the past empties place of its meaning and opens up a much larger social space. Within his genus of strangers (*ijin*), Inoue groups together mountain men, mountain women, mountain hags, snow women, hermit wizards, and celestial beings. While he cites from specific texts, he gives one or two examples of each type, thus emphasizing the prototypical nature of his examples. The stories of snow woman from regions throughout the archipelago are grouped together as a tale common among Japanese in mountainous and cold regions, opening the door for the story of Mosaku and Minokichi to become the prototypical version that represents all (Davis 1992, 149–53). The Historiographical Office played a similar role. By collecting data from all the locales on the archipelago, it set up the possibility for considering data differently, as autonomous from their site of production, and now meaningful to a Japan.

But what is interesting about this transformation is that this new space is being replaced by an idea of place that is no longer territorially defined. In 1890 the Office of Topography was transferred to Tokyo Imperial University and on March 31 of the following year was merged into the Historiographical Office. Certainly, territory is important, but this transfer signaled that it had become a malleable form, subject to temporal categories. The archipelago was given, but at this point, its features did not have specific meaning. It was reinforced by a new notion of foreignness. Foreigners were no longer in the category of strange (*ijin* and outside one's local knowledge system); they became human beings while those who abided by such inherited knowledge were looked down on as

children or the unenlightened. By reorganizing those beliefs according to scientific categories, the external world was transformed from the outside of local
places to externalities to the idea of the nation, Japan. But this new place was increasingly defined by the characteristic of the people who were defined to give
form, singularity, and unity to that place. They became internal to Japan yet remained separated from the present because of its distance from the ideal, the
"should" that dictates progress.

This new place was part of the cascade set off by the discovery of a different
temporality. The separation of nature from culture opened up the possiblity of
learning different laws and mechanisms that better explained the absolutism of
reality, the need to come to terms with one's lack of control. These new laws and
mechanisms, as well as the ways that the archipelago related to those laws, must
be written through the discovery of history. The next two chapters will examine
this fixation and regulation of time through history.

Chapter 3

NATURALIZATION OF NATION:
ESSENTIAL TIME

> The real thing is not, or is no longer available to us, and some-
> thing else is given to us in order to replace it. In this sense it
> can be said that we have historical writing in order to com-
> pensate for the absence of the past itself.
> —F. R. Ankersmit (2001)

THE ABSENCE OF the past is, interestingly, a result of the discovery and then separation of the past from the present. It leads to a rather interesting situation: the
inherited forms of knowledge that had organized society were now denigrated
because of a hope and promise that a better system based on science and rationality exists. But it was (is) a promise of improvement of which the immediate result was an uncertainty about what is given and created. Such dislocation
and uncertainty created by scientific and rationalistic ideas is described suc-
cinctly by Terry Eagleton: "Once the bourgeoisie has dismantled the centraliz-
ing political apparatus of absolutism, either in fantasy or reality, it finds itself
bereft of some of the institutions which had previously organized social life as a
whole. The question therefore arises as to where it is to locate a sense of unity
powerful enough to reproduce itself by" (1990, 23).[1]

The limitations of early Meiji attempts, like that of Ninagawa, to use artifacts
of the past to unify the people as Japanese indicate that artifacts alone are rather
ineffective without greater structure, something that locates that sense of unity.
David Harvey describes this problem: "The process of place formation is a process
of carving out 'permanences' from the flow of processes creating spaces" (1996,
261). In other words, the separation of past from present set off processes that neces-
sitated the reformulation of place; it was the beginning of the determination of
place through time.

Harvey is addressing a contradistinction with which numerous intellectuals
have struggled throughout the past two centuries, that between the simultaneity

[1] Eagleton continues: "In economic life, individuals are structurally isolated and antagonistic; at the
political level there would seem nothing but abstract rights to link one subject to the other. This is
one reason why the 'aesthetic' realm of sentiments, affections and spontaneous bodily habits comes
to assume the significance it does. Custom, piety, intuition and opinion must now cohere an otherwise abstract, atomized social order" (23). The centrality of aesthetics to the political and social system will be discussed in later chapters.

of mobility and stability in modern societies. This was raised by Marx and popularized by Marshall Berman in the title of his book, *All That Is Solid Melts into
Air*. If we place this within Blumenberg's absolutism of reality, while modern society is built upon the notion of change and improvement to allay that anxiety,
change also fosters the uncertainty of "perpetual perishing." A sense of permanence
ameliorates that uncertainty.

This problematic is compounded in non-Western places. Throughout the
Meiji period, numerous intellectuals expounded on the importance of progress.
But while they accepted this idea in the abstract, even proponents of enlightenment like Fukuzawa had a difficult time placing a Japan into this fluid framework. On the one hand, a Japan is already emplotted into a permanent place,
that of the Orient (Said 1978; 1993). The synchronization of Japan into the temporality of the Western powers involved the relegation of Japan to a temporal category of little or no progress. One of the fascinating aspects of the early Meiji
period is the extent to which intellectuals debated what should be discarded. For
example, articles in the famous journal devoted to enlightenment, *Meiroku
zasshi*, discussed the merits of components of society, from the rather obvious
political institutions to the sociocultural, such as language, the writing system,
concubines, and religion (Braisted 1976). The dilemma for intellectuals was
not only to extract a Japan from its already existing locus as a- or nonhistorical
(the Orient), but also (and much more difficult) to find a sense of unity that simultaneously forgets that past—those customs and habits that are deemed backward—
but also uses a past to demonstrate change while providing the permanence
necessary to become modern.

An interesting characteristic of the historiography of this process is the difficulty
that historians have had with this contradistinction. Most have generally characterized the significant rise of interest in the past as a conservative/nativist reaction
against Western enlightenment and a conservative reassertion of the nation.[2] This
narrative, which moves linearly from the moment of "opening," to enlightenment,
followed by a retrenchment, is one of the overstatements of our current understanding of history—and the process of modernization in non-Western places. On the
level of rhetoric, such movement is certainly evident, but when we examine the
considerable presence of inherited knowledge of the "Westernizers" (such as
Fukuzawa Yukichi, or Tokutomi Sohō), the extent of their transformation (or enlightenment) would seem meager by the standards of a later generation. Certainly,
the elevation of inherited forms was an important part of this process, but it is not a
turn away from Westernization or modernization. That is too self-congratulatory
and ignores the contradistinctions within the process itself.

This developmental framework ignores the fact that time, too, begins to take
on a historical quality. At this point it is important to consider Harvey's next sen-
tences: "But the 'permanences'—no matter how solid they may seem—are not

---

[2] See, for example, Pyle (1970); Pierson (1980); Gluck (1985).

eternal; they are always subject to time as 'perpetual perishing.' They are contingent on the processes that create, sustain, and dissolve them." Harvey is reinforcing the historical character of the process that formulates those permanences; it is crucial to look beyond the rhetorical component of the transformation as if it were solely within time. An emphasis on anti-Western reaction ignores the centrality of history itself in the process of transformation. Fukuzawa wrote in 1875: "All the history hitherto written in Japan has been merely a recital of the imperial lineage or a record of the virtues and vices of lords and their ministers . . . it has not been a history of the Japanese nation" (quoted in Keirstead 1998, 48). Fukuzawa's lament demonstrates a new idea of the role of the past; this new temporality requires the historicization of the archipelago in order to synchronize the place of the nation to modern time. He is moving toward the recognition that a relationship to one's past must first be defined before the identity or unity of the nation can be achieved (Ankersmit 2001, 261).

We must remember that the rise of a historical consciousness in nineteenth-century Europe and Japan coincides with the rise of the nation-state. This is not serendipitous. When we also include the historicity of history in our inquiry, we see that history provides the technology to establish that permanence of place and simultaneously a narrative of change (development). Japanese intellectuals needed to (and did) reevaluate the very basis of a past, the relation between nature and history. The German historian Johann Droysen describes the significance of this inquiry:

> Nature and History are the widest conceptions under which the human mind apprehends the world of phenomena. And it apprehends them thus, according to the intuitions of time and space, which present themselves to it as, in order to comprehend them, it analyzes for itself in its own way the restless movement of shifting phenomena.
>
> Objectively, phenomena do not separate themselves according to space and time; it is our apprehension that thus distinguishes them, according as they appear to relate themselves more to space or to time. (1967, 9)

My purpose is not to attempt some coverage of the vast philosophical inquiries into human apprehension of the relation between history and nature.[3] It is more limited to how this severing of the past forced a reconfiguration of objects, people, and ideas into the nation of Japan. This process is the historicization of the archipelago; in this effort to establish the given and created, intellectuals first removed different pasts from time, turning the nation into a transhistorical — that is, natural — entity. In addition, history provided the material evidence to prove this timelessness; pasts were transmuted into evidence that demonstrated that the nation has existed for a long, long time.

---

[3] For an account of the idea of nature in nineteenth- and early twentieth-century Japan, see Thomas (2001).

In a sense, this making of history is akin to the discovery of zero in thirteenth-century Europe.[4] To us, today, both are obvious things that are part of our thought and daily lives. But zero helped usher in a new epistemology that broke from the Aristotelian understanding that no void is possible. Without zero, concepts such as probability and infinity that are so foundational to modern science would be inconceivable. In a similar way history, that is, the writing of history, makes possible a linearity that opens up society toward some future. Dipesh Chakrabarty calls this move to free oneself from the past and establish a historical consciousness a "zero point in history" (2000, 244). The comment of Baelz's Japanese informant, "Our history begins today," speaks to the new possibilities: it both enables a logical progression to the unknown, a horizon of expectations that is characteristic of modern society, and has the power to nullify. Like the number zero, this zero point in history has magical qualities. It eradicates those denigrated pasts that were believed to have impeded progress, and, more importantly, it nullifies its own temporality, the making of history, by becoming a mere narrative of past events. In short, the idea of nation becomes that permanence of place.[5] This magic can be illustrated through a passage in Takayama Chogyū's 1897 essay, "Japanism":

> For the sake of our nation-state (*kokka*) I will advocate a Japanism—thoroughly considering the characteristics of our country's (*honpō*) culture, investigating the historical relationship of religions and morals, pointing to the general principles of human evolution, recognizing the laws of the interrelation between particular and universal in the progress of the nation-state and world development, and furthermore, seeing clearly our country's founding spirit and special national (*kokuminteki*) nature. (1970a, 23)

This passage indicates that there are a number of categories (conceptual spaces) that exist as if everyone understands those pasts as given; permanence is presented as "our country's culture," "founding spirit," and "special national nature." Each helps define a relationship to the past as if that connection between a culture, spirit, or special nature has somehow, naturally, always existed. Moreover, laws provide regularity for change. "General principles of evolution" and the "laws of . . . progress and . . . development" establish order, while at the same time pointing toward some horizon of expectations. These ideas themselves, the very basis of the history of Japan, are historical, established at the same moment as the narrative of Japan's unfolding. In this chapter I will focus on how, in the making of history, the very conditions of history were removed from history itself, thereby naturalizing the nation.

---

[4] For my use of the phrase "making of history," see de Certeau (1988). In 1202 Fibonocci introduced zero to Europe in his book *Liber Abaci*. For a history of zero, see Seife (2000, 78–81). I am thankful to Jim Ketelaar for bringing this book to my attention.

[5] For a fine essay that points out the historicity of the idea of the nation, see Geary (2002).

The Externalization of Nature

One influential intellectual who hinted at this reconfiguration of the archipelago was Katō Hiroyuki (1836–1916), a member of the *Meirokusha*, first president of Tokyo Imperial University, and intellectual perhaps best known for his advocacy of social Darwinism. In looking back over his career, Katō recounts the impact of natural science (progress) on his conceptualization of phenomena. "Thus, from around the age of 40 [1876] I became a virtually different person; my views after 40 were generally opposite those before. In other words, up to 40 I was a dualist, but afterward I became a pure monist" (1912, 4–5). For Katō, the transformation from a dualism, or the neo-Confucian dualism of matter (*ki*) and principle (*ri*), to a monism was less a philosophical issue than a problem of what kind of society Japan is and should be. The answer to that required rethinking of the relation between matter and a supernatural or transcendent idea.

Katō considered his *Shizen to rinri* (Nature and Ethics) as the best exposition of his monistic view of the constitution of society (1912, 1–23; 1959, 59.) It is the culmination of his thinking on how to merge human society with this new conviction in the universality of science and progress. This shift to a monism is indicative of Katō's acceptance of an idea of nature from the West, a separation of humans from nature that rested, interestingly, on the discovery of history in the natural sciences, and an analogy of the natural sciences with human history.[6] The former resulted in evolution, the latter in progress. Relying on the works of Haeckel and Spencer, Katō fully imbibes the merger:

> Why is it that myriad phenomena which are produced from the natural matter of the universe arise in the absolutely natural, absolutely causal, and absolutely mechanistic? It is because they are controlled by natural law, in other words, the law of cause and effect (*Das einzige Natur- und Kausalgesetz*). In the universe only one natural law, or law of cause and effect, exists, and it controls the activity of matter and all phenomena that are produced from this. This singular law does not need the intervention of a great magical or mystical being, but functions purely mechanically based upon nature and a series of causal links. (1912, 13)

This is an example of an early moment in the externalization of nature. One must be careful to point out that Katō was criticizing not only a Japanese society in which environment and the supernatural are imbued with life (the ghosts and wonders Enryō worked to exorcize), but also dualistic conceptual structures from the West that relied on some metaphysical ideal. He cited as examples Christianity, Schopenhauer's idealism, and the will of Wilhelm Wundt and

---

[6] R. G. Collingwood states, "The modern view of nature, which first begins to find expression towards the end of the eighteenth century and ever since then has been gathering weight and establishing itself more securely down to the present day, is based on the analogy between the processes of the natural world as studied by natural scientists and the vicissitudes of human affairs as studied by historians" (1960, 9).

William James, which, he asserted, rely on some kind of specter (*bakemono*) (1912, 5–6).

The key to Katō's conceptual system is the potential for social change. The monism removed phenomena from a fixed world established by some supernatural entity (neither Christianity nor Buddhism was suitable to his idea of modern society). Earlier in 1890, Katō directly addressed this separation of nature and culture in an essay distinguishing natural history from history (1890, 1–9). He argued that a history, that is the study of the past to understand the underlying laws that guide society, was not possible among ancients who did not separate nature and culture; they considered humans and creatures subject to natural forces as completely different, and the former, fortunately, half godlike (*hanshinteki*). He writes, "As I discussed above, in ancient histories there is no knowledge of reason, the same natural laws, because they believed that the deeds of human societies and the outcomes in the organic worlds are the same and are controlled from nature. They could not see that the rise and fall of societies and other changes are controlled by natural forces" (1890, 8). This shift removes attribution from what he calls magical (*fukashigi*) and mystical (*shinpiteki*) ideas and attributes all change to natural laws that structure the development of society based upon analysis of mechanistic relations of discrete parts. These natural laws are no longer human based; though constructed by humans, they claim a transcendent, universalistic quality that guides and orders society, yet remains beyond criticism (Polanyi 1944, 111–29). Natural law shifted emphasis from structure to function within the process. Rather than rely on some ontological difference between humans and other animals, Katō argues that it is the level of creativity and of development that is the cause of the difference. The difference, he argues, "is completely from the use of natural law, not any special power among humans" (1912, 21). In other words, the distinction among people is temporal, their position along a developmental continuum. But while he is imbuing human society with the potential for history, he is also removing nature, or natural history, to a static realm, that of an ahistorical law, the unchanging geophysiology, or the constant repetition of plants and animals. The change of nature into Nature offers the potential for stability in the changing world of modernity.

The externalization of wonders allows for the naturalization of a different nature, the idea of the nation.[7] Katō employs a familiar trope, the nation as organism, by drawing an analogy of cells to society. He finds three levels of cellular/social organization: humans are simple cells (*tansaibōtai*); they coalesce into groupings that are a compound cell (*fukusaibōtai*); and nations are complex cells (*fukufukusaibōtai*). He does not explain this analogy, but merely states its obviousness. The progression from the simple to the complex is natural; the fun-

---

[7] Katō generally used the compound *kokka*, normally indicative of nation-state. Occasionally he used it in this way, but more often he was referring to the nation; he often placed the German word *Volk* in parentheses.

damental tendency of the simple cell is self-survival. But because of the insecurity of competition that results (i.e., Spencer's adaptation of Darwin's survival of the fittest), individuals coalesce for security and stability; here, Katō states that individuals subconsciously choose groupings that best help them meet their self-tendencies. This trope allows for both universal comparability as well as difference: because each cell is different, each nation is unique, but relations among citizens within nations are similar. "When we see humans as the completion of this uniqueness, it is a matter of course that we must devote ourselves to the health and happiness of the nation" (284). Katō's invocation of cell biology masks the way that the state constitutes the individual as a member of a homogeneous body; the Japanese nation is turning into a natural (not historical) living object. This connection of the nation to natural law enabled Katō to use the past to provide a unified society with stability amid change. The philosopher R. G. Collingwood describes the efficacy: "The motive for asserting either of them [matter and laws as unchanging objects of natural science] arises from the supposed need for an unchanging and therefore, according to the time-honoured axiom, knowable something behind the changing and unknowable show of nature as we perceive it through our senses" (1960, 11).

My interpretation is not a cynical denial of existence of the nation, but a recognition of a variability of meanings throughout recorded time. For example, the Japanese word *kokka* (today translated as nation-state) signified the sphere of a lord's political control during the Sengoku and Tokugawa periods; Oda Nobunaga used the word *tenka* (heavenly realm) to signify his unification of *kokka* (Katsumata 1981, 112–24; Roberts 1998, 4–9). Amino Yoshihiko has described how the characters for Japan read today as *nihon* were also read *hi-nomoto* in the medieval period. What becomes clear is that those territorial and cultural boundaries that have demarcated "nihon" have changed over the years (Amino 1992, 121–42).

This naturalization of the nation depends on a rather subtle, but significant, inversion of the given and created. Katō makes a fascinating adaptation of Confucianism to natural science; citing Zi Si's (492–431 B.C.) *Doctrine of the Mean*, he replaces the laws of heaven (*tenmei*) with nature (*shizen*). He changes "That which is bestowed by Heaven is called man's nature; the fulfillment of this nature is called the Way" to "That which is from nature is called man's nature; the perfection of this nature is called the Way" (1912, 344).[8] This shift inverts the notion of humankind and the question of human agency. It is a shift from the idea that humans are inherently good and degenerate through the passage of time to the view that humans must overcome their rather raw and primitive natures (Soper 1995, 28–30).

There is a centrifugal potential within this formulation for individuals (simple cells) to act apart from the social whole. Katō writes, "Our unique characteristics

---

[8] For the Doctrine of the Mean, I have relied on de Bary et al. (1969, 1:118).

are not at all mysterious or miraculous, they emerge from pure nature. In other words, they are given by natural law" (1912, 345). But he also prioritizes the social body: "Those who act with such goodness are those devoted to the existence of nature and the nation" (284–85). By changing fulfillment to perfection (that is, cultivation), he emphasizes the need for human effort and allows for the perfection of uniqueness (*kōyūsei*), which he interprets as the Way. The result is the stabilization of a particular idea of change based on rational thought as a timeless quality that then transforms humans into progressive organisms. Differentiation among these organisms can be measured, that is, subject to analysis according to position along a temporal line of development away from a "natural" state. This framework removed the impediments that an old nature imposed upon society—it eliminated the supernatural and mysterious, as well as the morals and ethics that held society together. More important, the conflation of humans and nation also naturalized the latter as if it had always existed, though unknown to the primitive minds of its inhabitants. The potential of this system was to establish that beginning or zero point that facilitates a new relationship with the past.

LIKE A DRAGONFLY: THE INSTABILITY OF BEING OTHER

Interestingly, while Katō naturalizes the unit of the nation as a complex cell, and his monism and the progressive nature offer the possibility of development, it raises questions about the particularity of a "Japan" in the face of natural laws. In a statement that echoed Augustine's famous statement about time ("What, then, is time? I know well enough what it is, provided that nobody asks me; but if I am asked what it is and try to explain, I am baffled."), the intellectual Miyake Setsurei interrogated this problem in his famous 1890 essay *Shinzenbi nihonjin* (Japanese: Truth, Goodness, Beauty): "Who are Japanese? . . . When one ponders this, the meaning flickers before one's eyes like a mirage, and when one is about to describe it, one suddenly loses its image" (1931a, 216). Miyake's writings are indicative of many who seek to stabilize the idea of a Japan in this externalized nature. One of the interesting aspects of Katō's search for that unity of Japan is the absence of a geographical Japan. The organism was, of course, part of the archipelago, but during the course of the Meiji period, the archipelago grew to include Hokkaido, the Ryukyu islands, and eventually Formosa (Taiwan), Sakhalin, and Korea while the organism maintained its stability.

Miyake argues that Japan and Japanese culture are neither geographical nor material, but the accumulation of habits and sensibilities of a people in interaction with sites and objects. A fascinating outcome of this search for a Japanese past is the gradual removal of some pasts from time; they become ideas from a sensual experience. De Certeau describes the efficacy of this turn to aesthetics:

> Finally, nature is what is other, while man stays the same. Elsewhere we can observe that this metamorphosis, a product of the displacement generated by the text, makes of nature the area where *esthetic* or *religious* experience and admiration are expressed and where Léry's prayer is spoken, while the social space is the place where an *ethics* is developed through a constant parallel between festivity and work. In this already modern combination, social production, what reproduces sameness and marks an identity, posits nature, esthetics, and religiosity outside of itself. (1988, 220)

Miyake is one of many of this period who sought to define the natural and historical by turning to some kind of aesthetic experience. But interestingly, in this process of defining a past of Japan, Miyake and others began the removal of parts of that past from history itself, relocating them to some transhistorical category.

Miyake is one of the intellectuals who is frequently cited as an example of a renewed nationalism/conservatism that emerged during the late 1880s.[9] Like others of his generation, he was quite aware of the threat posed by the West, and he believed that Japan must respond to it. The goal of his writing was to elevate Japan out of the Orient, to show that Japan, too, could be an important and independent—not subservient or colonized—nation-state on the international level. He states that because Japan had been relatively isolated, it did not develop materialistic wealth as did many European countries, nor did it need to develop as strong a military force. Here, we again see the power of Orientalism; his interpretation elides much of the immediate past—the centuries of military rule, the concentration of wealth, and the rise of a mercantile/consumer society. The desire to expunge society of its anachronisms facilitated the relegation of wealth and power to external forces, the pressures of neighbors, not internal causes. The reason for the differential between Japan and the West was not that Japan is Oriental, that is, in this static category of the primitive, but historical.

Certainly *Shinzenbi* contains much to support an interpretation of conservatism; Miyake rails against the increasing mechanization of society, the disappearance of a Japan, and the shallowness of much of liberal capitalist society. He argues that to determine the true universal, data from more than Europe, in particular Asia, are necessary. The necessary components of this universal are truth, goodness, and beauty. First, truth (*shin*) is the quest to discover an ideal—reason and justice—beyond the particularity of Western universalism. It requires the full investigation of all sides of things. Second, goodness (*zen*) approaches Miyake's attempt to eliminate the monologic potential of truth. It is a self-critical quality in which one should doubt the correctness of one's own position when applied to others. (Truth and goodness suggest an acceptance of rationality, an idealism that thought leads to a perfect society.) And third, beauty (*bi*) is that

---

[9] Pyle's *The New Generation* has remained the most important expression of this interpretation.

universal that is prior to such human agency and cannot be measured or known only through the phenomenal.

These comments, however, should be read as a part of his overall critique, which also includes a criticism of many inherited ideas, habits, and institutions. These criticisms are readily apparent when *Shinzenbi nihonjin* is read alongside its companion piece *Giakushū nihonjin* (Japanese: Lies, Evil, Vulgarity). When read together, we find that Miyake, while employing dualistic language that fits within an Orientalist discourse, is seeking to rearticulate the relation between past and present. That is, he is seeking to relocate pasts to free Japan from the immaturities that persist from adherence to inherited ideas and forms, to allow for change to a modern society, and to establish the permanence of a modern state.

Perhaps the most troubling issue for modernizing places is the seeming effacement of the particularities of the inherited customs and practices for universalistic processes. Today, this is one of the compelling problematics of globalization; it is also one of the central problematics of modernity ignored in modernization theory. Miyake recognizes the particularity of the universality of Enlightenment and that full acceptance of the temporal narrative situates Japan in a category of incompleteness, inferiority, or, worse, a lack of distinctiveness:

> If we work to improve the country becoming completely Western—importing culture and texts, customs and habits even to the complete adoption of clothes, food, and drink—lamenting only that we do not have the skill to emulate rapidly, the result is a dragonfly state (*seiteishu*); one sees a Japan of foreigners—the beauty of mountains and water—not a Japan of Japanese. But when they look at our undisciplined people, we are compared with the mediocre of their country and with vulgar servants. Thus, in other words, emulation turns the country into only inferior Western ones (*Ōbei*) and the people into inferior Westerners; in the end it only increases the inferior tribes among Westerners. (1931b, 257)[10]

Throughout *Giakushū nihonjin* it becomes apparent that Miyake is directly addressing the complexity of alterity in the constitution of the subject of the modern place. *Giakushū* is the antithesis of *Shinzenbi*, and Miyake argues that such lies, evil, and vulgarity must be eliminated. When applied to Japan, those negative characteristics include over a thousand years of accumulated customs and habits as well as the superficiality of many fashions among people infatuated with the West. He concludes, "For this reason, when promoting truth, one must expose lies; when promoting goodness, one must crush evil; and when promoting beauty one must extinguish vulgarity" (1931b, 240). Many of his passages in this essay read like those who have been considered modernizers, arguing for an elimination of anachronistic parts of society in favor of the modern.

True to his search for a universal that considers both West and East, Miyake's criticism of the past, that is, lies, evil, and vulgarity, equally criticizes the inher-

---

[10] For a discussion of such hierarchical categorization, see Chakrabarty (2000, esp. 27–46).

ited knowledges of both Japan and the West. His most trenchant criticism is directed against Japanese whom he finds too passive. In *Giakushū*, he argues that one of the problems of contemporary Japan is the hold of anachronistic ideas and habits that limit the ability of Japanese. He writes, "Sad, isn't it? We Japanese are no longer overwhelmed by Reason and the intellectual abilities of Caucasians, but there is an obstruction that prevents us from fully developing our ability" (1931b, 240). Miyake is criticizing inherited structures—class and hierarchy, practices, and ideas that affect habits of mind. He is quite severe toward those sycophantic academics, bureaucrats obsessed with rank, as well as Westernized Japanese who advocate imitation of the West.[11]

Miyake's criticism of the West is less conservativism than recognition that the ideas of enlightenment, too, are of the past. He is railing against a propensity in Japan to follow the model of European countries. His criticism is the teleology through which people accept its components as valid without thinking about its applicability to the nation and about its purported universality. On the one hand, Miyake recognizes that many important ideas are coming into Japan, and that these ideas can be important because of the potential to improve society, not because they are Western. In this sense, the criticism against certain kinds of Westernization is not against modernity per se, but a tendency to look to the categories rather than the process of change.[12]

Moreover, Miyake recognizes that imitation of a model (by its very nature that of a past) will not lead to the goal of equivalence with Western nation-states. He complains, "Trying to emulate and transform everything, from left to right, head to toes, is itself uncivilized, it is barbaric" (1931b, 257).[13] In a sense, Miyake recognized the dilemma of adapting the ideas through which progress had been achieved in Europe. Trying to catch up and "follow" European nation-states was itself barbaric and fostered the lingering question whether Japan, as an imitator, can ever be an equal.[14] Miyake supports a strong military and industrial development, but he questions the relevance of these policies to the goals of a strong nation. He writes, "Railroads have been extended in all directions and telegraph lines stretch throughout the skies, we built the shiny surface of a civilized country; the merchants receive all the benefits" (1931b, 248). For Miyake,

---

[11] Miyake cites fathers who meddle in their son's education as an example. Today, of course, Japanese mothers occupy this role of stewardship. He also complains about contemporary scholarship: "However, through this enthusiasm for European scholarship, the so-called great scholar/technician (*sekigaku kyōshō*), in particular, responds to scholarly trends by continuing orthodox theories, appending new materials, and offering contradictory details. It is no more than a minor achievement" (1931a, 224).

[12] As an example of the need to distinguish content from the category, Miyake was often critical of some foreign scholars who taught at the imperial university. He singled out Bussé (philosophy) and Riess (history) as two mediocre, overpaid examples.

[13] Today we call this Japanese imitation.

[14] This issue was heavily debated at the time and is still an issue today. See, for example, Nakae (1984). The position of the *sensei*, in particular, is to leapfrog the West.

capitalism is leading only to uneven development. He likens it to the use of drugs; more money temporarily alleviates the symptoms of depression, but the more one uses drugs to mask problems, the weaker the body becomes. The metaphor of the body refers to the nation, the common people who, he believes, are becoming poorer. In other words, his collective unit is centered around the people, the nation as *kokumin*, not the nation-state (*kokka*).

This criticism of modernization as Westernization also recognizes that the Orient, too, is one of those anachronisms. Miyake's critique seeks to distinguish Japan's past from the Orient, that is, the position imposed by the West. In his discussion on ugliness, Miyake begins with an allegory of flattery and delusion: when an insincere man lavishly compliments a woman's beauty, despite being average, she becomes convinced that she is beautiful and adorns herself with gold and a conspicuous obi. (He frequently uses the word *mekki*, gilding.) In other words, she becomes fixated with a superficial spirit and vulgar (1931b, 252). The analogy is to the flattery of Western experts who have been assisting Japan's development. Here, he specifically criticizes foreigners (such as Ernest F. Fenollosa and William S. Bigelow), whose interest in "saving" Japanese art Miyake likens to a temporary infatuation with new things (1931a, 238). Their assistance is constantly conditioned by their view of Japan as a part of the fixed past of the Orient, a position from which Miyake is seeking to extract Japan. On art, he complains, "Today the word art (*bijutsu*) has virtually swept throughout the realm; when one says art, people somehow think of the sacred and refined and for this reason say they love art. When they claim to be engaged in the production of art they thinks of themselves as the chosen enlightening the vulgar masses" (1931b, 252). He does not deny that some of these objects are art, but he protests the emplotment of such art pieces, represented as an objectified past of the Orient, as representations of nation.

Miyake's goal is located in some future, the achievement of happiness (*enman kōfuku*). His truth, goodness, and beauty are directed toward a Hegelian idealism that assumes the perfect society can be reached only through rational thought. He concludes, "I have no doubt that if we understand the general path of development of the art objects from the past we can fulfill our hopes for the future" (1931a, 235).[15] For Miyake, the way to achieve that happiness was through a transcendent principle, what he calls reason (*rigi*). It was not the denial of any particular past, but the search of the archives of the past, recognizing the multiplicity of viewpoints: "One accumulates many divergent objects and ideas which one acquires from different experiences that depend upon circumstance. Analyzing the differences and similarities, and distinguishing between right and wrong is the great way to Truth" (1931a, 223).

---

[15] Miyake was one of the first students in Ernest Fenollosa's philosophy course. Fenollosa taught a version of Hegel's philosophy of history. For a description of Fenollosa's lectures, see Yamashita (1975).

The problem was not the existence of a universal nor the futility of achieving a universal ideal; instead, Miyake seeks to supplement that Western knowledge with knowledge about East Asia. He states, "Today Europeans and Americans have expanded to every part of the world and arrogantly extol the history of the Aryan race as world history. However, Japanese have experienced many hundreds and thousands of years always living on this small island country" (1931a, 221). In his description of truth, Miyake calls for Japanese to move beyond that partiality: "In other words, for Japanese the urgent task which cannot be put off for one day is to use the new resources of the Orient and discover new reason (*rigi*)" (227). This was to be one of Japan's major contributions, the presentation of knowledge about the East to create a universal based on the pasts of both East and West.

Miyake's writing brings out a sophisticated effort to rearticulate pasts into a structure that, in his mind, more closely approximates reason. His effort to expand the archive to include Asia recognizes the historicity of universalistic ideas themselves. He points out, quite rightly, that many ideas of modern society that have been presented as universal are historical. He cites the ideas of Newton and Darwin as recent discoveries; the theory of evolution, which has been used to formulate a hierarchical ordering of cultures, was only forty years old. Moreover, Europe, he argues, developed into a modern society relatively recently, from the fifteenth century, and even then drew upon India. Japan, which is two thousand years old, and China, four thousand years old, are rarely considered.

In addition, Miyake points out that the things that are proffered as universal might serve as explanatory moments, but not universal categories. For example, he questions the role of physique as an explanatory category for cultural development—in particular, the application of Darwin's survival of the fittest to society as an indicator of the superiority of Westerners. He argues that throughout recent history, Europeans have had to develop their military abilities because of the external threats they posed toward each other. "Those people who have survived using brute force for a long time have prevailed because of a large physique that is suitable for the use of weapons and fighting. They have formed a great tribe" (219). In contrast, Japan had been rather isolated, so the importance of the military was not as great as in Europe. But Miyake then turns strength and military prowess around and, perhaps drawing from Spencer, argues that violence is common to nomadic and warlike people, not the civilized; as societies develop, the need for raw physical strength declines—it is not as important in agrarian and industrial societies (220).

Miyake's point is to question some of the naturalized categories that grounded Western universalism. He argues that phrenological work that measures the cranium to prove the intellectual superiority of Caucasians cannot account for peoples who have larger crania, like the Ainu, but are less advanced. He then questions this logic by extending it to the absurd: in the animal kingdom, elephants should be among the smartest. But then, using these racial categories, he argues that the history of the Mongoloids, among whom Japanese are now the most advanced members, is rich, with the skills, commerce, and transmission of civilization often surpassing that of Caucasians (222). In short, the current position of Japan behind the wealth and technological prowess of Europe is a historical, not racial/genetic, issue.

This critique of race potentially removes Japan from the static category of the Orient, that is, the primitive past, and establishes the possibility of ordering the past to demonstrate its potential for change. To tap this potential, Miyake turns to a different form of permanence, what he calls characteristics (*tokushoku*) of the nation. This transhistorical category is juxtaposed to a linear temporality that can be analyzed through the ability (*tokunō*) of the nation. Characteristics (nature) provide the site for the preservation of certain pasts while ability (history) provides the framework to denigrate other pasts that had been a hindrance to development. By separating characteristics and ability, he has rearticulated the relation between nature and history or the given and created in the hope of synchronizing Japan with the international world, but outside of the static category of the Orient. This analysis bears some similarities to Herder's belief in both the universal and the particular:

> And is it ["taste"] not to be explained by the times, customs and people? and does it not thus always have a first principle that has just not been understood well enough, just not felt with the same intensity, just not applied in the correct proportion? and does not even this Proteus of Taste, which changes anew under every stretch of the heavens, in every breath it draws in foreign climes; does it not itself prove by the causes of its transformation that there is only One Beauty, just like Perfection, just like Truth? (Quoted in Norton 1991, 73–74)

Like Herder, Miyake believed that an inquiry into the particular, the accumulation of knowledge about one's cultural and physical development, would lead to an understanding of cultural difference within the same conceptual world. Because all humans are basically the same and bear the same potential, difference from Westerners is not based on some essential quality of the human being or of geography. Miyake's characteristics present an interesting alternative to the homogenizing tendency of the nation. His nation is not determined by some organizing idea but is composed of the various moments of the past that give content to this complex organism, the nation. In one sense, this is history. But his temporality fits neither our modern nor premodern notions. Past is not separate from present; it is the accumulation of experiences by people living on the archipelago. Miyake writes:

> It is not a place formed through human agency, rather it sprouts from a seed, grows, and becomes luxuriant, and over the thousands of years one sees development from this inevitable process. In other words, how could the country of Japan be a place

that organized itself naturally? From the legends of the *Kojiki*—chronicles which are probably not accurate—which depict much turmoil many thousands of years ago, there is procreation, reproduction, cooperation, and expansion. In this way, there are as many as forty million loving descendants, who exist over a long period and have a great variety of stations in life, this is smelted (porcelain), brewed (sake), and gradually forms the nation of Japan. The nation-state is not organized from desire and constructed like a company—planning, leisurely discussion, and the distribution of pamphlets (opinion papers). Each person in the nation of Japan with this history is called Japanese. (217)

Unlike Katō's nation, which is based on an idea, Miyake's nation is formed from the materiality of the everyday lives of the inhabitants. It is an interpretation that recognizes change, but his nation is the living accumulation of individual acts. It is important to remember that this notion of change is quite different from the earlier, pre-Meiji understanding of history—that is, the passage of time—as a devolution of the society from the ideal that can be recovered only through some apocalyptic or millenarian event.

An interesting outcome of this reorientation of pasts is the use of nature (specific sites) as a grounding for certainty in the construction of a transhistorical, national identity. The archipelago is transmuted into the nation, Japan, that contains the heterogeneous places of the archipelago, and people's experiences in these places in turn reinforce the idea of Japan.[16] But having opened the possibility of the historicity of this idea of Japanese, Miyake turns to another nature, one that blurs human characteristics and race, almost contradicting his criticism of Western distinctions rooted in race. He writes, "Race builds the nation; it does not happen without reason. Each person moves along with the trend of the times, or they might not know the reason, but race does what it is supposed to do and the nation does what it is supposed to do. Consequently, they ascertain truth, beauty, and goodness and seek to reach the realm of fulfillment" (223). Here, very early in the attempt to define the new nation-state, race has become synonymous with the nation in a way that ties the Japanese nation to nature. Importantly, for Miyake, this race is not a biological difference, but an accumulation of experience accrued in the same place; it is natural that Japanese comprise a nation (*kokumin*). Miyake draws an analogy to a deer in the mountain, the seagull and water, or stone and iron, which spark, creating fire, when struck together; people do not choose to belong; they have become adapted (217). This analysis is akin to the deterministic argument of Henry Thomas Buckle (1908), who uses geoclimatic conditions to argue that Nature gave Europeans their superior abilities. But unlike Buckle, Miyake's nature is not a fixed antithetical Nature, but sites—the mountains, rivers, lakes, ocean, heavens, the moon over Mikasayama

[16] This use of a historical concept to naturalize a historical form is certainly not unique to Japan. Dorothy Ross points out that, in the United States, natural law (a historical concept) has provided the certainty as Nature upon which a progressive history has been constructed (1991, 3–50).

(east of Nara), and the crying plovers at Awaji Island—through which Japanese continue to interact and make sense of phenomena (233).

This is one of the areas where history obscures its own historicity. Even though Miyake is using an accumulated past to constitute the people of Japan, this accumulation is not a series of events, but unconscious and repeated acts whose sum adds up to a transhistorical form, but possessing a materiality that people had and continue to experience. These accumulated practices establish the inhabitants' relation with the past, now part of nature. It makes possible the relocation of the denigrated and anachronistic senses into earlier or ahistorical categories. Miyake includes sites of everyday life—the inns along the major roads, the Tōdaiji, Hieiji, and Osaka Castle—as well as artifacts, such as helmets, swords, statues, *ukiyoe* (woodblock prints), paintings of Hōgen Motonobu, poetry of Hitomaru, and songs of peasants. In other words, Miyake's notion of beauty is in the familiar and intimate experiences of everyday life.[17] Importantly, though the artifacts skew this list toward the elite, Miyake's sites include both peasant communities—their environs and songs—and elite sensibilities—from the armor and tools of samurai to the prose and poetry of the learned (the invocation of Mt. Mikasa and Awaji Island recalls the poetry of the eighth-century *Manyōshū* and the twelfth-century Fujiwara no Teika).[18]

To establish the characteristics of the nation, Miyake has extracted from an exteriorized nature to elevate an aesthetic as the ideal of Japan; he calls that ideal *keimyō*, light and witty. Miyake's notion of *keimyō* is not just the frivolity of *ukiyoe*, the "floating world" of Edo, but an emphasis on gradual, natural change in accordance with the everyday life of Japanese. The nation is that accumulation of past experiences conditioned by the sites of the archipelago. These sites, though, are not a dead past that is separate from the present. Instead, many of his examples are of the past and the present. The import of this interpretation is to ground an idea of Japan in the interaction of people on the archipelago rather than upon the ideals of elites or historical categories. What makes inhabitants Japanese is the cumulation (learned and experienced) of these activities. Importantly, humans are no longer controlled by nature, but interact with and use it; it gives rise to culture. In short, this characteristic alters the relation with the past, formulating a transhistorical idea of Japan.

Miyake's idea was an important step in the rearticulation of the past from a denigrated past to a modern idea that is fundamental to the formulation of the nation or nation-state. The limitation of his argument, however, is that he is not able to articulate a way to claim authority in achieving his notion of happiness. His separation of ability from characteristics is useful to demarcate the present

---

[17] In the words of Arthur O. Lovejoy, "the 'natural' as that which is most congenial to, and immediately comprehensible and enjoyable by, *each* individual—this conceived not as uniform in all men, but as varying with time, race, nationality, and cultural tradition" (1948, 73).

[18] See, for example, the invocation of Mt. Mikasa in Cranston (1993, 304–5).

as new, that is, modern. But while he sets up the possibility for a narrative of Japan that demonstrates change, improvement, development, and/or progress, his discussion does not venture far beyond the liberation of the present from the "self-incurred immaturities." His appeal to ability is for smart men to open their minds and think (always an appropriate critique). Miyake is moving the discourse from rhetorical categories, such as East/West and traditional/modern, to the process.

Perhaps more than most, Miyake recognizes that time is gaining a historical quality. As I will describe below, Miyake is critical of those who seek to fix Japanese characteristics in some timeless, abstract idea. By defining the past as still present—the experience at different sites, such as Awaji Island and Mt. Mikasa—he is trying to limit this transformation of time into history. He is reluctant, here, to accept that modern society also occurs through time, that constant move of present to past, where the past is no longer a part of the present, only recoverable as some inert object. Miyake's rendition of the past retains a fluidity and heterogeneity that conceives of the nation as living and located in the experiences of the people. But while this everyday life, to repeat de Certeau, "reproduces sameness and marks an identity," it also "posits nature, esthetics, and religiosity outside of itself." His removal of goodness to a transhistorical idea potentially fixes these ethics as norms that Japanese must follow. That is, it sets up the possibility that culture is outside of history; this very problem is critiqued by Takayama Chogyū.

For those of us entrenched in the modern (as well as most postmodernists), this instability of pasts can be rather unnerving. For a modern society, such fluidity also perpetuates uncertainty and variability. Indeed, that is its difficulty: in Miyake's notion, it is still possible to envision the ghosts and spirits that had inhabited the lands. Indeed, many of his contemporaries sought greater stability, and it was from this impulse that the modern idea of Japan became naturalized. This instability would be reduced by entombing the past in an archive from which information and meaning can be extracted, something he resisted. For a different version of the same past, I will now turn to Okakura Kakuzō (Tenshin), whose writings Miyake often critiqued.

Spirituality from a Dead Past

Okakura offered a different configuration of the past. Both he and Miyake were among the first students of Ernest F. Fenollosa in the philosophy course at Tokyo Imperial University, and quite a hagiography has emerged surrounding him. He was truly a colorful and international figure. Wearing a robe, he rode his horse to work at the Imperial Museum (as well as to the Museum of Art in Boston), and he often published his ideas in English for an American audience. Together with Fenollosa, he is quite properly known as one of the discoverers of Japanese art and art history. Though there are important differences between Okakura and Fenollosa, the overall historical narrative of art that they advocated continues to serve as the prevailing framework for the field of Japanese art history.[19]

During the 1880s Fenollosa and Okakura worked hard to institutionalize their conviction that the Idea (Hegelian spirit) could be located in art and best expresses a Japan: they founded journals and clubs that promoted the appreciation of ancient Japanese art, took official trips to catalog and register ancient artifacts, were instrumental in ordering objects into a historical chronology, sat on various governmental commissions and review boards, and directed some of the most prestigious art institutions—the Tokyo School of Fine Art, the art department of the Imperial Museum, and the East Asian collection of the Museum of Fine Arts in Boston.

There are many similarities between Miyake and Okakura, especially in their turn to aesthetics. Like Miyake, Okakura cautioned that the past should not be separated from the present. He writes, "When people look at history, it is considered an account compiling traces of the past, in other words, dead things. But this is a major fallacy. History exists and lives within our bodies. After all, the tears and laughter of ancient people are the source of today's cries and laughter" (1939, 4:1). But despite Okakura's complaint of the past as dead, his selection of Buddhist icons and ink-brush paintings and the way he connected them to the present depended on an objectified past. His complaint notwithstanding, his interpretation led to the transference of the past from the people of the nation to the idea of the nation. And if we recall that he conducted his work through the sponsorship of the state, the homogenizing propensity of his formulation serves the needs for unity and obedience.

Okakura argues that art is the best source to understand some immanent Japanese spirit which, he believed, transcends the phenomenal and is the closest representation of a universal human spirit. He states, "Nothing is more hallowing than the union of kindred spirits in art. At the moment of meeting, the art lover transcends himself. At once he is and is not. He catches a glimpse of Infinity, but words cannot voice his delight, for the eye has no tongue. Freed from the fetters of matter, his spirit moves in the rhythm of things. It is thus that art becomes akin to religion and ennobles mankind" (1956, 81–82). The images and artists that Okakura singled out gave content to his version of the Hegelian spirit. Like Hegel, he argues that sculpture expresses the spirit in human form; paintings, poetry, and music present the spirit as an abstract visible (Taylor 1975, 478). The sculpture and paintings that he selected follow a developmental pattern— similar to Hegel's symbolic, classical, romantic—that celebrates the culmina-

---

[19] The longevity of this orthodoxy was recently raised by art historian Yashiro Yukio, who argued that the content and nature of Japanese art history has not changed significantly since the Tokyo Imperial Museum issued its compendium on important objects of Japanese art around the turn of the century (1987, 7–8).

tion of the Asiatic culture and spirit in Japan (I will describe this chronology in more depth in chapter 4). Art, not people's experience of it, is elevated to a spiritual level. He writes, "Art is a religion in itself. The mere fact of painting a holy subject does not constitute the holiness of the picture. The inherent nobleness and devotional attitude of the artist's mind toward the universe, alone stamp him as the religious painter" (1922, 191).

In contrast to Miyake, by emphasizing the spirit embedded in the object, Okakura and Fenollosa are giving meaning to the object, regardless of prior utility or historical significance. Okakura writes, "The very individuality of Art, which makes its problem so subjective to the artist, at the same time makes it defy classification in time" (1922, 181). In other words, it is up to the expert to classify the objects so that its "real" meaning can be discerned. Then these experts must tell the people what they should know; they must convert it into forms, in the words of an art historian in 1931, "easy to understand even for men living in that changing and rather uncouth age" (Ino 1931, 124). Okakura articulates this message:

> The strange tenacity of the race, nurtured in the shadow of a sovereignty unbroken from its beginning, that very tenacity which preserves the Chinese and Indian ideals in all their purity amongst us, even where they were long since cast away by the hands that created them, that tenacity which delights in the delicacy of Fuji-wara culture, and revels at the same time in the martial ardour of Kamakura, which tolerates the gorgeous pageantry of Toyotomi, even while it loves the austere purity of the Ashikagas, holds Japan to-day intact, in spite of this sudden incomprehensible influx of Western ideas. To remain true to herself, notwithstanding the new colour which the life of a modern nation forces her to assume, is, naturally, the fundamental imperative of that Adwaita idea to which she was trained by her ancestors. (1970, 222–23)

Here, Okakura has identified which past gives meaning to the present. His selection of Buddhist icons for this history marks a significant transition in the valuation of artifacts. Only six years earlier, the objects displayed at the 1875 Nara exhibition spanned time from the seventh century through the Tokugawa period; while many were religious objects, most showed the temple's connection to the imperial family. But Okakura ignored most of those artifacts, instead focusing on the large Buddhist statuary. Interestingly, he selected large Buddhist icons (still with their heads), especially from the Hōryūji; he omitted artifacts from the Shōsōin, more closely tied to the imperial family. One reason was the locus of these artifacts in the chronology that he was developing: he positioned the statues of the Hōryūji into an earlier period, Suiko (also Asuka, 552–645), than the artifacts of the Shōsōin, the Tenpyō (710–794) (this chronology will be discussed further in chapter 4). But this changing valuation is especially interesting when placed in the context of the emergence of State Shinto (Hardacre 1989). It seems to mark that contradistinction of modernity, the stable and mobile, now as timeless and timeful. Here, spirituality is one of those abstractions that would determine the subjectivity of the nation and establish the grounds for possession of objects. Buddhist icons gain a place in history; they are material objects that people can view and thus see the "reality" of this national past. They have become symbols of spirituality in the narrative of national development, while the imperial system becomes sacred and eternal, removed from history.

In contrast to Miyake's effort not to separate past from present, Okakura connects past and present using tactics of recovery and continuity. In short, past and present are severed and then reconnected through an immanent idea that serves as a medium to express a spirit in humanity that is simultaneously progressive, one that "ennobles mankind," and idealistic, transcending the phenomenal world on which it is dependent—materiality, class, history, and nationality. For Okakura, the history of art is a part of all Japanese because it was produced on the archipelago (the question of artist is often ignored); it is not only useful in depicting a Japanese culture, but also the means for revitalizing an Asiatic past that bears Japan's spirit. In a sense, this act parallels Inoue Enryō's ghost-busting and Kume and Shigeno's reformulation of history in the preceding chapter. Using the same icons, religiosity is transformed from the practices of the various sects that we now combine as Buddhism to a religiosity hidden within these pieces, the spirit of the nation.

The spirit that Okakura identifies maps the essential characteristics of Japanese. Okakura locates a spirituality—Buddhism; a sense of harmony—the naturalism and serenity of the objects; and adaptability—the keen sense of adapting important aspects of foreign cultures and harmoniously assimilating them into the culture. Old things are celebrated for a "patina of age" that Okakura defines through an immanent characteristic, the concept *kōtan* (refined simplicity)—his celebration of a lack of complexity in earlier periods. But spirituality here shifts from bodhisattva as part of a way of life to Buddhist icons as a reflection of an inner sense of the nation (1939, 4:86, 263, 172). This inner sense, though, is only possible because of the externality of nature from which he extracts a timeless idea of what Japanese should be.

The transmutation of these artifacts from a lived past to a past that informs the present can be illustrated through Fenollosa and Okakura's discovery of the Guze Kannon, one of the most famous statues in the archive of Japanese art history. Moreover, the difference between Fenollosa and Okakura indicates not only the separation of the past, but also its utility. The celebrated moment of discovery is in 1884, when a commission, sponsored by the Meiji government and headed by Okakura, Kanō Tessai, and Fenollosa, went to Nara to catalogue the important artifacts in temples and shrines. Although rather lengthy, their declarations are informative. Fenollosa describes a moment of discovery:

> I had credentials from the central government which enabled me to requisition the opening of godowns and shrines. The central space of the octagonal Yumedono was occupied by a great closed shrine, which ascended like a pillar towards the

apex. The priests of the Horiuji confessed that tradition ascribed the contents of the shrine to Corean work of the days of Suiko, but that it had not been opened for more than two hundred years. On fire with the prospect of such a unique treasure, we urged the priests to open it by every argument at our command. They resisted long alleging that in punishment for the sacrilege an earthquake might well destroy the temple. Finally we prevailed, and I shall never forget our feelings as the long disused key rattled in the rusty lock. Within the shrine appeared a tall mass closely wrapped about in swathing bands of cotton cloth, upon which the dust of ages had gathered. It was no light task to unwrap the contents, some 500 yards of cloth having been used, and our eyes and nostrils were in danger of being choked with the pungent dust. . . .

But it was the aesthetic wonders of this work that attracted us most. From the front the figure is not quite so noble, but seen in profile it seemed to rise to the height of archaic Greek art. . . . But the finest feature was the profile view of the head, with its sharp Han nose, its straight clear forehead, and its rather large—almost negroid—lips, on which a quiet mysterious smile played, not unlike Da Vinci's Mona Lisa's. Recalling the archaic stiffness of Egyptian Art at its finest, it appeared still finer in the sharpness and individuality of the cutting. In slimness it was like a Gothic statue from Amiens, but far more peaceful and unified in its single systems of lines. (1911, 50)

Fenollosa's account is an example of the recovery of a dead past, and its utility in the formulation of an idea of society can be described according to an abstract, universalistic, and temporal standard, that is, progress. Like Inoue Enryō, he is the authority, the expert, battling against the anachronistic priests rather than ghosts and apparitions. For the priests, the significance of the Kannon was in the meaning of the place, not the statue itself. It served as that sacred core that symbolized the connection between the spiritual and natural world—a magical connection between the hidden and the heavens. This space of experience depended on a principle of contiguity on two levels: first, the idea of the Kannon possessed meaning (and power) only for those who were aware of the legends that were transmitted orally by the Buddhist priests; those distant had no access to these stories. Second, the power of the Kannon was activated only by disturbance; too close contact, a direct gaze, was a transgression. That the local place bore meaning was evident in the punishment for the transgression—the wrath of the heavens would destroy the site, not the transgressors. Here, the place was inscribed with meaning that emanated from its proximate relations, not from that of Japan or its heavenly creators, unless one connects Japan's early society to Korea. Like the use of architecture in the Renaissance, visualization was important to maintaining its significance where "The effect of viewing magical shapes on the observer's memory and imagination was considered an important element in directing the heavenly forces" (Sack 1980, 161).

Fenollosa could make claims to have discovered an object that existed for a millennium, was known by local residents, and was protected by the priests because he emplotted it in a way understandable to a modern temporality. Fenollosa's Kannon has meaning in its relation to the world (Europe); he speculated on the connection to Greek aesthetics, compares it with Da Vinci's Mona Lisa and Egyptian art, and finds Han Chinese influences. This synchronization of the Kannon into a history of art reinforces the particularity of Japan. But, one must ask, whose definition of difference? The subjectivity is a Japan within the category of the Orient, that is, the past of Europe.

Okakura's account places Japan in a similar framework, but while employing the vocabulary of the Orient, it does not accept the locus as Oriental, instead elevating Japan's art above that of the West. He writes:

> In 1884 along with Fenollosa and Kanō Tessai I approached the priests [of the Hō-ryūji] asking that they open the door. The priests replied that if they did so thunder would certainly be heard. Recently, at the beginning of Meiji during the clamor over the separation of Buddhism and Shinto they did open the doors. Instantly the heavens clouded over and thunder roared; then the masses became frightened and fled. With such a memorable experience they did not easily acquiesce. But after saying that we would take responsibility for the thunder, they opened door, then immediately hid in fear. The mustiness accumulated over a thousand years almost overcame us. When we cleared away the spider webs we saw a table which is thought to be from the Higashiyama period; and beyond it, we could touch the statue. It was 7 or 8 feet tall and wrapped endlessly with cloth and pieces of sutra. Perhaps it was surprise of signs of life, we were startled when snakes and rats suddenly appeared. After we removed the cloth we reached white paper. This is where the masses [of the beginning of Meiji] stopped when they were frightened by the thunder. We could make out the statue's solemnity and serenity (*tangen*) in its outline. It was truly the most exhilarating moment of my life. Fortunately the thunder did not appear and even the priests seemed considerably relieved. Up to the middle of Ashikaga this statue was probably not a hidden idol, it accurately follows the features . . . as a life-size figure of a common person holding a jewel in the left hand and the right hand turned down covering the jewel. . . . On the face, the cheekbones were high and the lower cheeks drooped. This was a common form of Buddhist statues of the Suiko period: the head and limbs are large and muscles around the nose pronounced. (1939, 4:54–55)

Okakura, too, was operating in a very different conceptual world from that of the priests. His Kannon was also severed from their world and revived as art, but his art established an idealistic horizon of expectations, that is, the future, a national spirit, one that is intimately tied to a Japan. It is a spirit that expresses itself through the particularity of the statue yet transcended history.[20] From their for-

---

[20] A hint at the transcendent quality of art is evident in Okakura's definition of the Adwaita ideal; this ideal is the state of not being two and is the name applied to the great Indian doctrine that all that exists, though apparently manifold, is really one (1970, 235).

mer power as icons protecting those in the area from calamity, ghosts, and evil, the new value of bodhisattva is as artifacts that embody a national spirit, the otherness of nature, that is best seen and known through an aesthetic experience that could only be discerned by experts. Okakura writes, "We know instinctively that in our history lies the secret of our future, and we grope with a blind intensity to find the clue. But if the thought be true, if there be indeed any spring of renewal hidden in our past, we must admit that it needs at this moment some mighty reinforcement, for the scorching drought of modern vulgarity is parching the throat of life and art" (1970, 243–44). This is the site where Okakura seeks to return this art of a hidden past to the present. Fine art becomes an archive from which experts can extract visual reminders of the past as the embodiment of Japan's essential nature and future. His notion of that nature becomes a spirit that is removed from time and serves as an other of the human. Interestingly, this revived spirit reiterates the category of the Orient.

The different pasts of Miyake, Okakura, and Fenollosa demonstrate how different the nation might be, depending on one's definition. In the case of Miyake, the nation was more of a living organism that was centered in the inhabitants, while in Okakura and Fenollosa, it was an archive of artifacts to extract certain ideals that then needed to be taught to the people. But in each case, they began to transmute the archipelago into a place where history became possible. By working within a now accepted idea of Japan, and by giving the inhabitants certain characteristics that were connected to that site, they naturalized culture as either the accumulation of acts by people on the archipelago, or as a particular aesthetic that grounds those people.

The narratives of Okakura and Fenollosa are often interchangeable, but their differences bring out the utility of the past. Fenollosa was one of those Westerners whom Miyake criticized for being infatuated with his Japan. Fenollosa adored the bodhisattva for what was lost in the West. Japan was the repository of the best of Asian art that fit his Hegelian world. He did not notice (nor care) that that art remained at the symbolic stage of Hegelian development. He was (or sought to be) the interpreter of East Asian art. Perhaps Fenollosa's nostalgia for Asian art no longer exists today; the structure of meaning, however, remains. Okakura's main difference with his frequent partner was the locus provided by the West. Okakura's narrative is sprinkled with comparisons—within the same Hegelian stages—with European art, but he usually concludes that Japan's art is different—better—because of the secret, that Adwaita ideal.

Miyake is critical of this conceptualization of art as superficial. He writes, "In sum, art in our country today uselessly produces exterior ornamentation. There is no synthesis of interiority and exteriority. In other words it is as if both artists and viewers have abandoned without reflection the concept that is the basis of beauty" (1931b, 256). Even though Okakura and Fenollosa are seeking to connect past and present to establish some sense of permanence of the nation,

Miyake discerns that the imposition of spirituality is external and does not represent some interiority of a Japan. For Miyake, regardless of whether they are extolled as art, they must embody a concept of beauty (*bijutsu no shisō*), without which he finds only vulgarity and superficiality.

The superficiality of which Miyake complains is the overlay of this notion of aesthetic over the nation, removed from history. Miyake's notion of Japanese beauty is not the majesty, simplicity, mystery (*yūgen*), or melancholic characteristics that build upon the characterizations of Okakura and Fenollosa.[21] His beauty is in the familiar and intimate experiences of everyday life—elite and commoner. His past is more varied; it crosses class divisions and regions and includes the environment as well as products. But this selection is important, for Miyake locates permanence in the various peoples of the archipelago. His naturalized nation is more of a living nation, one that is evolving, naturally. I realize that there is a level of romanticism in this view, yet it is important to point out that the framework has some plasticity and that the subject is located in the people.

Both Miyake and Okakura sought to establish a "real" that transcends the reality of the present and of inherited forms and ideas.[22] In both cases, they appealed to an essential quality hidden and embedded underneath the surface of human/nature interaction and only discernible by examining ideas across time. But in the end, it was Okakura (or Fenollosa) who not only rescued Japanese art, but also established a unity that had much more stability than Miyake's characteristics. But it came with a cost: the "new" art objects, revived as art, now possessed meaning tied to the nation. These objects demonstrate a timeless or "permanent" quality that confirms that a Japan has always existed. This past is fixed, severed from the present and the masses. The wonders and spirits that had been an integral part of the lives of people were occulted; the *ijin* have been shorn from these icons. It is a spirituality that naturalizes the archipelago as a place endowed with certain immutable characteristics removed from history. It established, to repeat Eagleton (1990, 23), "a sense of unity powerful enough to reproduce itself by."

Nature and Nation

Katō, Miyake, Okakura, and Fenollosa were but a few of the intellectuals engaged in this search for some kind of essence. They were part of a sociocultural milieu that facilitated the production of this idea of Japan. They were joined by the hundreds of anonymous commoners and priests who prevented the destruc-

---

[21] These are the characteristics most cited when thinking of a Japanese aesthetic. See, for example, Keene (1969, 293–306).

[22] For a discussion of this quest in Bengal, see Chakrabarty (2000, 149–79).

tion of Buddhist objects that resulted from the policy of separation of Buddhism and Shinto; willing artists seeking patronage; and an audience in the West eager to discover their Orient in Japan. The greatest support, however, came from the state. At this point it is important to recall the purpose of these intellectual exercises: to formulate a unified place, the collective singular of the nation. Katō had been president of Tokyo Imperial University, and Okakura and Fenollosa had key government support from officials like Kuki Ryūichi. Through these and other scholars, the state was central to the constitution of the nation.

The penetration of the state is evident in the differing ideas of the nation in Miyake and Okakura. Miyake also criticized the emphasis on industry and saw its impoverishing effects on so many people. Instead he called for an economic development that would improve agricultural production, which would then foster industrial development (1931a, 231–32). This plan was more consistent with the idea of the nation as rooted in everyday life. Instead, ideas like those of Okakura that explain to the inhabitants what it is to be Japanese prevailed.

But while their versions are considerably different from each other, there is a key similarity. It is this familiarity that revolves around an idea of nature that is so intriguing. Many years ago Arthur O. Lovejoy pointed out that the word nature has a tendency "to slip more or less insensibly from one connotation to another, and thus in the end to pass from one ethical or aesthetic standard to its very antithesis, while nominally professing the same principles" (1948, 69). It is in this slippage that nature (or, more accurately, natures) was externalized in ways that reinforced a particular notion of the nation as if it had always been real. Nature became a convenient site for the domestication of pasts, necessary for the formulation of a modern society. Within this transhistorical category, anachronistic objects gained new importance by presenting, materially, the timeless characteristics of the nation.

An important outcome of this reconceptualization was the naturalization of space from locales to a unit within which subregions are connected directly to a center. In Miyake and Okakura, the naturalization of some essential idea into the basis of the nation turned the archipelago into the place, Japan. The explanatory power of this reconfiguration of the past was twofold: to establish the ahistorical character of the nation-state and to make the connections to the expanded world, ancient and contemporary. Harry Harootunian writes, "The discourse on the social was primarily ideological inasmuch as its primary purpose was to remove, conceal divisions, naturalize historical relationships, and eternalize them in order to declare the recovery of a lost unity and coherence outside of time" (2000, 215). One of the benefits of this formulation that concealed divisions (especially that of region and class) was to establish the possibility for a circulatory system of people and things within this place called Japan. People shorn from their locale, now homogenized as Japanese, could move about "freely" to participate in the labor market.

But importantly, place is not defined by geography, that is, the geophysical contours of the archipelago.[23] Place is defined by the characteristics of the inhabitants as they have unfolded in their interactions with the environment and nature. With the place of the nation defined through the products of people (no matter how abstract), the boundaries of the nation-state became defined as inner/outer or Japanese/foreign. But this idea remained vague—some spirit or practices that have existed throughout time. But it was in this vagueness that this "permanence" gained a naturalized significance. Okakura lamented the descent of stereotyped images into a caricature of art. Caricature in this sense is a "compact visual vocabulary" that captures the "essence" of some represented object.

This brings out the symbolic power of nature that has been able to absorb the heterogeneity that had resided on the archipelago. In spite of the differing ideas among these intellectuals, they were part of a milieu that recovered an idea that was located throughout the past; scholars and intellectuals discerned an inner meaning and then presented it to the people for them to know. Even though their respective "Japan" differed, the objects, either religious icons, landscape paintings, or important sites, could be used interchangeably because they had been stripped of their earlier significance and, within this broad transhistorical category of spirit or nature, served as evidence for the idea of the nation. As Karatani Kōjin has pointed out, it was only from the 1890s that the idea of landscape gained widespread use. It became a conceptual site to write about the interiority of both the individual as well as a Japan (1993, 11–44). But even though this interiority became an external form imposed upon the people and society as if it had always been theirs, the repetition of the idea and its visualization continues to give it form as if it is concrete and specific. Both Miyake's allusions to the mountains Awaji and Mikasayama and Okakura's call to a characteristic, *kōtan*, found in the statues as well as landscape paintings—especially of the Kanō school—fit a caricature of nature. The efficacy of caricature is that it accentuates the distinctive. For understanding, it needs no experts to mediate reception; the distinction between observer and observed is blurred by the experiential nature of apprehension (Hochberg 1972, 74–90).

This idea of Japan establishes permanence, but uncertainty remains. Possibilities of different interpretations of that past still exist, and the transhistorical status of a Japan does not readily account for change. These potential problems will be diminished through the formulation of a narrative of history that provides a template that gives order to the past.

---

[23] Robert David Sack contrasts territory with place in a way similar to the way in which I contrast place and space. Place (or territoriality) is a container that helps to organize the relation between humans and their environment. He states: "Territoriality for humans is a powerful geographic strategy to control people and things by controlling area. . . . It is used in everyday relationships and in complex organizations. Territoriality is a primary geographical expression of social power. It is the means by which space and society are interrelated" (1986, 5).

Chapter 4

NATURALIZATION OF NATION:
CHRONOLOGICAL TIME

> Recast in the mold of a taxonomic ordering of things,
> chronology becomes the alibi of time, a way of making use of
> time without reflecting on it. . . . Time continues to be expe-
> rienced within the productive process; but now, transformed
> from within into a rational series of operations and objectified
> from without into a metric system of chronological units, this
> experience has only one language: an ethical language which
> expresses the imperative to produce.
> —Michel de Certeau (1983)

THE FORMULATION of an essential time from the archive of the archipelago both naturalized the idea of Japan as a "collective singular" and removed that past from time. This is one of those continuities where such concepts and data become the constant, free-floating signifiers of the nation, whose periodic reappearance in time proves its timelessness. The formulation of an essence of this nation is a critical part of the unfolding of the modern nation-state. An essential time occults part of that past that was evil, those "self incurred immaturities" from which it is necessary to extract oneself. But even though the nation now possesses this transhistorical essence, it still needs history: history shows the unfolding and development of this place and also orders variation and difference (indeed, it depends upon difference).

During the 1880s numerous intellectuals were searching for and vying to establish some narrative that would give content to this nation. Koselleck offers an indication of the stakes in this debate: "[The collective singular] made possible the attribution to history of the latent power of human events and suffering, a power that connected and motivated everything in accordance with a secret or evident plan to which one could feel responsible, or in whose name one could believe oneself to be acting" (1985, 31). After the archipelago was reconfigured into a nation, a structure was needed to establish an orderly past, that "secret or evident plan" that determines to whom one should feel responsible, and in whose name one acts. We should remember that the constitution was promulgated in 1890, and during the early years of this constitutional system elections were heavily and bloodily contested. Margaret Mehl states the importance of history: "In the historical fever far more was at stake than the past: at a time when the present was confusing and the future a cause for fear, as well as anticipation, history was expected to provide orientation" (1998b, 80).

The "history fever" (*rekishi no ryūkōnetsu*) refers to a substantial increase in interest about history among the public between 1890 and 1893. This public obsession over the past changed the discussion from that among academics and elites to that of the general literate public. Up to this point, comments from intellectuals that there was no history of Japan but only accounts of the emperors and shoguns were common. It is important to recall that history as we know it today did not emerge until 1887, and it was not until the 1900s that a chronology emerged that narrated that history of Japan.[1] In short, the formation of the profession and institutions of history marks a resolution (not the beginning) of contestation over the representation and policing (or disciplinization) of the past according to a rather simplified notion of time—a chronology of a dead past, that is, History.

The contestation focused on establishing a particular temporality to provide that orientation. Koselleck describes the two primary forms of history in this contestation: "A dual difference thus prevails: between a history in motion and its linguistic possibility and between a past history and its linguistic reproduction" (1985, 232). Koselleck points to two different ways in which the past can be marshalled to orient the new place of Japan. A history in motion and its linguistic possibility is closer to the inherited understanding in which the past is not separated from the present. A past history and its linguistic reproduction is akin to our current notions of history. During the 1880s various intellectuals worked through these different temporalities. But in the resolution that leads to the modern nation, both temporalities coexist. Simplistically, and according to our current categories, disciplines such as Japanese literature (*kokubungaku*) and art history fill the temporality of the former, while history (*rekishi*) and notions of childhood give form to the latter. In the modern nation-state, these categories of knowledge resolve the potential contradiction of modernity between stability and change.

The coexistence of these temporalities is made possible because of a shared dependence on chronology. Chronology is a seemingly innocuous organizing device; it takes advantage of our reckoning of time as a linear progression, the continual advance of the second hand (or digital face), and the constant move of the present into the future and into the past. The developmental time that we use, organized chronologically, has been the dominant mode throughout the twentieth century.[2] Today the chronological passing of time is natural; it has be-

---

[1] For an incisive analysis of the "invention" of the medieval (*chūsei*) in Japanese historiography, see Keirstead (1998).

[2] For a fine essay pointing out the way in which the historical mode since the Enlightenment has become the dominant mode of constructing the past, synchronizing most of the world, see Nandy (1995).

come the principal way that time is experienced. This "common sense" of chronological time is possible because of the way that temporal measurements have imbricated our modern society and orient our lives. It gives the idea of the nation form, that is, a reality, through a narrative of unfolding, reinforced by verifiable data. But to use chronology as obvious and natural is, again, to overlook the transformation of time where it, too, is historical.

Chronology domesticates pasts, or those heterogeneous times, by placing select events, things, or ideas into a series of prior moments of the present. What had been common practices, that is, the "myths of yesterday," are turned into something historical, while what had been historical is removed to some detached realm, typically rendered within categories of modern, nature, and tradition, thus remaining within the epistemology of modernity. This is the compartmentalization of knowledge to which de Certeau points. The evolution of the discipline of history as an objective field, facts that recount the development of the nation-state as if it had always existed, certainly illustrates this reduction of time.[3] Childhood constantly reproduces this process among all the nationals. On the other hand, those texts that had been accepted as authoritative accounts become the domain of the new discipline of Japanese literature (*kokubungaku*), the icons that had possessed power for their spirituality become art objects that display the history of Japanese art, and childhood reinforces the perpetual presence of the past and the need to overcome the past through education and social reform.

Each of these fields—history, *kokubungaku*, art history, and the idea of childhood—emerged around the same time and, indeed, were part of the contestation that led to the historicization of Japan.[4] Where history depicts change and stability of the nation-state through political and economic development, Japanese literature focuses on the spirit and habits of mind, and Japanese art history focuses on the spirituality and ideas that are evident in the eras of Japan's past. In short, these, too, adopt a chronological narrative to describe the permanence of the nation. Childhood is also chronological, but whereas the above might be considered the structure that describes philogeny, childhood reinforces the stability of the nation through the ontogeny of the perpetually recurring development of Japanese. We must recognize that these new categories of knowledge helped formulate a certain kind of society, in the words of de Certeau, guided by "a rational series of operations and objectified from without into a metric system of chronological units." We must think again of the relationship of our (historians') adherence to the "linguistic reproduction" and the relationship of chronology to the "imperative to produce."

---

[3] For two recent accounts of the development of the profession of modern history in Japan, see Mehl (1998a) and Brownlee (1997).
[4] This list is far from complete. Peter Hughes (1995), for example, has written about the separation and interdependence of history and ethnology.

In this chapter, I will describe the reduction of time to chronological time. While the discussion necessarily starts in the debates on history, the implications are the reconstitution of society according to linear time. As historians were naturalizing such linear time, other fields of knowledge, such as Japanese literature and art history, also took advantage of the "imperative to produce." In these disciplines the separated past is rejoined to the present, but now as knowledge that citizens must know and feel. But, chronological time gains further credence as it becomes embodied in the ontogenic process of the human being; that is, the human is not born into a condition but develops (or does not) into an adult. This transformation of the idea of humans will be discussed through the idea of childhood, which also changed during this period.

HISTORY AS HISTOIRE

The early efforts to revive the past show the difficulty of relinquishing an inherited understanding that is closer to Koselleck's history in motion. During the 1880s, antiquarianism revived as witnessed through the publication of the *Kyūji shimonroku* (Record of Investigation of Old Things) and the *Edo kyūji kō* (Remembrances of Old Things from Edo). The nativists enjoyed renewed institutional support; in 1882 Inoue Yorikuni (1839–1914) and Konakamura Kiyonori, with the support of Katō Hiroyuki, established the Kōten Kōkyūjo (Center for Investigation of Ancient Texts, now Kokugakuin University) in the Faculty of Letters at Tokyo University. In addition, the first course on Japanese history (*nihon rekishi*) was added to the history curriculum (*shigaku*), which had consisted primarily of world history (*bankokushi*), at the Tokyo University preparatory school.[5] In the same year, Fenollosa, who was hired to teach philosophy at the Imperial University, presented his famous speech to the Ryūchikai, "An Explanation of Truth in Art." Also, in 1883, the Shigaku Kyōkai (History Society) was founded by scholars like Konakamura and Naitō Chisso. This society published the journal *Shigaku kyōkai zasshi* (Journal of the History Society).[6] By 1889, when the Shigakkai (Japanese Historical Association) was founded, history was becoming the reproduction of a distant past.

The standard historiography tends to place this interest in the past as a reaction against Westernization. The principal actors of this narrative shifted away from early enlightenment figures, such as Fukuzawa and others influenced by Guizot and Buckle, to the positivists (with Confucian training), such as Kume Kunitake and Shigeno Yasutsugu, the populist (*minyūsha*) historians, and some conservatives, usually unnamed and lurking in the background to sabotage the

---

[5] This course was recommended by Adolph Groth, a German hired to teach history, and implemented by Sugiura Shigetaka. Arai Hakusei's *Dokushi yoron* served as the text.
[6] Publication began in July 1883. Twenty-seven issues were published, until October 1885.

plans of these enlighteners. The transformation followed a similar trajectory, moving from a discovery of progress, to empirical research, and then the re-assertion of a conservativeness through both state institutions and traditionalists seeking to withstand the modern transformation. It is a story of hopeful trans-formation to the modern (to be like the West), only to be derailed by the non-enlightened. Interestingly, despite the centrality of history, historians are exonerated. The conservatives are usually indicted for an interest in an applied or political (mythical) history, while "populist" historians (as the label already implies) are derided. Iwai Tadakuma's evaluation of the populist historians gives a sense of the desire of recent historiographers to separate academic historians from the fray: "The strength of their history was in their sharp contemporary crit-icism, but there was no careful academic methodology" (1963, 81). In other words, methodology and rigor are guarantees against a slip to applied or popular history or something not objective. This narrative (predictably) ends with some evil (conservatives) hijacking history for the state, while historians become the unwitting victims. In applying this teleology to the study of history, historians (including myself) have generally followed the considerable interpretive struc-ture of Ōkubo Toshiaki.[7] In addition to the typological framework, this histori-ography has emphasized method as the litmus test to determine a modern history. In doing so, historians have emphasized how Japanese historians have (not) become fully modern.

The absences from this interpretive line remove from consideration the pos-sibility that the idea of history itself is historical. Interestingly, the intellectuals of the Shigaku Kyōkai, the first historical association in modern Japan, are not in-cluded in this historiography, and the positions of their students, those who founded Japanese literature, are also ignored. The history of Japanese literature also ignores history.[8] This is the moment when history gains an autonomous, ahistorical status; not only is data collected from throughout the land, separated from its locus, and entombed into an archive of Japan (the Office of Historiog-raphy, now the Historiographical Institute), it is gradually reorganized along a linear time, the universal time of progress. In other words, the creation of a his-tory of Japan entailed the reformulation of data into a universal temporal frame-work, not the organization of data according to its significance to place.

When compared with the interest in the past of the previous decade, scholars of the 1880s were trying to go beyond the particularity of old things, be it that of the emperors or of antiquities, to articulate that "secret or evident plan to which one could feel responsible." The principal actors were intellectuals with

---

[7] For essays on history, see Numata (1961); Duus (1974); Gluck (1978); Mehl (1998a); Brownlee (1997); and Tanaka (1993). Of these, Mehl has brought out the most detail on actors, especially those with *kokugaku* lineage, who have not commonly been included in these narratives.

[8] Interestingly, the histories of Japanese history and literature trace the emergence of each discipline without reference to each other. For essays that examine the canonization of classics, see Shirane and Suzuki (2000); Brownstein (1987).

a background in *kokugaku* (nativism) and empirical scholars trained in Confucian rationalism. Regardless of this background, we must recognize that this idea itself was new. Few disagreed with Katō Hiroyuki, who argued that history was the way to uncover the independent laws. "That which should be called history (*shigaku*) is, in other words, a search into the causes of past events, that is, the investigation of the phenomena that give rise to effects. In other words, it is in the research of the natural laws (*tensoku*) that influence the rise and fall and prosperity and decline of societies" (1890, 8). But those independent laws are also separate from society. Statements such as the "trend of the times" are evidence of the penetration of time as an autonomous actor in political and social discourses.[9] This interest in the trends of the times is evidence that history is occurring through time. It is the other side of the contradistinction of modernity—that while an essential time can establish permanence, pasts must also serve as the earlier, now anachronistic, moments of a narrative of development or progress. In this sense, the 1880s and 1890s can also be characterized as a search for and contestation over that past that successfully fulfills these demands, becoming the history of the nation.

In this recognition of the need for some narrative that orders the past, most intellectuals recognized that neither existing accounts nor current frameworks—Japanese, Chinese, and Western—could service the new idea of Japan, as the principal object of history. For example, the scholar Maruyama Sakura, whose intellectual lineage traced back to the nativist scholar Hirata Atsutane, complained in 1883 that the state of history of the country (*honpō no rekishi*) was lamentable; most histories were written in Chinese script, and few covered Japan as a unit (1883, 2–8). Maruyama acknowledged that inaccuracies existed in the classical texts. That is, these texts were no longer the truth, but some kind of vestige through which the past could be maintained or revived. They argued for the centrality of information about the past as the basis of good government and as a tool to build a sense of unity among the population. At the conclusion of his lecture to the inaugural meeting of the History Society, Maruyama beseeched his audience to participate in the formulation of a history that considered the country as the principal unit and was written in the Japanese language. His example of a national history was Kitabatake Chikafusa's *Jinnō shōtōki*, written in the fourteenth century.[10]

Today, we take for granted the function of history in society, even to the extent of denying it through claims to objectivity and neutrality. These scholars were trying to establish these functions. Konakamura, for example, points to the utility of history to the state in his essay in the inaugural issue of *Shigakkai zasshi (Journal*

---

[9] See, for example, Gluck (1985). Numata also noted this independence of history from politics and ethics (1961, 271).

[10] When the first Japanese history course was taught at the first higher normal school, upon the recommendation of Adolph Groth, Arai Hakuseki's *Dokushi yoron* was used as the textbook (see Maruyama 1883, 7, 5).

of the Japanese Historical Association). Konakamura was perhaps the most important figure in the History Society (the other was Naitō). He held an office in the
Jingishō (Ministry of Rituals and Rites) and in 1878 accepted positions at Tokyo
University and the Office of Historiography. In 1882 he became the first professor
of Japanese literature at the university. He cites three reasons to pursue historical
study: the fostering of a sense of patriotism; the importance of knowing one's past
to conduct government; and the possession of history by Japanese, not foreigners
such as Basil Chamberlain (who was translating the *Kojiki*) (1889, 6). Konakamura is clearly concerned about the Westernization of Japan and the diminution
of any distinctiveness. He warns that in this age of cause and effect, unless careful,
high-level (*kōshō*) discussions include the ancient texts, rational goals will not be
achieved. But we must be careful; for Konakamura, Westernization is a category
that symbolizes the decline of a Japan as known through the ancient texts. Iida
Nagao, for example, shared a similar worry, but read Western interest in Japan's
past differently. He wrote in the 1883 inaugural issue of *Shigaku kyōkai zasshi* that
foreign interest in the early texts was affirmation of their centrality to understanding the essence of Japanese culture (1883, 47–52).

Konakamura's arguments returns us to the tortuous contradictions that confront a place aspiring to become a modern nation-state: to value the new and
unknown, that is, some future, but through a system that is meant to limit uncertainty. That is, it must do it by ordering the simultaneous demands of permanence and change. Konakamura's arguments for the classics indicate his
skepticism toward a resolution using methods and modes of inquiry that are external to Japan and alter a cultural autonomy that he believed existed. His is an
idea of Japan in process of becoming; while he accepts the nation—the collective singular—his notion of change does not include the dislocation of the inherited knowledge, especially those ethical structures that were buttressed by
stories of exemplary figures. He already knows what that history should be, that
is, through a careful reading of the classics. Here, we return to Koselleck's distinction of "a history in motion and its linguistic possibility" versus "a past history and its linguistic reproduction." Konakamura's assertion of the classics sees
a history in motion, changing along with society—the linguistic possibilities. In
a sense, this debate was over what the old culture that should remain autonomous is.

In their effort to formulate a history of Japan, the limitation of the historians of
the History Society was that they were not willing to sever the past from the present. This past, however, was the increasingly denigrated past of the mythical
texts. This position is evident in Konakamura's remarks that prematurely celebrated the resuscitation of nativism (*kokugaku*) in 1882. He wrote:

> The two general paths of *kokugaku* are knowledge of reality and knowledge of po-
> etry and prose. In the case of reality, through the old texts since the *Kojiki* and

Nihon shoki, it is knowing the national essence (*kokutai*) and contemplating the accumulation of successive generations of systems and objects. In the case of poetry and prose, from the genre of ancient books such as the ritual prayer (*norito*), the *Kojiki, Nihon shoki,* and *Manyōshu,* we can consider the general transformation of poetry and prose that has come to be mixed with Chinese writing. (*Tokyo teikoku daigaku* 1932 [hereafter Todai50], 732)

Konakamura was writing through a knowledge system that did not distinguish between a field of literature and of history. He wrote histories of music as well as of law; in his mind they were not separate disciplines. But by seeing a reality in the classical texts, Konakamura was seeking permanence in the ethics that had been central in history as *historia magistrae vitae.* For Konakamura, history (*enkaku*) was more similar to *histoire,* stories about the past. He was worried about change away from what he saw as the core, that which is evident in the classical texts, such as the *Kojiki* and *Manyōshu,* where native language exhumed from poetry and prose illuminates the exemplary behavior of men before foreign cultures altered "Japan." He acknowledged change, but in this case, it was degenerative, not progressive. In assigning fault, his *kokugaku* background showed: the importation of Tang culture was instrumental in the separation of the military rulers from the people. By understanding this past, Japan could return to its essence; that is, permanence could be found in some cultural essence that has withstood the ravages of time. But that cultural essence presumes some pure beginning, a temporality that was increasingly questioned at the time, and a reliance on texts that were increasingly suspect. In short, Konakamura's history was a combination of the mythical and progress. But before we condemn Konakamura for seeking such simultaneity as conservative and nativist, it is important to point out, as I hope will become clear in the following pages, that modern historiography also subsumes such simultaneity in its writings.

Chronology: An Alibi of Time

In the modern nation-state, the mythical is embedded in history, which occults the contradistinction of permanence and change. Blumenberg describes this: "The mythical mode of thought works toward evidentness in the articulation of time; it is able to do this because no one ever asks for its chronology. Besides beginnings and ends it has the free use of simultaneity and prefiguration, imitative execution and the recurrence of the same" (1985, 100). On the one hand, the simultaneity and prefiguration can be found in the removal of the nation from history. Here, one chronology that goes unasked is the history of the formative moment of the nation in the nineteenth century. On the other hand, the recurrance of the same occurs through a chronology where the past is domesticated as an other of the present—it becomes the not yet, which provides that data to articulate both change and development. The unasked chronology in this case is the linear sequencing of dates. By accepting such temporality as natural, history need not deal with the myriad and undatable alters—the wonders, ghosts, and spirits—that had "named" the unknown, but certainly not made life more predictable or certain. These unstable forms would be separated and located in the fields of Japanese literature and folklore.

Konakamura and the History Society were vying with another faction of scholars also involved with the Office of Historiography and Tokyo University. These historians, who generally had a Confucian training, also envisioned history as a tool for the inculcation of inhabitants into citizens of the nation-state, but they argued for empirically based narratives that led them toward a history that became the linguistic reproduction of the nation-state. In an 1885 memo in defense of the Historiographical Office, Kume Kunitake began: "History (*rekishi*) is that which possesses the career (*keireki*) of a country. With the exception of places of ignorance, all countries have history. A country with literature but no history is like a wealthy family without a lineage" (1991b, 227). Here, Kume was distinguishing history from the narratives that had described the past; those texts are literature, not history. The problem with the recorded past in Japan, he argued, was that it had been limited to accounts of the ruling bodies. He acknowledged the importance of the Six Histories and the *Azuma kagami* of the Kamakura period. But these exhibited this narrowness, the separation of the elite from the masses. Then he pointed out that Japan and China developed a tradition of historical writing—public histories (*kansen*)—that was primarily produced by the imperial courts or ruling bureaucracies. In contrast, Europe also developed a tradition of autonomous scholarly production—private histories (*shisen*). He lamented, "Thus, when we recover nine hundred years of discarded texts, trace the deep past, and inquire into evidence (*jiseki*), surprisingly the official records are virtually separate from the thoughts of the subjects" (230). Significantly, these dates generally correspond to the ascendance of Chinese culture, especially in historical writings. By calling for a history autonomous from the state, he was also weakening the claims of the inherited historiographical practices, including his own. We cannot help but conclude that Kume's private history is also an example of a mythical mode of thought; he had been employed by the preeminent historical institutions of the state and was struggling to create a history useful to the nation. But while we might facilely dismiss this connection as his blindness, we must also consider the way that chronology, based on a separation of past from present, facilitates this mythical mode of thought.

In 1885 the History Society halted publication of its journal, and in 1886 the university was reorganized into the Imperial University at Tokyo. In the following year the history department (*shigakka*) was founded, and the young German historian Ludwig Riess was hired. In 1888 the Temporary Office for the Compilation of Historical Materials (formerly the Office of Historiography) was moved from the cabinet to the university, and in 1889 this office became the basis for a new department of Japanese history (*kokushika*), which existed alongside the history department. The researchers of the office, Kume, Hoshino Hisashi, and Shigeno, were appointed professors of this department.

In 1885 the department of Japanese and Chinese literature (*wakan bungaku*), which had been responsible for teaching about the past, was divided into the departments of Japanese literature (*wabun gakka*) and Chinese literature (*kanbun gakka*). Prior to this reorganization, the professors responsible for Japanese history, literature, and the classics were Konakamura, Naitō, and Mozume Takami.[11] In 1889 these departments changed their names to national literature (*kokubungakka*) and Chinese studies (*kangaku*). In short, this was the moment of separation of history (the reproduction of the past) from literature (a history in motion) in Japan.

This reorganization signaled the preeminence of a notion of the past where history became a scientific discipline, that is, a field of knowledge that objectively reproduced the past. The direction of this new discipline was clearly articulated in the 1888 memo of Watanabe Kōki, the president of the university, to the Ministry of Education, advocating the establishment of the department of Japanese history (*kokushi gakka*):

> Recently, we have realized that politics, law, and economics are subject to the climate (*fūdo*) and people (*jinsei*) of each land and each country. In order to clarify the relation of time and space, we will enthusiastically follow the research methods that establish the foundation of the history of that space, and in this way transform the methods of historical investigation. Today in order to understand social phenomena of a particular time and space, we will collect books, handicrafts, and other artifacts of those times; dissect and analyze them; discern their qualities; and research these things at a library just as science uses laboratories. Then for the first time we will have a scientific method of inquiry into history. Finally, we can refer all matters—political, legal, economic—for academic testing and decide accordingly. (Todai50, 1:1297)

Watanabe's memorandum indicates an idea of history in which the past has become an archive quite distinct from the present. Like Miyake (and Buckle), he connects activities of people in a particular climate as the context for a history of society. But this connection is not of an accumulation of experiences, but of artifacts, objects that need to be collected, categorized, and analyzed. Only after such a scientific treatment of data can a true history be known. A difference between these scholars is their understanding of time: Miyake's interaction of past and present is the accumulation of recurring interactions, Konakamura's past

---

[11] Konakamura taught Japanese literature, Japanese history, and ancient Japanese law; Naitō taught the classics, Japanese history, Chinese history, Chinese philosophy, Chinese literature, and ancient Chinese and Japanese law; Mozume was responsible for Japanese literature (Todai50, 1:1317).

embeds the ideals of the nation, and Watanabe's time is a series of definable, completed moments—events—and objects. The latter provides an aura that the past is real, recoverable through material artifacts—data. In the passage "history of that space," time and space are abstract concepts given form by history and nation. History is autonomous; it is a linear narrative that has to be given; texts, artifacts, and handicrafts are now objects that are to be housed and studied in a library, like a laboratory, where they are removed from their immediate surroundings and what they had represented. These objects become data categorized by date and era and verified according to chronological markers. The historian, the expert, creates that foundation of the nation, upon which it is reformed and its autonomy maintained.[12] Phrases like "history of that space" and "those times" suggest the naturalness and materiality of these structures that make up the development of place, the nation. This was summarized in an essay on history in the inaugural issue of *Shigakkai zasshi*:

> As the ideas which bring development and transformation from ancient times until today, the history of history (*shigakushi*) should be considered the historical narrative of that development. Moreover, in each period there is the particular historical idea; among historians of the Greek and Roman periods there is the thought of Greek and Roman eras. Historians of the medieval era (*chūsei*) hold the thought of the medieval era, historians of the early modern (*kinsei*) period hold the thought of the contemporary world. (Shimoyama 1889, 43)

This periodization is simplistic and would soon be refined. Yet the autonomy of the chronological era with particular definable characteristics is an example, I believe, of de Certeau's notion of "using time without reflecting on it." By framing one's study through a temporal categories, studies (literary, historical, art, etc.) can be written as a moment of the homogenized unit. On the one hand, a discussion of Japan is synchronized with a world (that is, Western) history, while a Japan is the assumed subject and referent. This is one of the differences between the academic historians and Miyake; Miyake's characteristics were always present in the interaction of people with their surroundings, whereas for these scholars, Japanese characteristics emerged during different eras. Miyake's characteristics set up the possibility for a latency in society that opens up to the exercise of abilities, while history establishes boundaries through the characteristics that have emerged to become ahistorical characteristics of the nation.

This segmentation of the past into different disciplines and the turn to chronology coincides with the "history fever" that peaked between 1890 and 1893 (Mehl 1998b, 67–83). On the one hand, this boom was fueled by the debates between scholars like Kume and Shigeno, who argued that exemplary figures of the past like Kojima did not actually exist and that tales like the *Heike monogatari* are not historical texts, and nativists, who argued for the value of

---

[12] For an interesting study on the archives and power, see Richards (1993).

those figures and accounts. Indeed, Kume's 1892 article that Shinto was an ancient form of heaven worship received little notice when first published in the *Shigakkai zasshi*. After it was republished in Taguchi Ukichi's popular historical journal, *Shikai*, it became the major historical controversy of that period. But on the other hand, the shortness of this boom also demonstrates the decline of that debate, and the rise of a more rationalized division of the past in which the acceptance of a chronological framework facilitates the segmentation of the past into different disciplines.

Of course, the idea of formulating a new historical chronology preceded the 1890s. Numerous proposals existed that predated the Restoration, and numerous intellectuals who were familiar with Western scholars, such as Buckle, Guizot, and Spencer, also attempted to write a linear history of Japan. Taguchi Ukichi's *Nihon kaika shōshi* (A Short History of Japanese Civilization), published between 1877 and 1882, is the best example of an early adaptation of progress to Japan. But we must remember that these texts, attributed to an "enlightened" attitude, were common during the 1870s and early 1880s, while the proliferation of research and writing on chronology began in the late 1880s.

The relatively late development of chronologies of Japan suggests that some permanence of the nation is required prior to the writing of a linear history (Keirstead 1998). Droysen's (1967) sage comment that facts are stupid without interpretation also reminds us that some interpretive framework, both the unit of analysis as well as a mode of organizing information, is a prerequisite for the formulation of history.[13] Miyake's ability did not quite make the shift to chronology; his characteristics did not provide a stable enough container through which ability could become a history.

The historical chronology that emerged follows the key political developments of the imperium; it moves from the age of the gods, to the ancient period, the medieval period (*chūsei*), the early modern, and finally the modern. This transformation of society as chronological opens up possibilities for relationships that had not been previously possible. In this new, national space, regional differences are increasingly dissolved and replaced by temporal categories within which moments within Japan become interchangeable. The new interchangeability is now organized by time.

The new temporality of modernity provides a different kind of release from those "self-incurred immaturities" to which Kant refers: it is an interchangeability, or, more accurately, circulation of people and comparison of places.[14] Certainly, migration was prevalent in pre-Meiji Japan; this is not new. But the notion of development also provided different categories to orient people, now

[13] Droysen's statement is much more elegant: "It is only in appearance that the 'facts' in such a case speak for themselves, alone, exclusively, 'objectively.' Without the narrator to make them speak, they would be dumb" (52–53).

[14] A related condition to interchangeability of people, especially in capitalist society, is their expendability.

according to their level of cognition. This is evident in Kume's likening of the *Heike monogatari* to a children's story, and in Inoue Enryō's attribution of early understanding of the world to emotion, rather than abstract reasoning.[15] This interchangeability is different from the simultaneity of past and present of earlier societies. Now temporality uses the distinction of present from past, to combine and order what had been heterogeneous forms into the same chronological moment. It becomes possible to comprise a unit based on stages of development, regardless of date or place. For example, it is possible now to categorize children together, regardless of their social milieu. Moreover, children, the uneducated, and aboriginal cultures can now be grouped in the same general category as primitive. To get ahead of my narrative, this interchangeability established a vital condition for the rise of liberal-capitalist society.

By reorganizing data according to year and date, historians were able to extract events, people, and ideas from the specificity of a local place, now in the space of Japan. Material that had been "real" could be verified and called into question. It became possible to combine those of the same moment even though there was no contact or interaction; for the first time information from throughout Japan was organized by period rather than place. This was one of those transformations that forced the release of society from those "self-incurred immaturities." The exorcism of ghosts and the debunking of heroic figures such as Kojima and Kusunoki helped domesticate the alterity of spirits, wonders, and exemplary, but mythic, figures. But while history destroyed what had been known as the "real" past, a new real emerged through the writing of history.

This demand that history be a science using only verifiable data of the nation to formulate a "national history" points to Koselleck's linguistic reproduction of the past. Verifiable data predisposes the new history toward the elite (literate) who were concerned about affairs of states; the category of the nation orients history toward the important moments of that unit, that is, earlier political events that lead up to the present. History (that is, academic history) on Japan has become a story of the political and economic progress of the nation-state (I include both factions of Marxist historians as well). This was especially true of the pre–World War II period. Fact and objectivistic methodologies dominated the field divided into developmental categories. Chronological time fosters a mechanical production of history seemingly separated from the specificity of time and place.

The significance of these chronological studies is in the potential for a narrative of change that reinforces that "permanence" upon which it is built; they become mutually reinforcing. The first moment establishes that originary point for a progressive structure—ancient, medieval, early modern, and modern. These chronological units gained historical specificity and "reality" when connected to political periods—Nara and Heian; Kamakura to Tokugawa; Tokugawa; and post-Meiji *ishin*. These periods become containers, alibis of time, that facilitate

---

[15] According to Kami, the genre of children's literature emerged around the 1910s (1994, 9).

the production of history. Interestingly, once the chronology had been established, historical accuracy did not necessarily alter the significance of the object of study to Japan's history. For example, Naka's revised chronology of the age of the gods, published in 1888 and revised in 1897, though potentially devastating to the originary myths of "Japan," was generally accepted. In contrast, Kume's essay, published in 1892, "Shintō wa saiten no kosoku nari" (Shinto Is an Ancient Custom of Heaven Worship), led to protests by supporters of *kokugaku* scholars and his firing from the Imperial University. In 1893 Yoshida Tōgō resolved this seeming contradiction as a technological transformation of history as a domain of experts: "*Nihon shoki* chronology is a public one for general use by all imperial subjects. The revised [Naka] chronology is a private one to be used for reference purpose only" (quoted in Young 1958, 95). Yoshida's notion of the private was perhaps internalized by historians, but it was not the private advocated by Kume. Kume's private was the public participation of intellectuals autonomous from the state. History becomes a form of knowledge about the public that is to be conducted by experts. This separation of the past into a domain of experts is certainly an important part of the nation-building process. Kuno Osamu, for example, has built upon this idea to describe a bifurcation of knowledge between the governed and the governors (1978, 60–80).

This bifurcation exposes the importance of chronology to the ideology of the nation-state. Yoshida's statement rationalizes the break between meaning and the production of history; this language was the technology of locating verifiable data into dates and places. From the 1890s, the historical discipline was filled with heavily contested debates over chronology. For example, the location of Yamatai *koku*, the kingdom in the land of Wa mentioned by the *Wei Zhi* in the third century, was the object of considerable historical labor during both the 1890s and 1910s. The stakes of this debate were to locate the origin and site of protohistoric Japan, but historians increasingly focused on the accuracy and validity of the limited information at hand. In architectural history, the debate over whether the Hōryūji was reconstructed consumed the efforts of many. The Hōryūji, too, has become an originary site, the archetype of a Japanese aesthetic.[16] This obsession with chronology facilitates the occultation of the historicity of history, where the ideas to which history helped give form became naturalized even as the production of history continues, even today.

Of course, we now realize that Jimmu is mythical, but the collective singular remains a Japan dating back over 2,600 years. In his evaluation of *Kuni no ayumi*, the first textbook written in post–World War II Japan, John Brownlee cites it as evidence of a more "universal and human" history, away from the emphasis on imperial divinity. In place of the mythical emperors, the authors of this textbook wrote: "It was in very ancient times that our ancestors settled down in

---

[16] For an overview of the debate over *yamatai*, see Young (1958). I will discuss the Hōryūji in chapter 6.

this country. We do not know just when it was, but without a doubt it was at least several thousand years ago" (1997, 205). What I find so interesting about this statement is that in the desire for rationality and objectivity, we have moved from mythical emperors starting from 660 B.C. to "ancestors" who settled in some "very ancient time" that preceded that mythical date. The subject remains an always existing Japan; chronology is the neutral structure that maintains it. Interestingly, Japan now is older under the rational and secular approach than that through the *Kojiki*. Which is more mythical?

A cynic would describe the institutionalization of history as the act of wise officials creating the possibility for historians to produce knowledge and gain prestige through this elevation of the discipline of history. Indeed, this is a criticism that Yamaji Aizan leveled at historians and scholars at Tokyo Imperial University during the latter half of the 1890s (1965b, 402, 404). But even in a more positive light, more recently, Peter Duus commented on the mechanization of the past as history, that is as objective and scientific:

> These academic historians were as much in revolt against the praise-and-blame approach of traditional historiography as men like Fukuzawa and Taguchi, but they fought not by seeking out general laws of civilization, but by careful verification of historical facts. . . . They were capable, critical, and dedicated scholars, but basically uninspiring, without an axe to grind or the passion of political commitment. (1974, 419–20)

The issue I would like to emphasize is not which history is more objective, neutral, or mythical, but that these historians, espousing objectivity, have adapted a chronological framework that is at the center of efforts to constitute the nation-state. In the assertion of empirical historians of a "real" beyond the stories (fiction), these elite historians were separating themselves (and history) as knowers of the past. The ordinary, those who "only" know or tell stories, cannot really know. Erudition now shifted to the expert, with the requisite tools of analysis. By emphasizing objectivity, empirical historians eliminated the "free use of simultaneity and prefiguration" from those accounts of the past. In this way chronology facilitates the constriction of the historical field to the timefulness of politics and economics. Chronology is seductive, for it seems natural, so commonsensical. Dates provide an aura of certainty, those measured markers to arrange data in a logical order.

Chronology enables scholars to write about the past as if they are speaking of the same subject and referent. The discussion of a particular era implies that the principal unit of analysis is a Japan, even if the object of study might be an individual or event. But to accept this "natural" form, huge chunks of the past are eliminated from history. De Certeau describes the process that must occur before chronology gains such a natural status:

> In history everything begins with the gesture of *setting aside*, of putting together, of transforming certain classified objects into "documents." This new cultural

distribution is the first task. In reality it consists in *producing* such documents by dint of copying, transcribing, or photographing these objects, simultaneously changing their locus and their status. This gesture consists in "isolating" a body— as in physics—and "denaturing" things into parts which will fill the lacunae inside an a priori totality. (1988, 72–73)

There are two parts to this "gesture of *setting aside*": that of the individual text and that of the discipline. The work of historians, like Kume and Shigeno, is an example of the transformation of texts into documents. The debate over the veracity of Kusunoki was about the changing locus and status of these forms of knowledge. Critics like Konakamura were correct to point out that the result is a denatured understanding of the past. Subsequent interpretations of history as pure, as contrasted to applied or objective vs. some ideological demon, work within this gesture of setting aside. This brings out the second part of this gesture: chronology occults history from its own moment of formation; it obscures the utility of academic history to the state (more accurately, historians have exonerated themselves). In this contestation over which has more utility, history is ideological. Whereas in the past the mythical existed because no one asked for chronology, in the case of the nation-state, chronology is employed, but no one asks for the temporality that is masked by chronology. In this sense, chronology, too, is mythical, like ghosts and exemplary heroes.

SPECTERS OF HISTORY: NATIONAL LITERATURE AND ART HISTORY

The interpretation that the modern historical discipline was (is) objective, without political commitment, and separated from the nation is a different way of saying that history has become a technology and historians are technicians who reinforce the materiality of the nation-state. This separation from the past, as well as from history as a means of conveying that past, is summarized in Margaret Mehl's observation, "the historians at the Historiographical Institute did not become interpreters of the nation; their lives and works did not help shape the Japanese empire" (1998a, 159). But we must ask whether it is even possible to examine objects for their inert properties, independent of their surroundings. This indifference to natural objects, events, and how they are understood is not (or should not be) easily applied to the study of humans. Drawing from Erich Rothacker, Blumenberg writes, "In man's historical world of culture things have 'valences' for attention and for vital distance different from those they have in the objective world of things that is studied by the exact sciences, in which the distribution of subjective value to phenomena that are studied, tends in the norm, toward zero" (1985, 67). If one accepts these statements, one can only shudder at the thought of a valence of zero (we seem to be moving in that direction).

Even though the discipline of history does turn toward increasingly mechanistic and antiseptic approaches to the past, others proposed chronologies that were not as mechanistic and absent of any subjective value. Indeed, an important part of the history fever was a concern for these valences and the presence of different pasts. We must remember that the formalization of history as a discipline was part of the amelioration of those pasts in which disciplines such as Japanese literature and art history also emerged. Whereas history took possession of the new riches of the archive created by the centralization of materials to describe the political and economic change of an always existing nation-state, national literature and art history took possession of and resuscitated the discarded texts and artifacts emphasizing the character, sensibility, and spirit of the nation.

These disciplines also emerged at the end of the 1880s. The department of Japanese culture (*wabungakka*) split from that of China (*kangaku*) in 1885 and changed its name to national literature (*kokubungaku*) in 1889, and the ideas of Okakura and Fenollosa were legitimized when they convinced the government to close the Technical Art School and establish the Tokyo School of Fine Art in 1888. In fact, *kokubungaku* was founded by the students of scholars like Konakamura who "lost" the fight to determine the history of Japan. As history tended toward that valence of zero, national literature and art history were formulated into fields that emphasize the human sensibilities of the past. They compensate for the increasing fragmentation and mechanization of knowledge of the past, including (perhaps especially) in history, by turning those formerly authoritative texts into canonical aesthetic objects of Japan. What we now think of the humanities, here literature and art history, emerged from the reduction of the past to historical time.

In 1890 three texts were published that sought to outline this new field of literature: Haga Yaichi and Tachibana Sensaburō's *Kokubungaku dokuhon*; Ueda Kazutoshi's *Kokubungaku*; and Mikami Sanji and Takatsu Kensaburō's *Nihon bungakushi*.[17] In *Kokubungaku dokuhon*, Haga and Tachibana argue that national literature emphasizes the particularity of the individual author and the importance of his context; they write, "In some way, each piece of prose and poetry conveys a sense of the writer; each writer conveys a sense of the literature of the era; the literature of an era conveys a sense of a national literature, and the national literature conveys a sense of world, that is human, literature" (199). In their emphasis on the individual, ideas, and sensibility, it is possible to find in literature a sense of openness and heterogeneity. But an interesting move in this structure is the transition from the individual to the era. Temporal categories have replaced the spaces of experience. We have moved from the context as the site of production to the generality of a historical period. Periodization becomes

---

[17] These scholars were the students of the earlier *kokugakusha*, such as Naitō and Konakamura. Mikami had just graduated from the Imperial University, while Haga was still a student. For a description of the rise of *kokubungaku*, see Brownstein (1987).

a way to naturalize belonging into that of the nation. *Kokubungaku dokuhon* offered a chronological division of literature: ancient period (0–1305 [to 645]), middle period (*chūko*) (1305–1845 [645–1185]), Kamakura (1845–1996 [1185–1336]), Muromachi (1996–2264 [1336–1604]), Edo (2264–2527 [1604–1867]), and post *ishin*, (2527– [1867–]).[18]

A similar chronological structure emerged in art history. Okakura organized art in the following chronology:

> We can indicate that rise and fall linearly. In other words, following the above chart, gradually from the protohistoric period, we ascended in the Suiko period and directly progressed through Tenji to the prosperity of Tenpyō. And then we declined, rose during Kūkai and again in Kanaoka, declined a little during Genpei, but rose again during Kamakura. In the Ashikaga we reached the prosperity of Higashiyama and experienced the short Toyotomi period; then the Genroku which was opposite the Toyotomi emerged, turned to the Tenmei and finally continued to today. (1939, 4:16)

This chronology corresponds to the three periods in Hegel's notion of aesthetics. Okakura groups the Suiko, Tenji, and Tenpyō as ancient; Kūkai and Kamakura as medieval; and the Ashikaga and after as modern. This, too, is a movement from the Symbolic, where the actualization of the Idea is no more than a "*mere search* for portrayal*" (for Hegel, the "pantheistic cultures of the East" best represented this level); to the Classical stage, best exemplified by the art of Greece and Rome; and finally to the Romantic stage (Europe), where a recognition of the inwardness of self-consciousness leads to the perfection of the heart and spirit (Hegel 1975, 1:76, 77). As in national literature, Okakura and Fenollosa were keen to organize and describe the key characteristics of each stage.

These chronologies have important differences, and I am not arguing for the sameness of the narrative structures of history, art history, and national literature. Indeed, their differences further this imperative for reproduction, as well as a lack of reflection. (This further sets up the possibility for scholarly "innovation," that is, the poaching from another discipline.) But they share enough similarities that they reinforce each other as well as their differences. In the case of history, a simplified von Ranke and the positivistic goal of Comte dominate, while a strong Hegelian presence structures art history, and in national literature scholars like Haga were working from Hippolyte Taine, who is famous for his use of milieu, race, and moment to discern the habits of mind of a nation (Brownstein 1987, 435–60). As in the similarities of Okakura and Miyake, the chronological eras gain generalized characteristics, a caricature, that obscure the differences and reinforce each other.

[18] *Kokubungaku* dated the beginning of Japan at the ascension of Jimmu (year 0), 660 B.C. according to the Christian era (in brackets). Haga and Tachibana (1989); Mikami and Takatsu (1982). For modern attempts to establish periodizations of these disciplines, see Keirstead (1998).

It is in this acceptance of chronology that the national literature scholars differed from their mentors and were very much a part of the transformation to the modern. Indeed, they were no longer seeking to represent history; instead, they decided to carve out a part of the past. Mikami and Takatsu recognize the trend within Japan toward a labor society, that is, its specialization and mechanization; they see opportunity. They write that the world of knowledge is increasingly being divided into disciplines, such as law, politics, economics, ethics, aesthetics, philosophy, history, and literature. They agree with empiricists like Watanabe and Kume that the purpose of history is to recount the past mechanistically, "using accurate facts, to investigate the cause and effect of change and clarify the vestiges of our country's ebb and flow" (1982, 22). The role of literature, on the other hand, is to reintegrate the sensate—the human, the ideas, sensibility, and imagination—that has been denigrated by mechanistic forms of knowledge: "Literature stores within a kind of originary spirit; even more, it is that which influences politics, religion, feelings, and customs" (2). In other words, national literature explains the historical formation of the permanence of a nation, those ahistorical characteristics of the nation-state.

Mikami and Takatsu define literature as follows: "Through certain literary styles, literature is the skillful expression of the ideas, sensibilities, and imagination of people, and adds utility (*jitsuyō*) and pleasure by conveying a general knowledge to a majority of people" (13). Haga and Tachibana argue that this is the foundation of the sciences, just as the earth is the medium from which plants thrive. Their national literature was much more open-ended, and they argued against a definition that would unduly restrict it. They write: "In discourse it interacts with the world of principle; in narrative accounts it parallels the world of facts; and as the sensibility of morals and aesthetics it instills the world of values" (1989, 198).

Haga and Tachibana, like their mentor, Konakamura, were less willing to cede a part of the past to history (Hisamatsu 1957, 234–39). Instead, they sought to historicize this trend and point out that the realm of knowledge was not fragmented prior to the craze on civilization (*bunmeikaika*). They are correct to point out the homogenizing tendency of the new disciplines, what they call *hyakka no gakumon* (catch-all disciplines). Progress, they argue is not natural and inevitable: "The enlightenment of humans and the civilizing of society is not the superficial progress of mechanization. In other words, we should understand that because it is nothing other than the development of an holistic knowledge and ethics, the development of ordinary knowledge and ordinary feelings are the most critical elements to the enlightenment of a country" (198).

One of the interesting things about this notion of permanence is the connection to chronology. Haga and Tachibana ask the question, "How can we bring forth and develop an everlasting literature that has such value? It is only by returning to the origins of literature, where we see how the character of our race has acted and developed in accordance with the direction of the world and the laws of nature" (199). This is a fascinating statement that exhibits the temporality of this field of national literature. The language is that of a return to and preservation of an essential Japan. But the framework is that of the abstract laws of modern society: the laws of nature, synchronization with a world history, and the primacy of the era in a narrative of development. National literature highlights those transhistorical characteristics by extracting the key characteristic of each era. In short, through chronology, national literature is able to further separate the past from history, giving more authority to an idea of Japan.

This utility of the chronology of Japan to national literature can be illustrated through a summary of the period that Haga and Tachibana call the middle period (*chūko*), 1305–1845 [645–1185].[19] By focusing on the texts that we now regard as the classics, these scholars unearth the ideals and emotions that characterize this period, which ranges from the Taika reforms, a series of major political acts that rationalized political power among the aristocracy, to the rise of the Kamakura bakufu. They highlight the transformation of culture from a pure Japan that was characterized by a brave and energetic will (evident in the *Kojiki* and *Nihon shoki*) to one that increasingly adopted from the continent, especially Chinese and Buddhist ideas. Haga and Tachibana describe this period as one of the high points of Japanese literature. Poetry, especially *waka*, developed out of the oral traditions of the ancient period, and prose began to emerge, illustrating the development and "virtual perfection" of an aesthetic sensibility. Mikami and Takatsu write, "From the reign of Emperor Shōmu and along with the gradual spread of Buddhism the brave and energetic will [of the ancient period] became lost and an indecisive and effeminate spirit emerged. This spirit and climate is somewhat evident in the Nara period, but became pronounced during the Heian period" (1982, 98–99).[20] They acknowledge its contributions, but also its limitations; Mikami and Takatsu summarize the characteristic of the era, "The spirit of Heian was like a flower or the moon, beautiful (*enrei*) and elegant (*yūbi*). But it was effeminate, not vigorous, profligate, and lacked principle" (209–10).[21]

The power of this characterization of chronological periods is evident in a revision of the Heian era by Hisamatsu Sen'ichi, who argues for greater complexity in this interpretation of the Heian as effeminate; he suggests that some women writers, such as Akazome Emon maintained the earlier characteristic of the Yamato (ancient) period, a soul and energy (*kihaku*), making the Heian less

---

[19] They used the system of counting years from the ascension of Jimmu, the mythical first emperor. Today this word is translated as medieval, but at that time, the use of *chūsei* as medieval was not yet common. See Keirstead (1998).

[20] I will treat the books by Haga and Tachibana and Mikami and Takatsu as part of a whole. I do not mean to conflate their differences; but for my purposes, it is sufficient to accept the interpretation of more recent specialists of the field that these texts are complementary. See Hisamatsu (1957).

[21] Exemplary literature of this era are the *Manyōshū*, *Taketori monogatari*, *Sumiyoshi monogatari*, *Utsubo monogatari*, and *Hamamatsu Chūnagon monogatari*, as well as *Genji monogatari*.

effeminate (1957, 240). I do not mean to belittle the revision, but this revision ultimately reinforces the already existing periodization and characteristics; debate is over the dating—especially emergence—of the same characteristics. Chronology makes possible the production of this scholarship, while keeping it within the bounds that had been historically produced.

I have already described many of the features of art history in relation to history and literature; to reiterate the chronology would be a virtual repetition of the chronology of national literature.[22] At this point I would like to emphasize that Okakura's art history is the beginning of a canonical form that presents visually this permanence of Japan. This essence is presented through the combination of the diverse pasts into a single history. One of the characteristics Okakura mentioned as a part of Japan's self-conscious (modern) art is a respect for ancient methods. This respect allows him to merge the characteristics of different moments—the majesty of Nara, feeling of Heian, and self-consciousness of Ashikaga—into one. He laments that observers, especially Western, see only the refined simplicity of the Ashikaga as representative of all Japanese art; they do not see that majesty, elegance, and virility are also part of that same refined simplicity (1939, 4:172). "The art of Nara," he states, "became meditative; it avoided unnecessary elements and concentrated its power on only the important things"; for the Heian period, he claims that the art of Fujiwara "demonstrated thorough simplicity and reached the epitome of elegance" (86); and the Ashikaga "brought a change from the feelings of the Fujiwara to one of self-consciousness" (172). Like the national literature narrative, Okakura organizes Japanese art into eras that bear particular transhistorical characteristics. Words like majesty (*sōrei*), spiritual (lit. "miraculous" [*reimyō*]), beauty (*enrei*), elegance (*yūbi*), and virility (*kōken*) describe the art of these periods.

This essence is then conveyed in the display of objects; despite (or because of) the vagueness of the universal, the distillation into an essence provides a chronological map by which others see the object. As David Lowenthal (1985) has shown, the past is highly malleable, and one's mode of preservation and presentation tells much about the present. The presentation of these icons as art history allows for one to depict the timefulness—different characteristics of that past—and timelessness—the essence embodied in all objects. Bruno Latour describes the power of these objects: "In sum, you have to invent objects which have the properties of being *mobile* but also *immutable, presentable, readable* and *combinable* with one another" (1986, 7). Because they are also mobile and combinable, they allow the "rational series of operations" of each discipline also to claim possession and ownership. The particularity of an object, text, or event as a part of the unfolding of Japan justifies the specialized knowledge of art history,

---

[22] For an overview of the relation between art history and the nation-state, see my "Imaging History" (1994). For a more detailed study, see Satō (1999).

literature, or history. The operational phrase that demonstrates the occultation of any reflection on time is "the unfolding of Japan." The permanence of Japan and the developmental mode of organizing the past have been naturalized through the production of scholarship into a chronological framework. An example of the interpretation involved in presentation can be shown in the following caption describing a wooden bodhisattva of the Tōshōdaiji: "The combination of swelling volume with brooding, austere energy reflects new criteria of beauty in the arts which began to appear at the very end of the Nara period. The image was originally coated with thin plaster and painted, but the flaking away of the paint has revealed a beauty in the carving which surpasses that of color" (Noma 1967, 73). This caption brings out the immutable mobility of this piece of sculpture. The interpretation creates, maintains, and reproduces a specific cultural vision. In this passage, experts—historians, art historians, critics, etc.—place it in categories of the past that reveal its true essence, "a beauty" that surpasses the original piece itself and is only understandable through time (Price 1989, 22). It is the expert who knows, more than the artist, the true meaning of this artifact; it is in the piece shorn of the decoration, the plaster, paint, and possibly gilding that the expert has discerned as the essence and true beauty of this piece.

In both national literature and art history there is an important transformation of the significance of the text or object; using the language of preservation, the inherited artifacts shift from authoritative documents or spiritual icons to material evidence into a past that is now dead and valued. The old, or inherited, were not forgotten after being debunked and exorcised from historical discourse; in this act of preservation, there is always the possibility that the artifacts might be used to destabilize this new history. But the potential of this specter is delimited by re-emplotting these artifacts as part of a temporal category, some earlier stage of development. In this way, they reinforce the idea of history by occulting the fear of uncertainty from history, they become a part of the dead past, confined to particular eras or categories. What had been an alter, *ijin* or stranger/supernatural, is now domesticated as an earlier moment of the Same (Japan), confirming the newness (and progress) of the modern present. It is now a past that becomes a datum for the way that "Japanese" thought and felt long ago.[23]

The writing of history in the last decade of nineteenth-century Japan is not the narrative of history as much as the historicization of society as the nation-state. In an interesting way, Miyake's idea of truth, goodness, and beauty gain a materiality through these disciplines. By reorganizing data according to year and date, historians, art historians, and national literature scholars were able to transmute the past. That is, they were able to take the material that had been "real" but could not survive an expanded, abstract conceptual realm and place it

---

[23] Many sculptures were produced by artisans who migrated to the archipelago from what is now the Korean peninsula. Moreover, many of the canonical texts of Japanese literature were written either in Chinese or using Chinese ideographs.

within a new category of knowledge that complemented the mechanistic and progressive time of modernity. The decapitated Buddhist statues, the exorcized ghosts, and the debunked heroic figures were rescued as examples of art, folklore, and literature. History transformed the past into the truth of the nation-state; national literature formulated the stories of the classics into a chronology of the ethics or goodness of the nation; and Japanese art history rescued the icons of an earlier wealth and power. This linear narrative has turned them into symbols of the sublime beauty of a national spirit. They have become foundational forms of knowledge to the understanding, the identity, of the nation-state.

FROM GHOSTS TO CHILDREN: THE IDEA OF CHILDHOOD

Up to this point I have argued that the transformation of time on the ideational level gained a materiality when resituated to constitute the nation. But this temporal transformation also altered the very constitution of society. Childhood, too, is one of those sites where the interiority of the nation-state is naturalized through a chronological time. It has become a common symbol and metaphor in modern society, and it has penetrated to the level of everyday life, a part of our common sense that resides in our memories (Aries 1962; Kessen 1979). In this sense, it is like history: it possesses clarity, the certainty of an early or originary stage—a separable site—within a developmental process that fulfills the demand of modernity for mobility. It is a site where the ambiguities and contradictions of modernity are ameliorated into a coherent whole personified through the child. But whereas those chronological disciplines naturalize a national progress, in childhood, the human body serves as an object that naturalizes the developmental time of modern society.

Childhood has become a symbol for several aspects of modernity. The constant regeneration of the new and the subsequent development emphasizes mobility, that is, a progressive society, one looking forward to a seemingly better future. The human being becomes a microcosm of some collective—the community, family, or nation. The child provides a site for the affirmation of the autonomy of the self; the formulation of a developmental idea (ontogeny) suggests the potential for development of the self, of improvement. It parallels the idea of history, of an originary state (an idealized past) that must learn, must be guided, and is transformed. In this suggestion of interiorization, nature is combined with society. While the individual child demonstrates the potential for mobility, the idea of childhood suggests the interchangeability of the child, not the individual child, but of the same age group. Moreover, while childhood is useful in constituting the nation, it is also a metaphor used among nation-states. Here, it is especially problematic among nonmodern places that must confront their position as a child. Descriptions of nonmodern places and people as childlike—always connoting a lacking, the category of "not yet"—are common within scholarly discourse. In this sense, the child naturalizes unevenness—in human development, in society, in the nation-state, and globally.

The transformation of the child accelerated during the Meiji period and was part of the reorientation of communities reconceptualized according to abstract categories that symbolized this new temporality. Just as historians were preoccupied with locating Japan's origins in a protohistoric period, children, too, filled that signifying function for the idea of a Japanese people (*kokumin*). The child became that originary point (mythic) that unifies all Japanese as the same; it is simultaneously one's own past, the present (through contemporary children), and a hope and prescription for a better future.[24]

In the *Meiroku zasshi* Nakamura Masanao wrote in 1875, "Rather than changing the political structure, therefore, we should aspire instead to change the character of the people, more and more rooting out the old habits and achieving 'renewal' with each new day. . . . Should you ask how to change the character of the people, there are but two approaches—through religious and moral education and through education in the arts and sciences" (Braisted 1976, 373). That renewal was the imposition of a totally new system where rationality and knowledge would bring the objects of modern society while ethical codes would bring the social responsibility and "civil" deportment of a liberal-capitalist society.

Such a rupture brings to the surface a fundamental issue in human apprehensions of time. Sociologist Thomas Luckmann (1991) describes this as the interplay between an inner time of the individual and the intersubjective time, the social interaction. Inner time is embedded in the body; it is a "natural" time of everyday habits and bodily rhythms. It is also tied to the social, for our awareness of time is through socially objectified norms.[25] Luckmann is exposing a common problem in modern scholarship, the use of socially objectified temporal categories as normative knowledge. Childhood becomes one of those sites of social interaction that is apprehended as something natural and experiential, thus prior to the social. Because children have always existed, childhood also comes to stand for something timeless, that pure state before learning (of good and bad) occurs. Childhood becomes a socially objectified site, a permanence that gives procedure and meaning to social interaction. The socially constituted is then naturalized (or turned into inner time) by our everyday experience. It is seemingly universal because it is tied to the body and "experienced" by everybody.

---

[24] Michel Foucault writes, "It is no longer origin that gives rise to historicity; it is historicity that, in its very fabric, makes possible the necessity of an origin which must be both internal and foreign to it: like the virtual tip of a cone in which all differences, all dispersions, all discontinuities would be knitted together so as to form no more than a single point of identity, the impalpable figure of the Same, yet possessing the power, nevertheless, to burst open upon itself and become Other" (1973, 329–30).
[25] Luckmann states, "The rhythms of inner time are the basis of experience, and all other structures of time in human life are erected upon it. The latter, however, do not *originate* in the (pre-predicative) inner time of a solitary self. They originate in social interaction" (1991, 155).

The potential of childhood to the nation-state is as the site to turn the idea of the nation into material practices, in both the idea of edification and the educational institutions. The centrality of the child in the formulation of the new nation-state was most evident in the Imperial Rescript on Education (1890), one of the most important decrees of the Meiji government. The rescript, on the one hand, has been characterized as a conservative document that keyed the reaction against the Westernization of Japan. If one's goal is to exalt an idealized liberal society, this is true. It is a document that uses the emperor to establish filiality and loyalty as the foundation of a communal patriotism that, in Inoue Tetsujirō's words, "return[s] the dignity of the Japanese nation before decades pass" (1974a, 156). Inoue was professor of philosophy at the Imperial University of Tokyo and contemporary of the intellectuals discussed above. If we stop our analysis here, his reputation as a conservative ideologue is warranted. But to label this as traditionalistic and anti-Western denies the possibility that these are conditions inherent to the process of becoming modern.

The power of childhood, in contrast to the abstraction of nation, is that it is a temporary position through which all people pass; it potentially unites people to the idea of nation. Childhood embodies the physiology of a group of people and cuts across other existing divisive categories, such as class (hereditary), wealth, or region, as well as new categories, such as class (economic), knowledge, or putative ability. For a place attempting to establish its unity from a mass of local communities to a developmental whole, childhood also provides a language for the naturalization of a national space, for integrated within it is an expectation of reproduction of society as well as of a better future, a horizon of expectations. Difference is now altered into temporal hierarchies of the Same—that is, through the diachrony of human growth and progress—and childhood signifies the synchrony of ethnicity or race. Childhood becomes the originary moment of the race, but unlike history, the child perpetually recurs as if the past and present are not separated. It orients society around a diachronic epistemology, and at the same time, the child is also a visible form (body and images), the "like us," that facilitates the construction and maintenance of a national "we." Inoue describes such a role of the child in the "*chokugo engi*," the official commentary to the rescript: "If all children receive this national education, there is no doubt that our land will coalesce into one country" (156). The combination of learning and children turns childhood into an experiential site for the nation-state. In this sense, the rescript is also a quite modern document, one that envisions the unity of a nation-state. But such a function is possible only with the presence of Western nation-states, an alter that validates the national idea in conjunction with geographic boundaries.

As Inoue suggests, childhood is always a category of the past. Few, if any, children understand childhood until after they have left it. As a temporal category in a developmental structure, it also reinforces change; people must leave childhood. This developmental notion of the human body appeared earlier in the

Meiroku zasshi; Mitsukuri Shuhei foresaw the changing role of the child. "From infancy until they are six or seven, children's minds are clean and without the slightest blemish while their characters are as pure and unadulterated as a perfect pearl. Since what then touches their eyes and ears, whether good or bad, makes a deep impression that will not be wiped out until death, this age provides the best opportunity for disciplining their natures and training them in deportment (Braisted 1976, 106)." A key age (seven) that signifies a life-course change remains the same, but the child has been transformed from the godlike, or "among the gods until seven," to an infant as an empty vessel to be trained as a proper citizen. Today this proverb is used to justify spoiling children who will be disciplined into "good" citizens after entering school. It is also the early beginnings of a ritual that today is symbolic of childhood, the 7-5-3 ceremony, where parents dress their children in elaborate kimonos (sons at three and five, daughters at three and seven) and take them to a temple or shrine. This ritual is a good example of the transformation of age from practices tied to immediate exigencies to rather commercialized observations of abstract (age-based) categories.[26] In other words, the child changes from an uncertain being—between nature and culture—to the preparatory stage where its externality is molded into the Same, the interiority of the nation-state.

Now, childhood is a temporal category for a future good. The modern child offers the nation (and parents) a hope that it controls its future, that it can create a better future.[27] Whereas in the past, initiation rites—the ritual at seven years of age—recognized the child as a member of the world whereupon he or she would go off and work/learn, the modern child should go to school. Inoue writes, "In the first place, human life is like climbing a mountain: the climb is remembered as long, but we know the second half, the descent, to be very fast. In this way, people need to study hard during their youth. Actually, one's life is determined by one's diligence in the first half, just as the organization of a day is determined in the morning." Inoue is describing the space of childhood: a temporal site in which deferred work, the acquisition of knowledge (discipline), is not considered wasted time, but an asset more important than material resources (1974a, 169).[28] By highlighting this early time of each national, Inoue is

---

[26] Prior to the Meiji period, children were considered godlike and not yet subject to the rules of human society. Seven, as reflected in a proverb that children are "among the gods until seven," was a watershed year, marked by recognition paid to the gods. This observance was conducted in the home. Children were generally naked, keeping warm within the clothes of the caregiver until the age of three. Samurai usually marked changes at the third year by no longer shaving children's hair; at five, boys received a *hakama*, the traditional skirtlike pants; and at seven, the girls began wearing the *obi*, the girdlelike sash (Kuroda 1994, 10; 1989, 89–94).

[27] Foucault reminds us that within this disciplinary structure, "the child is more individualized than the adult" (1979, 193).

[28] Interestingly, Inoue's and Mitsukuri's division of childhood is not different significantly from today: infants are dependent upon parents and society for basic needs, then at the age of six or seven

placing children in a similar temporal role of early historical eras of the new history. The difference from history, though, is important; because it perpetually recurs, it is a rare site of an early stage where adults can not only study and "know" (like history), but also correct for a better future. In this sense, Inoue, who is considered a conservative ideologue, is working within a progressive linear concept. The child who goes to school represents the hope of the nation-state as a key producer (i.e., laborer) for its wealth and power.

CONCEPTUAL MAP

The result of this historicization of society is what Julian Hochberg calls a map, a conceptual system by which people encode their experience (1972, 63–66). It reestablished that internal coherence that was lacking after the old institutions had been demolished. This map, however, is not that of any one person or school, for the sociocultural and international milieu facilitated its production. Moreover, it is not a map that depicts a geographical space; instead, it delimits and provides structure to the open space and universal time of modern society. I think of it similarly to Poulantzas's material practices, "embracing the customs and life-style of the agents and setting like cement in the totality of social (including political and economic) practices" (2000, 28).

These chronologies are fundamental to the material practices by which the state unified Japan. By the mid-1890s this map was increasingly accepted. After the debates of the 1880s abated around 1893, it seems that the different sides were no longer vying to be the purveyor of the past; each seemed to accept a different domain of the modern temporality. This is the setting aside that de Certeau describes. In each of these timeforms, the focus was on the components: in history, the data; in literature, the texts; in art history, the artifacts; and in childhood, children. Each was concerned with how their component fit into a developmental narrative of Japan, now, the a priori totality. Indeed, chronology facilitates this setting aside, providing a structure as if the object it describes is natural.

Perhaps one reason for this naturalization of chronology is the substantial change in personnel during this period, which led to new specialists who were more attuned to the complementarity of history and literature. In 1891 Shigeno resigned from his professorship to become director of the Historiographical Institute; in 1892 Kume was fired. On the other hand, in 1891 Konakamura resigned

---

the child goes to school, and by age twenty he or she is generally capable of becoming autonomous. Again, this is less something that was introduced from the West than a process that was catalyzed. For example, Kaibara Ekken described a somewhat developmental educational structure beginning at six, which bears some resemblances to the ideas Japanese in the Meiji period were to pick up from Pestalozzi and other educational reformers. For the latter, see Lincicome (1995, esp chaps. 1 and 2).

from his professorship in national literature and Naitō was fired. In 1893 Tsuboi Kumezō and Naka held the chairs in history (Riess did not have a chair), while Kurita, Hoshino, Kurokawa, and Mozume taught Japanese language, literature, and history in the department of national literature (Todai50, 1:1318–22). In addition, the Historiographical Institute was abolished in 1893 and reorganized in 1895.

The abolition of the Historiographical Institute can be seen within the context of the earlier debates. According to Mikami (1992), the reason that Inoue Kowashi, the minister of education, abolished the institute stemmed from public criticism. This criticism echoed the complaints and charges directed against Shigeno and Kume for close to a decade. There were four major charges: first, by 1893 the emphasis on the Japanese language (*kokugo*) and on national literature was strong and was quite critical toward the compilation, which was still written in classical Chinese (*kanbun*). Second, the institute historians were criticized for combining their Confucian rationalism with the empiricism of German historiography. Third, Shigeno and Kume were the targets of attacks against objectivistic history; Shigeno was called professor obliterator (*massatsu hakase*), and Kume was heavily criticized for his work on the fourteenth century and protohistoric Japan. And fourth, rumors circulated that historians at the institute were writing the above essays rather than compiling the chronologies (Mikami 1992, 58–59). Some credit Konakamura for influencing Inoue Kowashi. In other words, even though the separation of history and literature gave the positivists control of history at the academy, the nativists had enough influence in the state apparatus that they could depose some of their competitors, especially Shigeno and Kume.

The reopening of the Historiographical Institute shows, however, both the complementarity of the two disciplines and the centrality of the state. After the office was terminated, Inoue solicited opinions widely. The common response was that the work of compilation of historical data is the most important work of the institution. Indeed this became the primary task of the institute, and this limited role is usually cited as evidence of the further retreat into objectivity of the historical profession in Japan, to the extent that the historians at the Imperial University have often been described as innocents in the ideological minefield of Japanese politics.[29] But rather than a retreat into objectivity, there is a retreat that hides behind its own moment of formulation.

The plan for the reopening of the institute debated before the Diet stipulated that its members come from the department of Japanese literature, not the department of history or Japanese history. In the end, Hoshino, Tanaka Yoshinari, and Mikami were named editors. Hoshino became the nominal director, but

---

[29] Numata, for example, cites this as an important moment in the formulation of a "Tokyo [the Imperial University] tradition of historical writing" (1961, 286). Mehl (1998) and Brownlee (1997) are the most recent to exonerate history and those historians.

because of his ill health Mikami served as de facto director until 1899 when he became director. He held this position until 1919 (Mehl 1998a, 133–40). Mikami's reputation straddles the boundary between history and literature. Because of his writings on Tokugawa history and position at the Historiographical Institute, he is generally categorized among the academic, positivistic historians. But while Mikami completed his graduate work in the history department under Riess and Tsuboi, he earlier studied with Konakamura and Naitō, and he wrote one of the foundational texts of *kokubungaku*. He himself claims that he was most influenced by Naitō, making his authorship of *Nihon bungakushi* an important part of his career, not an early aberration. Indeed, his recollection of this period indicates a careful and shrewd figure who worked with both camps (Mikami 1992, 42–60). Despite his reputation as an objectivistic scholar, one gets the impression of his dislike of historians like Shigeno and Kume and support for the position of Konakamura and Naitō.

Under Mikami, the new institute's sole task became the compilation of data, which are being published as the *Dai nihon shiryō* (Chronological Source Books of Japanese History), the principal project of Shigeno and Kume, and *Dai nihon komonjo* (Old Documents of Japan). The Chronological Source Books are based on the Tokugawa document collection of Hanawa Hokiichi, which is organized chronologically by event from 887, the accession of Emperor Uda. It is because of this focus on chronology and data that historians have described the institute as objective and neutral. But rather than evidence of objectivity, this is one of those areas where "denatured" documents located within an a priori totality, the nation-state, reinforce that totality. The Source Books incorporated a much wider range of data into events, including the tales, than in previous collections. The additional material, rather than being merely more, altered the subject of the chronology from the imperial institution to the nation-state. Objectivity, or the pretense to objectivity, allowed historians to produce as if they were autonomous from the state. Institutions and great men became the objects of inquiry.[30] There was a shift in the subject of history where the privileging of progress of the nation-state "causes the condition of its own possibility—space itself—to be forgotten" (de Certeau 1984, 95). Thus, while the subject of history has become the nation-state, the objects of historians are the data that speak to that progress, while the referent is modernity, that is, the West.

National literature and art history, too, were part of this conceptual map. Those aspects of the past that had to do with culture, that is, the ideals of the nation, were located in disciplines like art history and literature (in the twentieth century, folk studies [*minzokugaku*] would become an important discipline that preserved a Japanese culture). *Kokubungaku* took those texts that were of questionable historical status and gave them a literary status as exemplary texts that

---

[30] I hope that the gendering of this history will become more apparent below. At this point it is important to point out that the histories turned to male figures as the important objects of history.

described the spirit of the people of the nation, what Taine calls the "genius of a race." In other words, national literature became the domain of *historia magistrae vitae*. Mikami and Takatsu write, "Literature reflects people's hearts. For this reason, through the history of literature we will investigate by era the vestiges of the progress of knowledge and morals from ancient times, and we will know the ideas, sensibilities, and imagination of high and low" (1982, 5). But this elevation of national sensibilities still distrust the human senses. Mikami and Takatsu argue that the literary is formed by three agents (katakana: *ezento*) that give rise to a national literature. The three agents are the special characteristics of the nation (*kokumin*); external phenomena, that is, nature—geography, topography, climate, weather, mountains and streams, and flora and fauna; and the changing times. Interestingly, these three agents locate the forces for change and influence outside the human, simultaneously closer to that "inevitable mechanism" and a force that was weakening the social ethics of community. Their formulation is reminiscent of a statement by Pierre Nora: "history is perpetually suspicious of memory, and its true mission is to suppress and destroy it" (1989, 7).

In this return of sensibility to modernity, an interesting shift occurs in the human relation with nature. Here, we return to the role of nature in the amelioration of the absolutism of reality. But now, it is nature, the inert, external influences. Nature is the environs that is a major, external influence on literature, through which people's feelings are expressed and habits and customs formed. Watsuji Tetsurō would build upon this idea in his influential book *Fūdo* (Climate) thirty years later. Nature is shorn of the spirits and wonders that had populated it. In short, it becomes landscape; the mountains, moon, and flowers that have gained such a central place in a Japanese sense of Japan. Also, because it is external and part of those unseen natural laws, it is incumbent upon experts to uncover the influences upon society and tell people what they had or should have experienced.

Art history literally rescued many artifacts from destruction and organized them into a narrative of the greatness of Japanese culture as a part of the world. But here, too, the objects of study became inert artifacts from the past. Okakura identified the early part of the Nara period as the classical era of Japanese art. Outside influences stimulated this development—Buddhism from Tang China and India brought statues that had been influenced by the art of Persia and Greece, synchronizing Japanese art with the history of art in the West. The height of this classical art appears between the reigns of Shōmu (r. 724–49) and Kōnin (r. 770–81).[31] The Buddhist statues of this era best present the idea or spirit in a sensuous form. Okakura states: "When one summarizes the special features of the art of the Tenpyō period, first, it is idealism, the height of which has not again been achieved in any period of Japanese art since" (1939, 4:96, 79, 88). This is an example of a new locus and value of the Buddhist statues which

---

[31] For a fine discussion on the Western debate to define a Greco-Buddhist sculpture and its implications for an Orientalist construction, see Abe (1995).

were moved from the temples to museums, from sites where they were rarely seen to institutions where they are always on display to show the development of "Japanese" sensibilities.

Childhood, too, played a central role in the reorientation of locales into the nation. As an originary point of a developmental sense of time, childhood is a conceptual category that reinforces the linear time of society that history maintains for the nation. It becomes a temporal abstraction in this transformation from a heterogeneous to progressive time, which all modern societies have experienced. By turning the child into the focus of a developmental notion of human life, intellectuals merged ontogeny and phylogeny as if they were an "underlying essence," the mysterious and hidden, now placed in the realm of science rather than that of the supernatural (ghosts). This blurring of the distinction between ontogeny and phylogeny turns a certain kind of social time into a natural progress where individuals and nations are used interchangeably. As a metaphor for development, childhood is something temporal and temporary, now a category that determines human activity, not the reverse. While childhood recognizes the individuality of each human being, it also provides the framework to develop each child into members of the social body, the nation-state. This occurs, of course, through the educational edifice. But the efficacy of childhood goes well beyond the child; just as the maturity of the nation-state is measured by its distance from its early moments, the adult is measured by the extent to which one distances oneself from childhood toward socially objectified ideals—notions of civility, ethics, and morals. Distinctions occur by measuring the extent to which one improves from that pure state, that is, to what extent one is a good, productive citizen. In this sense, the child naturalizes an asymmetry—in human development, in society, in the nation-state, and globally. The word maturation suggests norms that are separate from the child; what is natural is in those norms, not its actions.

But the child exists only through the body of "the Japanese," reconnecting the abstraction of developmental time to each human being. Far from being universalistic, the constant birth of children establishes that synchrony of nation, the same passage of all Japanese since the beginning of time. Childhood provides those characteristics that combine into a coherent image that reoriented society around those abstract forms of knowledge, something seemingly common that could give a point of sameness to all people of the archipelago, despite the considerable differences by region, class, occupation, and so forth. This synchrony fostered a different form of interaction where certain past codes could be retained as something inherent. The child became a site of that new temporality that established "specific dispositions" and demonstrated "ways of assimilating experience."[32]

---

[32] Steedman describes this role: "Developments in scientific thought in the 19th century showed that childhood was both a stage of growth and development common to all of us, abandoned and left behind, but at the same time, a core of the individual's psychic life, always immanent, waiting there to be drawn on in various ways" (1992, 129).

While it is a chronological structure within the place, Japan, that connects these separate fields of knowledge together, they are separated, or isolated, in their different roles in relation to that nation-state. The purpose of the histories of literature and art was not to support the historical narrative, but to unearth the underlying spirit buried in these artifacts. Their descriptions are filled with judgments of the nature of the whole of each period. The ancient is known for its purity; the Nara and Heian are exemplary of an elegance and majesty. Despite the decline of the Kamakura, elegance continues, as does the virility and simplicity that emerges among the military rulers. Each period is set apart from the others to show both change—a change in which there is a strong connection between the past and the present—and continuity. Childhood provides the structure for ensuring that the bodies understand those ideals; it facilitates the constant reproduction of the national ideals through the education of the child.

In the case of history, literature, art history, and childhood, each serves a particular, useful role in establishing and reproducing the nation-state, as if it has always existed. It reconnects what had been a denigrated past to the modern present. Chronology reunites the dead past (the other) with the present (the self). The events, texts, art objects, and children are particular to Japan, depicting national progress. The newly formed archive holds documents that recount the political and economic development of the nation-state; pieces of art or works of literature that facilitate the imagination of the great aristocrats of the nation; and children remind all of their own maturity and constant need for collective and individual development.

There is a vagueness to this conceptual map. But that, I believe, is its power and source of continuity as if it is "permanent." It is an idea that transcends history and expresses itself through the particularity of the past.[33] This is one of the keys of mobilization of belief of a nation-state: the inscription of belief in such a way that it is very difficult to challenge the part; this is the power of what Latour points to as immutable mobiles. At one point, Okakura lamented the descent of stereotyped images into a caricature of art. But his caricature was the careless reproduction of images. Caricature in another sense is a "compact visual vocabulary" that captures the "essence" of some represented object. The efficacy of caricature is that it accentuates the distinctive. It needs no experts to mediate reception; the distinction between observer and observed is blurred by the experiential nature of apprehension (Hochberg 1972, 74–90).

The power of this map is to transmit knowledge and behavior indirectly, or Foucault's "government at a distance." The historicization of society relegated the very disciplines that were central to the process to a disconnected, but supportive, status. In the case of history, most recent interpreters argue that the his-

---

[33] A hint at the transcendent quality of art is evident in Okakura's definition of the Adwaita ideal; this ideal is the state of not being two, and is the name applied to the great Indian doctrine that all which exists, though apparently manifold, is really one (1970, 235).

torians were not central to the formulation of the history of the nation-state. Mehl echoes the common refrain: "the historians at the Historiographical Institute [the academic, orthodox historians] did not become interpreters of the nation; their lives and works did not shape the Japanese empire as those of the German historians shaped the German empire" (1998a, 159). Though I disagree that these historians were not central to the formulation of the empire, Mehl's statement indicates a disconnect between the practice of history and the utility of the past to the formulation of society. Literature and art provide a simple and enjoyable way to transmit a complex idea. Mary Carruthers cites psychologist George Miller: "'Some of the best 'memory crutches' we have are called 'laws of nature,' for learning can be seen as a process of acquiring smarter and richer mnemonic devices to represent information, encoding similar information into patterns, organizational principles, and rules which represent even material we have never before encountered, but which is 'like' what we do know, and thus can be 'recognized' or 'remembered'" (1990, 1–2). For example, Mikami and Takatsu and Okakura believed that the aesthetic pleasure set their fields apart from history. The utility of literature, argue Mikami and Takatsu, is not only in transmission of information, but also the way that the lesson is transmitted. For example, they point out how people have often learned indirectly through songs and poetry: "When one listens to the words and deeds in poetry and songs of wise rulers, wise counselors, loyal retainers, filial children, virtuous wives, faithful servants, heroes, and scholars one is not only pleased by the rhythm and voices, the tune and tempo, one is probably moved by the deeds." It is this use of literature as a tool of instruction, especially because people learn better through pleasure rather than didactic instruction, that they find particularly efficacious. "There is nothing better than literature to instill spiritual pleasure in so-called ordinary life" (1982, 22).

But lest we think that Mikami and Takatsu would allow this interpretation to create a space for freedom and consumption, they restrict this pleasure to that of a spirit of the nation (*kokumin*), not individual choices that might be harmful to the body (22–23). It also facilitates the development and operation of a liberal-capitalist society. They argue that literature is an anesthetic for this tendency toward the mechanization of society; just as one forgets a hard day of work with a drink at the end of the day, a song gives pleasure to work and can also dissolve depression. In a society that is becoming increasingly mechanical and specialized, literature and art as forms of pleasure that retain some human element in life are like a salve or placebo that anesthetizes an inevitable pain. At this point we must question this term pleasure; Ashis Nandy's statement that "once you own history, it also begins to own you" brings out the naturalness of chronology and the way that it, as both historical structure and anesthetic, dictates the constitution of life in Japan today (1995, 45).[34]

[34] For a discussion on the predictability and banality of Japanese society, one that raises questions whether history "owns" Japanese, see Miyoshi (2000).

Chapter 5

SOCIALIZATION OF SOCIETY

> Nothing matters much nowadays. As long as a craftsman does
> his work fast, he is good enough.
>
> —Yokoyama Gennosuke

> In Marx's analysis, social domination in capitalism does not,
> on its most fundamental level, consist in the domination of
> people by other people, but in the domination of people by
> abstract social structures that people themselves constitute.
>
> —Moishe Postone (1993)

THE WORKER'S STATEMENT above that "nothing matters" suggests a transformation of neighborhoods and societies based on immediate and overt human relations to abstract ideas governed by time. Indeed, this is an outcome of the new
temporality on the archipelago: the loosening of local, place-based ideas in favor
of a national space oriented toward economic growth and military power
(*fukoku kyōhei*). It is the transformation of the craftsman into a unit of input
(labor) and a part of the "abstract social structures that people themselves constitute" that Postone sees as an instrument of control. Long ago Karl Polanyi
identified the moment of this separation:

> The circumstances under which the existence of this human aggregate—a com
> plex society—became apparent were of the utmost importance for the history of
> nineteenth century thought. Since the emerging society was no other than the mar
> ket system, human society was now in danger of being shifted to foundations utterly
> foreign to the moral world of which the body politic hitherto had formed part.
> (1944, 115–16)

As Polanyi suggests, this "discovery of society" in late-eighteenth and early
nineteenth-century Europe and mid-nineteenth century Japan is tied to the
changing political economy, the rise of the market and capitalism.[1] But within
this discovery of society, history provides the permanence, a conceptual realm of
the nation-state, that has become distinct from that change. History has established the general contours of the place that also facilitate a mobility and inter-

---

[1] Numerous scholars have written about this discovery of society: Polanyi (1944, esp. 111–29) and
Barry, Osborne, and Rose (1996, 1–17). The latter draw upon Foucault and his essay on governmentality. Moscovici (1993) writes about an "invention of society."

changeability that had not been possible before.[2] People and goods are now freed from their previous ties to place, class, and so forth to move around and seek opportunity (in theory).

The 1890s and 1900s witnessed an intense discussion on the nature of the individual and his or her connection to a whole. It was called the "social problem" (*shakai mondai*). We must remember that liberalism both liberates from the past and imposes new restrictions that, I will argue, are integrated into the new temporality of modern society. This change often leads to actions and decisions that are certainly at odds with inherited norms and to fragmentation, new inequities, and new forms of conflict. This autonomy is made possible because now experience is determined not by what is around the individual, but by how that environment connects to abstract criteria—knowledge, be it objectified by texts, artifacts, or a national common sense.

The connection to the temporal transformation I have been discussing is described, albeit rather obliquely, by Agamben:

> Within this perspective, ghosts and children, belonging neither to the signifiers of diachrony nor to those of synchrony, appear as the signifiers of the same signifying opposition between the two worlds which constitutes the potential for a social system. *They are, therefore, the signifiers of the signifying function,* without which there would be neither human time nor history. Playland and the land of ghosts set out a utopian topology of historyland, which has no site except in a signifying difference between diachrony and synchrony, between *aiōn* and *chrónos,* between living and dead, between nature and culture. (1993, 84–85)

The combination of children and ghosts as unstable signifiers is fascinating. Agamben reminds us of what was eliminated through History—the ghosts, spirits, and superstitions that pervaded the myriad communities on the archipelago (see, e.g., Hearn 1971). The child becomes that "potential for a social system" that sets out a "utopian topology of historyland [Japan] . . . between nature and culture." It articulates that magical zero point in history that stabilizes the idea of the nation, cuts across regions making possible different forms of social organization that facilitate unification, becomes the concrete form to prescribe development, and also serves as the metaphorical idea to proscribe deviance. But this idea of the child is also a fantasy; as the potential for a social system, it suggests that the individual and the private is separated from the public. More important, it displaces these conflicting, even contradictory, demands onto the individual. The child stabilizes the idea of the individual as an autonomous actor as if he or she is free to succeed or fail. Yet as Jacques Donzelot (1978) has so powerfully shown, the child is surrounded by an edifice, the tutelary complex, that ensures that it is free to act only as long as it stays within the norms of

---

[2] For a powerful argument that the transformation of time is tied to the rise of capitalism, see Sohn-Rethel (1975) and Postone (1993).

bourgeois society. This is one of those places that the state intrudes into the lives of the inhabitants; it is one of those places that scholars, working from Foucault's idea of "governmentality," have called variously "government at a distance" or the "materiality of the state." Nicos Poulantzas writes, "The State here presupposes a specific organization of the political space upon which the exercise of power comes to bear. The centralized, bureaucratized State *installs* this atomization and, as a representative State laying claim to national sovereignty and the popular will, it *represents* the unity of a body (people-nation) that is split into formally equivalent monads" (2000, 63).

This ambiguity between the idea of enlightenment and liberalism and the constraints required by their very structures is at the core of this social problem. Typically, scholars have characterized it as the need to fully implement modern structures and ideas (that is, the elimination of anachronistic forms) or as temporary and unfortunate costs of change. During the 1890s and 1900s, elites focused on the increasing gap between rich and poor and proposed a number of reforms that sought to help the poor and limit the extraction of wealth by the rich; that is, it was seen as "merely" a technical problem of distribution. Numerous scholars have written about these important issues in relation to labor or the socialist movement (see, e.g., Garon 1987; Gordon 1991; Kublin 1964).

However, to accept the social problem as one of labor, zealot reformers, or socialists accepts the temporality of modernity, especially the displacement of the materiality of the state to the realm of culture or some nonpolitical (and thus less significant) realm. As Postone (1993) points out, the problem of distribution is but a part of the total reconfiguration of society centered around a socially constituted (not transhistorical) labor.[3] To be sure, the social problem properly focused on labor and the rising poverty in urban areas. But that labor is both socially constituted and constitutes the social. Postone writes, "In capitalism, labor itself constitutes a social mediation in lieu of such a matrix of relations. This means that labor is *not* accorded a social character by overt social relations; rather, because labor mediates itself, it both constitutes a social structure that replaces systems of overt social relations and accords its social character to itself" (151).

In and of itself, this is a difficult enough problem to resolve. But it is compounded in the non-West; what Postone describes as the objectification of labor and labor's objectification of social relations is part of the naturalization of capitalist development. In the West, this transition is progress and universality; in the non-West, it is progress, universality, and Westernization. That is, in Western societies, labor's objectification of society leads to the naturalization of capitalist

---

[3] For example, Postone writes, "Though his critical analysis of capitalism does include a critique of exploitation, social inequality, and class domination, it goes beyond this: it seeks to elucidate the very fabric of social relations in modern society, and the abstract form of social domination intrinsic to them by means of a theory that grounds their social constitution in determinate, structured forms of practice" (6).

modes of production, and the social forms that emerged in tandem with capitalism have become common sense. In the non-West, while labor is objectified, indicating an acceptance of capitalism, the objectification of society through labor, the new, is easily transposed to the worst of Westernization—greed, self-interest, impoverishment, alienation, and so on. This representation of problems of capitalism as Western, that is, external to Japan reinforces the unity of the nation. The newly constituted past then becomes a ready archive to establish a formula for the resolution of this social problem. That is, culture, or some national essence provides a "matrix of relations" that is emplotted to correct the problem. In the case of Japan, it is an idea that is imposed upon the nation as an "internalized" notion of being Japanese.

THE "SOCIAL PROBLEM"

In the last few years of the nineteenth century, the popular press began to write about a "social problem." What was called a problem was part of the transformation to a modern, liberal-capitalist society; the new urban spaces, the concentrations of poverty, squalid living conditions, and the wretched working conditions drew most of the attention, even though poverty and horrible working conditions in factories were widespread in rural areas. Conditions were desperate, pay was below subsistence levels, unions emerged, and strikes increased. News of these horrid conditions appeared in Matsubara Iwagoro's popular and sensational *Saiankoku no Tokyo* (In Darkest Tokyo), which appeared in 1893, and in Yokoyama Gennosuke's reports in the newspaper *Mainichi shinbun* and his 1899 book *Nihon no kasō shakai* (Working-class Society of Japan). Others, of course, were well aware of these conditions, but after Yokoyama's exposé, the government began its first survey of urban conditions, which was published in 1903.

However, this "labor problem" was but one aspect of the social problem. In examining this transformation, I prefer to follow the lead of Ogi Shinzō (1980), who examined the transformation of Edo to Tokyo. Ogi shows the complexity of this transition, for it was a transition not of the premodern to the modern, but of the ebb and flow of different populations and of different forms of social organization. Above all, those who wrote about the social problem were worried about the absence of social ties—the objectification, fragmentation, and loneliness of the increasingly crowded city. But we must also remember that this absence is also the freedom from self-incurred immaturities. Though Ogi does not go as far, the transformation is an example of Postone's observation that labor constitutes a social structure.

Throughout the early Meiji period, the population of Tokyo declined rapidly as many samurai returned to the provinces and merchants and artisans who catered to these aristocratic consumers lost their principal source of income. Ogi argues that these merchants, artisans, and shopkeepers formed what he calls the neighborhood societies (*chōnai kanketsu shakai*), akin to what I have been calling a space of experience—those inherited practices and human relations built from contact and the immediate surroundings. On the other hand, migration to Tokyo began to rise as peasants, now laborers, entered the city. These migrants saw Tokyo as a place to work, sleep, and advance, but they still felt a connection to their home village. Ogi calls Tokyo "Tōkei," a name that designates this transition (what Koselleck [1985] calls a *sittelzeit* [lit. "saddle time"]) from Edo to Tokyo.

The new inhabitants began to change the demographics and, more important, the consciousness of the city. From 1887 Ogi documents a rise in migrants changing their registered domicile (*honseki*) to Tokyo. He argues that Tōkei became Tokyo in 1889, when a different consciousness among residents became evident; the neighborhood societies began to wane, being overwhelmed by the large number of people living at or below poverty. These were "men of the world" (*sekensama*), indicating a disconnection from their immediate place. According to Ogi, these worldly people were atomistic; they did not have the same social manners nor ties to the locale. They had a level of simplicity—they lived as they felt and apart from social ethics. Indeed, this was the social problem, the absence of those ties among individuals that hold a community together. While progress is one outcome of the removal of self-incurred immaturities, the severing of the inherited past also loosens the ties that bind people together, and abstract ideals of liberal capitalism do not provide a replacement. The worker's declaration at the beginning of this chapter exemplifies this new society.

Few were satisfied, but it was (is) unclear what should replace those ethical ties. On one level, Ogi points to the rise of antiquarian societies, for example, the Edokai (Edo Society), where the interest in preservation of aspects of Edo is a reaction to the change. This antiquarianism (or romanticism) coincides with debates over the nature of history of Japan. But on a different level, Ogi points to the reorientation of pasts among these new residents of *shitamachi* (working class quarters, lit. "downtown"); the migrants and workers who moved to fill the jobs of the new economy took on some of the characteristics of Edo—the liveliness (*iki*) and pretense (*tsū*) of the spirit of *Edokko*—but shorn of the social connections that had also been a part of those characteristics (204). The latter part is interesting, for in the change of *shitamachi* to the modern, the new workers who filled the factories and assimilated some of the characteristics of Edo are using the past to celebrate their newfound autonomy. This is an example of Postone's comment that labor accords its social character to itself; but from the perspective of an elite or reformer, it is evidence of customs (i.e., the primitive) that need to change.

In 1893 and 1894, the *Rikugo zasshi* published essays by Kanai Noburu and Ono Yōjirō on an emerging "social problem." Both drew heavily from their readings of the problem of the social in Europe (especially in German); they acknowledged that it was not yet a major issue in Japan, but they were confident that the problem was emerging. While labor is a principal focus, especially the growing gap between rich and poor and the rise of urban poverty, both recognize that it encompasses the whole of modern society, rather than a particular segment, that is, labor. Kanai's fear of the chaos and conflict that would emerge if not addressed is evident in the fourteen categories he outlines as research themes. His topics indicate that labor is central, but that the resolution of this problem requires the implementation of social reforms. The issues include protection for workers, relief legislation, establishing a minimum wage, profit sharing, insurance, and unionization. But he also includes more general or "social" reforms, such as education of workers, emigration, social legislation, and an investigation of political attitudes and aesthetic sensibilities.

The recognition that this problem is related to a very different mode of social organization, but one tied to labor, is more apparent in Ono's essay. Ono argues that the freedom of the individual and state power are the two parts of social progress. Indeed, the role of the individual, the connection to society and to hidden laws, and the possibility of autonomous action became key concerns. Ono argues that enlightenment is a social, not individual, phenomenon. He writes, "Civilization is not in the activities of an individual; it develops from the power of social cooperation." This social cooperation gives rise to progress and is connected to the trends of the times. Ono argues that deeds of great men—scholars, politicians, inventors, and explorers—are a product of the trend of the times, that is "by a majority of people cooperating" (7).

This cooperation requires the involvement of the state. Ono argues that individualism has increased over the past two centuries in Europe, and more recently in Japan, but because of the sociality of progress, it is important that the relation between state and individual be balanced. In other words, Ono sees the rise of individualism as threatening the balance between state and individual. He argues, "We will not be able to resolve the confrontation between rich and poor unless we, on the one hand, enhance the abilities of individuals and reform the ideals of everyday life that determine their behavior, and on the other hand, reform the spirit of the laws of the state" (3). Ono cites the public railroads, postal service, factory laws, intervention in labor disputes, and laws for compulsory insurance as evidence of the swing of the pendulum toward an increased role of the state. The state, then, should control the exploitation of natural resources so that they benefit the whole of society; it should provide assistance as well as protection to labor; and it should promote the development of the individual, especially in education, health, arts, and fine arts. In particular, he writes, in a constitutional state, policies must have the consent of the people. He concludes, "For this reason, unless the ideals and feelings of individuals evolve considerably, one cannot even expect the development of state power. I consider the progress of individuals and the development of state power as both sides of the evolution of society" (8). In short, the social problem was not an issue of distribution, but a problem of the very constitution of the social. Ono's resolution was for the state to take on a more active role to establish that social.

While many argued in 1893 that Japan did not yet have a "social problem," the concerns of Kanai and Ono for the need to fashion social ideals and feelings among the populous indicate that problems were already apparent. Ono located the problem in the heterogeneity across the population, now divided by class (economic), not region. His ideal is a bourgeois sensibility; he argues that the upper classes indulge in luxury, the middle classes are tied to manufacturing, and the lower classes are not yet self-conscious. While he recognizes that the issue requires attention from diverse sectors, he encapsulates the problem, quoting Lujo Brentano, the German historical school economist: "The social problem is a problem of human education" (9). For Kanai and Ono, education is more than the research into all aspects of the problem, it is the unification of all people as nationals; it requires the cultivation of people to recognize the sociality of individual pleasures. Echoing Miyake, Ono argues that pleasure transcends physical pleasures, such as food and drink; it is a social pleasure that is also connected to metaphysical ideals—truth, goodness, and beauty (within the nation-state). He writes, "If there is progress in the ideals of nationals beyond their everyday life, a social pleasure becomes the principal motive force of society; the benefits to the individual will be harmonized and the social problem will naturally disappear" (10). In short, in this reconfigured world, now a Japan, intellectuals sought to determine those norms that connected individuals, society, nation, and state, thereby constricting the possibilities of individual autonomy.

In 1897 this debate became less abstract. In that year, the Shakai Mondai Kenkyūkai, the Social Problem Research Group, became one of several organizations established to discuss the "social problem." Others established in the same year were the labor groups, Kyōdō Shinwa Kai, Shokkō Giyūkai, and Rōdō Kumiai Kisei Dōmeikai, and groups advocating universal elections, like the Futsū Senkyō Dōmeikai. While today we might identify the organizers—Nakamura Ōhachirō, Yokoi Tōkichi, and Nishimura Fukamichi—as early socialists, the membership, political perspective, and topics discussed at these meetings varied considerably. About two hundred men were listed as members, and about thirty members attended the monthly meeting. The list of members and their interests indicate the newness and uncertainty of the social. Shinagawa Yajirō, a conservative Diet member, spoke about the need to protect labor and establish banks; he advocated the reform of society around Japan's unique characteristics. Taguchi Ukichi discussed the single tax and the need for a tax increase. Matsumura Kaisuke, a member of the Salvation Army, advocated spiritual uplift. Miyake Setsurei and Kuga Katsunan participated, as did many reporters from various newspapers; Kōtoku Shūsui was a rather quiet participant. (Yamaji Aizan [1965a] observed that at the time no one would have imagined that Kōtoku would become a figure embroiled in the Great Treason Trial of 1910–11.) Iwamoto Zenji discussed the women's problem (*fujin mondai*) and education of whom we would today call mentally disadvantaged; the economist Tajima Kinji was a follower of the Wagner school of economics; Yamaji talked about the inequalities and problems of the primogeniture system for second and third sons. Sakuma Teiichi, a factory owner, discussed the conditions of labor and sought reforms. Katayama Sen was initially concerned about urban conditions and advocated urban reform. Sakai Yūjirō, who had studied in France, was well versed in the writings of French socialists, such as Florian and Saint Simon. Others debated the differences between Marx's world socialism and the national socialism of Lasalle. In short, participants ranged from conservative politicians to future labor activists (Yamaji 1965a, 370–72).

In a sense, this discovery of the social emerges from a fear of social disintegration that accompanies the transformation of the natural world that became subject to the regularity of laws and analyzable as discrete components and objects. Just as in the rise of science, the separation of nature from the human, or the elevation of the social to norms, begins a move that turns agency over to a particular segment of the human, the experts. These intellectuals believed that the human being, who is separated from animals because of knowledge, is thus a social being. In their debates on the nature of this social, they searched for some regularity, some way to make sense of and give order to this new phenomenon. One common characteristic is the belief of these men (the members were all male) in the importance of study and analysis; in other words, this is also the beginning of a science of society.

A CRY FOR EXPERIENCE AS EXPERIENCE

This recognition of a "social problem" marks an important moment in the transformation of the archipelago into a Japan. At this moment, development was not linear; there were multiple paths, perhaps even a confusing maze. But gradually the problem became reduced to the contradiction of separation and totalization, which Lefebvre points out is a condition of modernity:

> The socialization of society goes on unabated. As the networks of relations and communications get more dense, more effective, so at the same time the individual consciousness becomes increasingly isolated and unaware of 'others'. That is the level on which the contradiction operates. We must begin our analysis by grasping both aspects one by one, seeing them as antithetical. Once the dialectical movement has been caught, the drama is revealed: separation and totalization, the former working on the individual and his life, the latter made effective by means of the state, the global society, communications, norms, culture, etc. (1995, 190)

Takayama Chogyū and Inoue Tetsujirō are two key intellectuals who sought to resolve the relationship between the individual and society. Inoue is the conservative, German-trained philosopher who wrote the commentary to the Imperial Rescript on Education; Takayama, his protégé gone wayward, became one of the most influential and widely read intellectuals until his suicide in

1902. While Takayama sought to understand the freedom and responsibilities of the individual within a social unit, Inoue molded the individual into the social defined in terms of a national community.

In his short career, Takayama was a sharp critic of the materialism and rationalism of Meiji civilization. He advocated what we translate as Japanism (*nihonshugi*) as well as the primacy of individual happiness, what Hashikawa Bunsō calls bourgeois individualism (1962, 387–93). These are not two poles, but parts of a dialectical process. Even though Takayama committed suicide at the young age of thirty-one, his brief career was filled with rich and varied experience: he graduated from Tokyo Imperial University in philosophy, co-authored an early ethics textbook with Inoue, edited *Taiyō*, the most popular journal at the time, and in his final years was very influential in bringing Nietzsche's ideas to Japanese readers.

Takayama's writings savor the rise of Japan as a world power and also increasingly question the makeup of society, especially the role of the individual. He, too, did not question the nation of Japan, and instead sought to ameliorate the new relationship between the inhabitants and the new nation-state. For example, in a statement reminiscent of Agamben's reaccession to infancy, he commented on the possibilities of freedom in childhood:

> Ah! What is the spirit (*kokoro*) of the child? Like a brilliant jewel or like pure water, it is completely separate from the bonds of a world that demands fame, seeks to aggrandize the self, and is filled with form, means, and habit; it is not bound to all artificial (*jin'i*) morals and learning. That which completely opens up the inherent goodness and discloses one's true heart, alas, that is the spirit of the child. (1970f, 100)

Here, Takayama identifies the child as a site when humans are unrestricted of the modern structures and categories that guide individuals and society. He is searching for a unified nation that does not subject individuals to fixed constructs that impose new restrictions or codes that are divorced from human immediacy. Indeed, a characteristic of his writing is the search for some balance between the autonomous individual and the social unit, the nation.

It is in this seeming juxtaposition between his support for the nation and later writings that emphasize individual subjectivity that has led many scholars to conclude that Takayama underwent conversion (*tenkō*). During the 1930s ultranationalists extracted from Takayama's writings evidence that furthered their nationalist and imperialist ambitions. For example, Takasu Hidejirō finds in Takayama's writings a "prognostication of the Greater East Asia War and annihilation of Britain and America" (Hashikawa 1962, 389). But we should remember that the essay "Japanism" was written in 1893, not only a year before the Sino-Japanese War, but also coterminous with the founding of history and national literature. That is, he was writing at the same time that intellectuals were seeking to determine the nature and content of the nation, an entity that they acknowledged was still only an idea.[4]

To argue conversion ignores the fact that individualism and freedom are possible only through a defined and regulated space. In his reappraisal of the politicality of Michel Foucault's writings, Nikolas Rose points out that government must not only make "visible the space over which government is exercised" (1996, 36), but also that the "achievement of the liberal arts of government was to begin to govern through making people free" (69). This freedom is structured; freedom is possible in various prescribed realms. These spaces can be that of the nation (as opposed to other nations), the city, the family, a child, oneself—all defined domains with specific characteristics, limitations, and horizons. Instead of reading Takayama's article as evidence of nationalism, his quite conscious separation of the nation-state from the nation suggests a different concern, the reorganization of society where individuals constitute the whole (nation), rather than being subject to it (nation-state). Takayama's nation is not a spatial unit, but the accumulation of activities of the people of the nation. To elevate the nation, Takayama tries to recover the historicity of ideas; that is, he tries to release ideas from an essential nature by recovering their historical specificity.

Takayama is pointing to problems that emerge from the historicization of society, that is, the reconfiguration of pasts into ahistorical categories that facilitate sociopolitical order—the materiality of the state. He writes, "I believe that today's reform of civilization must eradicate the bonds of a secular nationalism that pervades all society" (1970e, 97). That secular nationalism is the prioritization of the state or nation-state above the people. For Takayama, knowledge, whether Western or Japanese, and morals become that exteriority that diverts development of Japanese from their true nature, and this constraint makes people crazy. In this criticism of the nation as an idea defined by the state, his definition of Japanism is similar to Miyake's idea. Japanism is "a moralistic principle whose purpose is to manifest the aspirations of our country's founding through a subjectivity based on the particular character of the nation" (1970a, 23). Takayama, too, does not question the unit, a Japan or Japanese. At this point it is possible to see a reaction against enlightenment qua Westernization that resembles the conservatism of Inoue or even the ultranationalists.

Takayama's principle, however, is not a transcendent spirit; it is historical, that is, in the practices of the people. He writes, "Japanism designates the spiritual peace and enlightenment of the nation (*kokumin*). Japanism is not religion; it is not philosophy. It is the practiced ethical principle of the nation" (26). Takayama's distinction between the nation and the nation-state is a different way of recognizing the social. By rooting the principle in the everyday, the "practiced

---

[4] Takayama argued that Japan must develop a consciousness of itself as a nation and acknowledged that this was a new era in the culture of Japan (1970a, 23).

ethical principle" of the people, he is seeking to locate the nation in the activity of people, not some abstract ideal or spirit. Takayama's principle is different from earlier societies, for it is not akin to Ogi's notion of a neighborhood society. It, too, is an abstract idea (bounded by both place and practice) within which people exist, not a lived place. At this point, this practiced ethical principle is vague; it eventually evolves into his notion of happiness. But it might be better understood through its antithesis—those ideas and forms that fix life.

This practiced ethical principle becomes apparent in an essay, "The Relation between Goodness and Beauty," published in 1896. This essay brings out his differences with Miyake; he questions the wisdom of combining beauty and goodness, arguing that they are quite distinct, though often merged (he attributes this conflation to Eduard von Hartmann). He exalts beauty as an expression of feelings; it is the highest form of subjectivity as opposed to truth, which is the highest form of objectivity. Goodness, which he values for its role in social relations, falls between truth and beauty and establishes the norms, which he argues are always historical. He acknowledges that these norms seem to be truth and fixed. He emphasizes, "In every country and time there are fixed norms that unifies people's behavior; they are in the constitution, laws, customs, and habits. These fixed norms that serve as objective criteria of good and bad, the consciousness of goodness, resemble that of truth. When decisions are made based upon objective norms, a consciousness of goodness is close to a consciousness of truth and resembles an aesthetic consciousness when it is close to one's awareness of absolute reality" (1970b, 56–57). Takayama astutely exposes limitations of Miyake's idea of nation: by removing goodness—those ethical ideals that guide individuals in society—from its specific historicity, what should be a practiced ethical principle becomes an ahistorical ideological construct that through norms dictate what people should be and do.

This criticism becomes more direct in his famous "An Aesthetic Life" (*Biteki seikatsu o ronzu*). In this 1901 essay, Takayama points out that the combination of truth, goodness, and beauty serves as the basis of a rationalist philosophy. The tie of truth, goodness, and beauty is an expression of a public good, and thus itself an extrinsic idea that relies on knowledge (truth) and morals (goodness).[5] Though subtle, Takayama's recovery of history has potentially major repercussions for the state. From his perspective, the contestation between academic historians and national literature scholars at the Imperial University was inconsequential. Both sought to determine the character of the nation through some fixed past; they did not look to the nation (that is, the people), but the ideals of their chosen pasts. For Takayama the nation-state is completely instrumental, the necessary institution that maintains order and facilitates the goals of the nation; it should not define or determine the nation.

---

[5] His criticism of religion and philosophy is directed toward transcendent, ahistorical ideas, like Buddhism, Christianity, and Confucianism.

Takayama also sought to free the idea of beauty from the dictates of the state. He argues that it is not some external ideal, but an internal feeling to all people. He writes, *"German scholars have placed the concept of beauty on a lofty plane. I see it as common experience"* (1970b, 58). This sense of beauty is located in the masses, not the icons, paintings, or other objects of fine art exalted by Okakura and Fenollosa. By separating truth, goodness, and beauty, Takayama is distinguishing ethics and knowledge as historical, those external ideas and rules that facilitate social order and advance society, from feelings and instinct, which are internal or natural. In short, Takayama has formulated an understanding of a Japanese past that maintains the historicity of those ideas that organize society.

Takayama's interpretation has the potential to remove Japan from its perpetual dilemma of being both modern and Oriental. The idea of an Orient conflates two categories of knowledge (rational/West vs. moral/East) usually separated as Western and Eastern into one category. But as Takayama argues, if both rationality and morals are artificial, that is, historical, then the distinctions of Orient and Occident must also be historical. Domestically, this distinction allows for the possibility of a different kind of history from those of the new disciplines that were turning parts of the past into inert objects of a chronological narrative. For example, he exposes the selectivity of the chronological narrative of art history. In the essay "Hibijutsuteki nihonjin" (The Unartistic Japanese), he writes rather caustically, "Those Japanese who brag of a rich artistic spirit must admit that it is empirically clear that throughout history independent creativity and growth are truly rare, and that the high points of that history of art were generally influenced by foreigners" (1914a, 583–84). Here, Takayama exposes the way that chronology obscures much of the past; in the case of artifacts, many were not produced by "Japanese." By doing so, he questions the ideal, the spirit, that the objects are claimed to represent.

He is equally disparaging of historians and writers; the following passage, reminiscent of Nietzsche, is an example of his critique: "We of the late nineteenth century cannot overcome the grandness of history (*rekishi no ōki*). It is history that subsumes subjectivity (*shukan*), oppresses the individual (*jinkaku*), and ignores innate ability. It is history that obstructs the development of individual freedom, homogenizes (*heibonka*) all races, and places a curse on all genius" (1970c, 63). Takayama probably included national literature with history, but he also attacked novelists. He writes, "They have much that is called poetry, songs, and novels, but from what I have seen it is only *gesaku*, words with no significance. They [writers] still have not opened their hearts to humanity; if they have ears they do not listen, and if they have eyes they do not see. It is as if they have chosen to scribble almost like children. It is without principles of place: without vision, without spirit, without honor, and without ideals" (1970c, 64).

In short, Takayama is critiquing the historicization of society where historians, literary scholars, philosophers, and so forth are endowing elements of the past with an ahistorical status. On one level, his distinction facilitates an attack against things imported into the archipelago. Often his statements echo with the language of nativists, like Konakamura. For example, he wrote in "Nihonshugi," "[Japanism] is nothing other than the clearest public expression of an authentic self-conscious spirit that is based on a 3,000-year verified history of the nation." To accept a verifiable past on the archipelago for three thousand years is to accept the myths in the *Kojiki* and *Nihon shoki* (many of the myths in these texts were being questioned at this time). In his criticism of religion, philosophy, and art, he points out that Japanese have not been religious (especially during the ancient period). Moreover, he criticizes religion, with its penchant for metaphysical truths: "Is it not a type of creed that one achieves through metaphysical laws and by yearning for a type of supernatural ideal, not through the course of contemporary life?" (1970a, 23). Buddhism and Confucianism were imposed (the passive is important here), Christianity is foreign, and the fine arts are drawn from the continent and Korean peninsula. At this level, Takayama is following a line of argument similar to that used by many nativist scholars. There is an idea of some pure Japan that is still recoverable if only one can penetrate all the fixed historical layers.

But he also applies this criticism to modern society. He belittles contemporary knowledge as instrumentalist and false science and identifies its problem in its fixity and restrictions. The categories and forms lose their heuristic character and become static, often sufficing for or replacing the meaning that had given rise to the unit. These categories of knowledge then become divorced from principle and ideals, curtail initiative, and foster complacency. His attack on morals was directed toward the codification of behavior. In a criticism of ethics teachers as a contemporary evil, he writes, "Do they not turn things people have made into creations of heaven? Thus, do they not vest morals which should readily change with an omnipotent power?" (1970d, 84). Takayama consistently places the accumulation of actions of the people before the institutions or ideas that seek to order those people. Thus, when he criticizes scholars as charlatans (*gigakusha*)—he mentions moralists such as Inoue Tetsujirō and aestheticians such as Okakura—he is attacking the imposition of a homogenizing idea upon the multiple possibilities of the people on the archipelago.

By pointing to the externality of knowledge and morals, Takayama opens up the possibility for criticizing those constructions, Western and Japanese, that seek to define, especially those ideas that extract from the past as if they are timeless. For example, he calls Confucianism a decayed Confucianism, which is devoid of life. In a discussion on the five relations he writes, "Morals are customs that have suppressed consciousness, inquiry, and effort" (1970d, 81). On the other hand, he leaves no doubt about his dislike for the new science. He emphasizes that knowledge and morals "*often injure the body; moreover they make people bigoted, obstinate, and dejected, and rob their common sense. In the extreme, they make people mad*" (1970b, 62). He also points out that even those who sought to correct for such fixity, such as Miyake, who tried to eliminate

Western mediations in the formulation of Japan's character, often failed. Miyake only eliminated the hierarchical framework of Enlightenment (no small feat). Takayama is quite right in pointing out that Miyake's ideals fit into a rationalist framework, even if one that is now centered in Asia rather than the West. Miyake did expose the particularity of the West, but he still replicated the Occident/Orient distinction. This criticism of the effort to use Orientalism to authorize a unique Japan also calls into question Okakura's and Fenollosa's aesthetic where their definition of beauty naturalized a Japanese aesthetic that draws from objects tied to the continent.[6]

Takayama also differs from the historians, national literature scholars, philosophers, and others in the way that he conceives of the relation between the nation and the state (or people and government). His criticism is directed toward the way that history has made itself into a tool of the nation-state; as such, it robs people of their own natural instinct, to seek happiness. In "Kangai issoku" (A Bundle of Emotions), he is quite explicit in his criticism of the bonds that the emperor system, ancestor worship, and *kokutairon* have imposed on society through the elevation of ethics to the status of norms (1970e, 92–99). Many scholars have attributed this elevation of social individuals over the collective whole to his reading of Nietzsche. But as Maeda Ai points out, this prioritization of the individual over the nation-state was also apparent in his earlier writings (1989, 113–30). But this distinction between the nation and the nation-state is crucial; without it, it is easy to overlook his emphasis on the human, rather than the unit. For Takayama, the difference is between a historical processual nation grounded in the accumulated activities of the masses and an ahistorical idea of what the nation should be through examples from the past. Takayama argues that the nation-state (*kokka*) exists for the individual (*kojin no tame*); the latter is in the soul, where an inexhaustible supply of energy exists. His criticism of the nation-state as inhibiting recalls Raymond Williams's description of different natures (processual and essential) as fixed. Williams writes, "Each of these conceptions of Nature was significantly static: a set of laws—the constitution of the world, or an inherent universal, primary but also recurrent force—evident in the 'beauties of nature' and in the 'hearts of men,' teaching a singular goodness" (1976, 188). Williams (like Takayama) is pointing to one of the fascinating sites of circularity in modern epistemology: it is built upon the denigration of the past to enable change as well as demonstrate progress, yet it reformulates certain pasts as transhistorical ideas or conditions that, in the name of order, unity, cohesion, and so forth imposes another "self-incurred immaturity." Takayama then

---

[6] Takayama raises a fascinating question in his essay "Rekishi o daimoku to seru bijutsu." He asks why Shinto objects are not part of this new archive of art history and complains, "Did the people of the divine land not vainly dislike their submission to the foreign cultures as in the Buddhist statues from ancient India. *The nation (kokumin) must strive to produce art that corresponds to national ideals*" (1914b, 464–65). In the early surveys of old artifacts, objects tied to the imperial household, tombs, and Shinto regalia were included, but sometime in the 1880s, these disappeared from the catalogs.

returns to Descartes to question the idea of enlightenment as practiced in Japan, asserting, "We must first awaken our consciousness to our own existence and establish our own foundation." Moreover, it is in this inquiry that raises the uncertainty of Blumenberg's absolutism of reality that Takayama finds hope: "It is because we are appalled, doubtful, tormented, and troubled that for the first time it is possible to conceive of a human nature" (1970e, 96).

That awakening took Takayama to what he called the aesthetic life. His best essay expressing this relation between the individual and society is his "An Aesthetic Life." He explains this idea: "After all, a sense of aesthetics is the locus that harmonizes feeling (*kankaku*), thought (*shisō*), and emotions (*jōcho*). It does not favor any one element" (1970b, 59). Thought, emotion, and feeling recall Miyake's truth, goodness, and beauty. But for Takayama, these three ideas do not constitute an ideal. Instead, they are brought together in his notion of aesthetics, which is located in every human. Aesthetics or beauty (*biteki*) is not visual, but the attainment of supreme happiness through the satisfaction of instinctual needs; morals and knowledge are the means to achieve that end. He writes:

> An aesthetic life is completely different. Prior to those values it is absolute; it is intrinsic. There is no derivation, it is not bound [by anything], and it harmoniously transcends the boundaries of Reason. It is a place of peace of mind; it is a place of peace. It is a place that possesses perpetual power, and *it stores the energy for development of the universe. Where else can one find this sphere of supreme human happiness.* (1970d, 82)

Here, Takayama too is grounding his concept of Japan in nature, but it is an essence rooted in the human organism, not some metaphysical system. His goal is supreme happiness or an aesthetic life, which he defines as the satisfaction of instinctual needs. In other words, it "resounds equally throughout the body"— the unity of mind and body—of all Japanese, but is prior to history (1970b, 59).

In defending Takayama's position, Tobari Chikufū points to the centrality of nature in modernity. But this nature is that of human instinct and the senses that have been denigrated in this march to establish a modern society. Tobari states, "Today is a world of almighty science, it is a world of the absolute power of knowledge, and it is the golden age of moral education; it is an age that condemns the instincts particular to humans, especially those that bring freedom" (312). Takayama's emplotment of an innate human desire—the fulfillment of happiness—as prior to knowledge and morals inverts Miyake's faith in an abstract rationality. Instinct is the basis of life, where people have choice and freedom. He calls instinct the lord, as opposed to knowledge and morals as the retainers (1970d, 81). In other words, the latter is the means, a history, created by humans to achieve happiness.

By moving nature to instinct and the fulfillment of happiness, Takayama is attempting to formulate an alternative modern temporality that is part of, but not beholden to, progressive and chronological time. His origin is not some originary condition or primitive beginning; it is a biological need. Moreover, his horizon of expectation is in the fulfillment of this human need, not some improved future (usually defined materialistically). On the other hand, by placing knowledge and morals as the means, change, development, progress, and so on are also possible and even desirable; however, they are not the goal. Above all, this shift also returns the past to history. That is, he denies the possibility of naturalizing those social forms as some trans- or ahistorical idea.

In this turn to the individual body, Takayama is bordering on individualism, but his self was not the unbridled ego, but a self located in a social nexus where knowledge and morals are necessary to fulfill (but do not determine) one's happiness. Through this tie to the social, Takayama's self was not the self-interest of a "world that demands fame, seeks to aggrandize the self, and is filled with form, means, and custom." That, too, is an artificial world of capitalism that imposes desire on people.[7] In this sense, Takayama's idea of happiness parallels Ono's notion of pleasure. Both tie it to the social, but Ono's is tied to an ahistorical ideal that is conflated with the state; Takayama's happiness is the fluid accumulation in the nation. Lest one think that he leaves room for a definition of happiness as the acquisition of wealth, Takayama would respond that that is an individualism that does not respect the social and is a false consciousness where one is only accumulating an empty form. He writes, "A man with only money is not wealthy; a man with only power is not noble. By recognizing your kingdom (ōkoku) in your heart, for the first time one can speak of an aesthetic life" (1970d, 83).

Takayama's reliance on happiness depends upon a belief in the fundamental goodness of humans. In his "An Aesthetic Life," he sees the goal of achieving a supreme good as part of that instinct: "Morals anticipate the supreme good. The supreme good is a conception that holds the highest purpose of human behavior as our ideals" (1970d, 79). Achieving this good requires both consciousness of it and expression of that good through one's behavior. But in general, he finds that Japanese lack this goodness; even though he praises the ethics in *Chushingura* (Story of the 47 Rōnin), he argues that these samurai followed public morals: they adhered to a moral code but they did not act from internal understanding of that good (1970d, 80). Had he lived another decade, he probably would have condoned the suicide of General Nogi following the death of the Meiji emperor.

At this point, it is important to remember that while Japan was "catching up" with the more economically and militarily developed nation-states, the emergence of this "social problem" was coeval with a similar recognition in European states.[8] This does not mean that Japan is the same, but that up to this point,

---

[7] Maeda differentiates between individualism and a self initiated by pride and sentiment (1989, 121).
[8] Rose, recognizing that it is an accumulation of changes occurring during the latter half of the nineteenth century, dates the emergence of the social at the beginning of the twentieth century (1999, esp. chap. 3).

the process of transformation is more similar to other places dealing with modernity than we have described it in the past.

Takayama's critique of modernity was not directed against the failure of the masses to progress and learn. Instead, he identified the problem as the blindness and superficiality of scholars, intellectuals, and writers, the charlatans. His hope is in the people themselves: "The individual has always had an inexhaustible supply. The honor and essence of humanity is in developing this inexhaustible supply. The so-called way of humanity (*jindō*) is nothing other than connecting this limitless process as the primary effect of this development to a time and site. Thus the methods of everyday life that impede the development of this inexhaustible supply is a public enemy of humanity and must be reformed" (1970e, 97). The problem is the "methods of everyday life," the ideas, forms, and institutions that give order and constrict individuals in modern society. His microcultures of the everyday served to counter those methods, the rationality and instrumentalism of capitalist Japan. His idea of enlightenment, then, was not the transformation to the liberal-capitalist nation-state that Japan was becoming, but to a nation of autonomous, harmoniously interacting individuals. His aesthetic life placed greater reliance on the will, variation, and heterogeneity of humans.

But Takayama's dilemma is a difficult one: a recognition of knowledge and morals as a form of power that impedes the growth of the people, the necessity of a nation-state in the modern world, and the belief in the customs of the race. But this is not a transhistorical notion of race, but the collective bodies of Japanese. That collective body is not the physiological/racial being; instead, it is an idea of Japan grounded in the accumulated habits of the human organism, not some metaphysical system or essential being. The difference is a fine one; it has to do with the locus and understanding of a history of that collective body. It is a past to be respected, but one that does not bind the present to it. He concludes, "At the same time that we value this great bequest of our ancestors we must respectfully continue this valuable heritage and ceaselessly strive for that happiness that is born from this heritage" (1970e, 82). To do otherwise would objectify the idea of Japan and Japanese according to a fixed past.

CONTESTATION OF WILLS

Although Takayama's desires might not have resolved the social problem, his writings do indicate a sophisticated engagement with the processes of modern society, rather than one that follows a path to modern society. But his elevation of the individual was too discomforting to others troubled by the fragmentation of society. His mentor, Inoue Tetsujirō, for example, turned to the issue of will as a way to tackle this interrelation between the individual and the social. There are many similarities in Inoue and Takayama's thinking.[9] But a key difference is the temporality of history: Inoue transformed the historicity of society that Takayama so carefully formulated into an ahistorical ideal of the nation-state. This is one of those moments when a national past was reemplotted as that matrix of relations that uses culture to objectify social relations.

Inoue is best known for his criticism of Uchimura Kanzō, which is frequently cited as evidence of his anti-Christian conservatism. But this criticism of Christianity was part of a broader endeavor to expose the specific sociohistoric conditions of institutionalized religions and ethics, which were at odds with his notion of modern society. Like Takayama, Inoue is seeking to retain a historicity of knowledge forms. He argues that religions and ethical systems, such as Buddhism, Confucianism, and Christianity, are artifices that make claims to a transhistorical idea that grounds their doctrines. He was quite aware that, to paraphrase Kant, the first two are institutions that are also responsible for the self-incurred immaturity of Japanese. Inoue does not deny the moral and ethical contributions of Buddhism and Confucianism to Japan's past, only that adherence to religion does not ensure ethical behavior. Instead, he argues that morals are prior to religion, "Morals have a much wider scope; they are much broader than any religion. It is something that must exist in all humankind" (1915, 734).[10]

But at this point, Inoue turns away from the processes of modernity to a dualism of modern society, that between the objectivity of modern science and rationality and the subjectivity of social worlds. In contrast to Takayama's faith in the goodness of humans, Inoue seeks to find the basis for regularities in conduct that parallel the scientific world. He locates those natural-like laws in the idea of will (ishi), which he situates between individuals and the social. Will, now, has the potential to appropriate and control desire.

Inoue identified human will (ningen no ishi) as that universal that is inherent to all humans and is the basis of a progressive spirituality. He states, "There is a thing called will in humans, and when one possesses will there is definitely purpose" (1915, 714). The connection of purpose to will leads humans beyond a survival instinct where purpose and the accumulation of experience endow humans with a progressive nature. He writes, "However, by gradually accumulating experience, the power of will develops on its own, and humans always try to establish purpose beyond the present." Will is that source of progress that separates human nature from nature. It is prior to knowledge and without will, such as in animals which are limited by their endowed capabilities, there is no improvement: "When the complete human being is not led by will, there is no

[9] Many historians, such as Hashikawa Bunsō, see a marked change in Takayama's later writings, arguing that he "converted" from the more nationalistic writings of his mentor (1962, 389).
[10] For a challenge to Inoue's elevation of morals, see Nolte (1983).

development as a human being" (743).[11] In other words, will establishes a horizon of expectations as an inherent part of human beings.

Inoue's notion of will not only accounts for the difference between humans and animals, that is, the separation of culture and nature; it also serves as the basis to explain social variation—why some societies develop and others have not. He writes, "In the regulation of humankind, there is a gradual movement—the extrication from narrow religions to the adherence to a general spirituality. I see this as today's new religion" (735). Here, it is possible to read a development toward Hegel's spirit. Individual development comes from gradually overcoming nature, nurturing the spiritual abilities (*reimyō na seinō*) through which one overcomes the material and corporeal. "We must nurture the power to control one's carnal desires with spirit. It is not succumbing to a fleeting emotional desire, rather, it is the power to control oneself for a future goal" (748–49). Like Inoue Enryō, Tetsujirō also denigrates the senses for the cognitive. In the natural world there is inevitability; in the human world, there is selection and what should or must be. The identification of the inner self, then, facilitates the separation of humans from culture—or, more accurately, the inversion of "inherited traditions," what had been common sense, into "textual products," that is, anachronistic historical ideas and institutions.

Up to this point, Inoue, like Takayama, is pointing to the externality of ideas that had masked themselves as transhistorical. And like Takayama, he does not accept the potential for an unrestricted self-interest and sees the individual as a social being. But they differ in the nature of that sociality. Where Takayama was not willing to delineate those regularities and intrinsic laws, Inoue identified a great will, that of the good for a whole, that transcends individual will. He states: "That final goal, in other words, an ultimate goal that unifies each individual goal, is the ideal (*risō*). This ideal is the source and basis of morals" (719–20). Thus, instead of a will that sees the individual as the basic human unit, Inoue argues that the fundamental sociality of humans, those intrinsic laws, are located in this great will. In this naturalization of human sociality, Inoue recognizes the diversity of individual wills, but they are combined and superseded by an ultimate will, or the "ultimate ideal as a human being." In other words, it is natural for individuals to work for this common goal. Like Katō, Inoue's invocation of a great will draws upon the trope of the nation as an organism. But he goes well beyond Katō's metaphor of the complex cell; he is extending this organism to one also endowed with norms of behavior. Inoue states, "because for society the ultimate ideal of mankind (*jinrui*) is to strengthen brotherly feeling and gradually to strengthen mutual love, one must clarify more the common characteristics of all mankind" (728–29). By subjugating individual will to a great will, Inoue begins the transformation of will into the "force of habit" of being Japa-

---

[11] In contrast, Katō Hiroyuki argues that it is not creativity that differentiates humans from animals, but the level of that creativity (1912, 19–20).

nese.[12] This is one of those sites where the state has formulated what Poulantzas calls a "material substratum" (2000, 30–31). It is the emplotment of behavioral norms within the very body of Japanese themselves.

Inoue's turn to this great will complements the release from "man's self-incurred immaturities" and the interchangeability that results. He is building upon what Postone identifies as a dual nature of labor to that of individual roles, as private and social. He makes clear that this embodiment of norms is tied to the modern economy. He states quite emphatically, "Time, in other words, is an asset (*kazai*)" (1974a, 169). Workers and inhabitants are still released from inherited forms of constraint, but now, they work for a common goal of the nation because it is natural. This unity also functions to limit the mechanistic rationality of modernity. Inoue prioritizes this spirituality over knowledge. He writes, "The development of all knowledge is determined by will, and one cannot control emotions without will" (1915, 742).

Inoue is countering social activists and reformers, such as Yokoyama Gennosuke, who sought to elevate the private, that is, labor. Yokoyama's critique was directed toward the problem of distribution. By limiting his attention in this way, he facilitated the objectification of the private (labor). Because he saw a transhistorical labor as the central element of the new social, his movement helped to objectify the capitalist social relations he was hoping to correct. On the other hand, Inoue turned to the past, to a Japanese culture, to objectify those social relations opened up by the emasculation of the socialist and labor movements. Where the social is the rearticulation of knowledge and technique, culture becomes the way to localize the social by encompassing and using the past to stabilize change. It is an ahistorical and ambiguous thing that becomes divorced from the political and economic, that is, change, yet it ensures the interchangeability of labor and goods.

Inoue then gives this great will historical specificity: he concludes that the ultimate will in Japan is *bushidō*. He does not deny the historicity of bushidō but essentializes a part—the spirit of acting decisively at the risk of one's life—as the whole. This is the moment when the idea is separated from its history and history gains multiple temporalities; bushidō transmutes from a historical practice to an ideal of the nation, but it is proven and demonstrated through historical facts and chronologies.[13] While religions are anachronistic, bushidō becomes that permanence that determines Japanese human nature; it both is historical and, as a new "ethical religion," transcends the human. For Inoue, that spirituality has existed in the everyday throughout Japanese history; Inoue's appeals to

[12] Nikolas Rose writes, "The extent of this faculty of control, the degree of consciousness involved, the presence of the force of habit rather than will: all these criteria were also utilized to differentiate—the child from the adult, the man from the women, the normal person from the lunatic, the civilized man from the primitive" (1999, 44).

[13] Takayama, too, turned to the warrior, extracting the idea of self-initiative (*jiga jitsugen*). While the difference is quite fine, it leads to a very different idea of society.

the body—masses and everyday—served as a way to essentialize the idea of a collective body. It is an idea that determined that body, rather than an idea that emerged from it. In the end, this human nature constrains the realm of individual action supposedly made possible by modernity.

By giving this sociality (*daiishi*) greater weight than individual will, Inoue turns a past into a norm that now objectifies society. This is one of those sites of slippage; because everybody learns some conception of this past, a narrative of continuity turns it into a timeless ideal of a collective will. The social becomes both historical (as chronology) and timeless (as idea). Inoue presents the ultimate will as transcendent of man, yet it is used to reconstitute society, where past, present, East, and West provide an archive for a narrative of the nation-state. By incorporating pasts into this human nature, Inoue naturalizes the nation, not as the accumulation of individual acts, but as the ideals that his expertise "knows" has guided life throughout the history of a Japan.

In this quest to deal with the social problem, Inoue turns to what will later become popularized as a national culture.[14] He does recognize the historicity of the nation-state, but the events he cites, such as the anti-Japanese immigrant movements in the United States, are political events, data of the nation-state. In other words, the removal of the past from history (as cultural) is accompanied by the provisioning of a site for history (as political), the data that becomes the chronological narrative of the nation-state.[15]

THE SOCIALIZATION OF A NATIONAL SOCIETY

Inoue Tetsujirō's writings were much more central to the constitution of the nation-state than Takayama's. Indeed, his commentary on the Imperial Rescript on Education became virtually the official interpretation of this important declaration, and he continued an active scholarly life until World War II. His ideas readily fit within a narrative of the forty years of Meiji as the emergence of technologies for the suppression of movements to foster mass participation. In the first few years of the new century alone, the government constricted labor and public gatherings. In 1900 the Diet passed a Police Regulation Law that became an effective tool for restricting union activity as well as political activity deemed socialist. In 1901, shortly after Kōtoku Shūsui, Abe Isoo, Kinoshita Naoe, Kawakami Kiyoshi, Nishikawa Kōjirō, and Katayama Sen founded the Social Democratic Party on May 20, the government suppressed it. Also in that year,

---

[14] I agree with Tessa Morris-Suzuki (1998, 60–78) that the popularization of a national culture occurred later, around the 1920s. One of the earliest writers to use this phrase, Haga Yaichi, was a contemporary of Inoue Tetsujirō.

[15] Inoue, too, was concerned about the formulation of history; see, for example, his speech to the newly founded Japanese Historical Association, "Tōyōshigaku no kachi" (1891–92).

the government sought to restrict a rally of workers at Mukōjima Park on April 3, 1901 (30,000–40,000 attended).

The application of state power on the side of capitalism is a common story at this time throughout the industrial world. But we must remember that the transformation of this idea of society in Japan, the uncertainty of the social problem, is compounded by the foreignness of the West. The new ideas of society, rather than being new and modern, are also Western and subject to facile labels as un-Japanese.[16] The uncertainty of the new is compounded by the specter of becoming Western. Resolving the social problem was compounded by the omnipresent need to maintain a national unity in the face of Western imperialism.

Inoue's turn to the national community is a common move among nationalists in the non-West. It is a rather easy move that homogenizes the myriad communities into one that fits within the conceptual space of the Orient, but with a positive spin. But it also raises the problem that Maruyama Masao sought to answer, the absence of a sense of individuation in Japanese society. Maruyama argues that in the drive to modernize, the state instilled a sense of loyalty to the nation but did not reform "traditional social consciousness": "With the democratic front silenced, the Meiji leaders zealously injected national consciousness by a full-scale mobilization of irrational attachments to the primary group. Above all, this meant that feudal loyalty and traditional devotion to the father as family head were centralized in the Emperor, the concrete manifestation of Japan's national unity" (1963, 145). Maruyama is correct to point to the suppression of popular political movements and the indoctrination of a national consciousness that many call the emperor system. Indeed, that is the object of this chapter. My difference, however, is that this transformation to modernity is not a removal of tradition in favor of the modern; instead, it involves the transmutation of past forms (rather than any continuity of irrational anachronisms) now removed from politics through the removal of their temporality. (I will discuss Maruyama's identification of the family as central to this lack of individuation in the following chapter.) This transhistorical time is usually categorized as values, emotions, or culture. It is the catch-all for what Rostow (1990) dismissed as a vague "psychological and sociological orientation."[17] This trivialization (and continued maintenance through various academic disciplines), though, serves the goal of the state to establish and secure the unity of the nation; the materiality of the state that is embodied in individuals, now Japanese, has become a norm, not a historical political condition. By removing this materiality from politics, the state is able to rely on an orienting (more often control) mechanism that facilitates a rather mechanistic participation of citizens in the liberal capitalist system.

---

[16] Ono, Takayama, Inoue, and Miyake were all careful readers of contemporary Western social critics.

[17] For a provocative effort to reintroduce the psychological into our appraisal of modern society, see Moscovici (1993).

One of the interesting aspects of Japan's modernization that is different from the experience of the West is not that it was late, but that a compression existed where changes were simultaneously after, coeval, and prior to those occurring in Europe and the United States. Certainly, the scientific revolution, the Enlightenment, and the Industrial Revolution occurred earlier, especially in France and England. But while we can see the discovery of the social also occurring earlier in England and France, many of the reforms as applied to the nation-state were coeval. In addition, if we are to accept Nikolas Rose's location of the emergence of a "third space" of government, a community-centric idea, in the post–World War II Anglo-American orbit, then the turn to community as a corrective to the social occurred earlier in Japan, as well as the non-West.[18] Rather than being a peculiar "Japanese" thing, it is more probable that a non-Western tactic in the formulation of the modern is to reemplot the culture that Orientalism separates as anachronistic into an idea of the collectivity as a corrective to the social problem. The use of this process to support the peculiarity of Japan, however, results from a tendency to reify the national unit as transhistorical and its self-professed characteristics as normative.

A critique of this formalization of the social was offered by Yamaji Aizan, a popular and rather prolific critic. He criticized the excesses of laissez faire capitalism as well as the socialist movement for their adherence to transhistorical ideas that were not grounded in the local place (Japan). Both, he argues, reemploy the instrumentalist framework of capitalism because of their separation from any past that might stabilize the process. In contrast to the two-dimensionality of socialism, he proposes a national socialism (*kokka shakaishugi*), which he argues is three-dimensional because it operates in the historical setting of the nation. He writes, "The national socialist party does not stop with applying the research results of one wing of Marxism. It inquires into the cooperative living conditions in the history of both Japan and China (*nikan*), and seeks to construct a Japanese style socialism using an understanding of freedom and independence as the foundation" (1985, 212).[19]

To create this nationally rooted socialism, Yamaji creates an alternative national history that locates antecedents to socialistic policies. He turns to the eighth century and finds the beginnings of private property during the reigns of emperors Genshō and Shōmu; he also finds a rare example of the state acting to reduce the exploitation of the masses by the aristocracy during Emperor Kanmu's reign. In other words, he was arguing that many socialist principles are

---

[18] Rose dates the emergence of this phenomenon around the last decades of the twentieth century (he is certainly aware of the vast literature on a loss of community dating from the nineteenth century) (1999, 167–96). I am also thinking of books that examine the ways that the colonials, especially from the subcontinent, were key to framing the space of the imperium. See, for example, Viswanathan (1989) and Mehta (1999).

[19] For an English translation of Yamaji's attempt to write a history of Japan that shows an indigenous development of rights, see Squires (2001).

not alien to Japan; evidence for the maintenance of private property as well as restrictions on a policy of laissez faire existed as early as the Nara period, the same era that the Meiji government was invoking to support its claim of a restoration.

His ideas certainly share similarities with the fascism of the 1930s, but there are important differences, and it would facilely exonerate other aspects of modernity to place Yamaji within such a teleology of unfolding. The resolution of the social problem, the constriction of desire, was effected by turning not to history, but to a transhistorical practice located in the Japanese past, as if it is natural behavior of all inhabitants. Inoue Tetsujirō, for example, used ideas of Japaneseness to establish those "natural extra-political human relations" that localized the social problem, was a positive evaluation of participation in the nation, and remained external to politics. This tactic serves two purposes: history established the container for that society; it uses the space provided by the West to demarcate the national whole. Second, history also provides the archive upon which the social problem can be resolved (no matter how imperfectly); transhistorical norms are emplotted to constrict the individual by encouraging him or her to believe that limitation is a natural part of the national being. In the end, culture, not labor, has objectified social relations. Nevertheless, both culture and labor have taken on a transhistorical characteristic that separates history from the social. Within this realm of society, citizens are free to participate in society, as long as they adhere to the norms of the nation-state. Though that culture serves as the link for the individual to the whole, it is a link of the alienated to that using abstractions that are also part of what one is alienated from. Again, the denigrated past is revived, but in a way that supports the totality, but from a distance; the public has infiltrated the private.

Chapter 6

SOCIALIZATION OF NATURE:
MUSEUMIFICATION

> Finally, we shall look at museums as they appear in the de-
> constructed cultural landscape, poised between a ghost town
> and a child's play pen.
> —Susan M. Pearce (1992)

> In short, the debate boils down to whether history is con-
> cerned with life or the petrifaction of life.
> —Didier Maleuvre (1999)

IN HIS 1917 appraisal of Japan, after decades of admiration through his friendship with Okakura, Rabindranath Tagore writes, as if betrayed:

> I have seen in Japan the voluntary submission of the whole people to the trimming of
> their minds and clipping of their freedom by their government, which through vari-
> ous educational agencies regulates their thoughts, manufactures their feelings, be-
> comes suspiciously watchful when they show signs of inclining toward the spiritual,
> leading them through a narrow path not toward what is true but what is necessary for
> the complete welding of them into one uniform mass according to its own recipe.
> The people accept this all-pervading mental slavery with cheerfulness and pride be-
> cause of their nervous desire to turn themselves into a machine of power, called the
> Nation, and emulate other machines in their collective worldliness. (38–39)

Tagore's criticism came after years of praise and admiration of Japan for the way
that it was both preserving its culture—speaking for an Orient—and becoming
modern. Along with Okakura, he supported the transformation of the archipelago into a nation based on the more rational, Hegelian idea. As in the previous
three chapters, we have moved increasingly away from the material toward abstractions that provide a historical framework. But as Tagore's critique suggests,
a vexing problem of this elevation of abstractions is how these new ideas are to
be integrated into the lives of the people they profess to describe.

Although Tagore's statement suggests a betrayal or turnabout, rather than a
deviation from the years when he partnered with Okakura, it should be considered a continuation, where the ideals and artifacts they praised became integrated into the social structure of modern Japan. In his discussion of the museum,
Didier Maleuvre writes, "The paradox of museums lies in their representing the

progress of history through diversity, yet doing it from the standpoint of a suprahistorical, transcendental notion of what this history is" (1999, 11). The same unified nation that Okakura and Tagore sought also inscribes objects according to that suprahistorical, transcendental notion of history that facilitates the "cheerful mental slavery" that Tagore lamented decades later. The art work that they extolled and museums that they helped found are examples of this reinscription. But if we push this analogy a bit, we might ask to what extent does the idea of the nation, the space of the nation-state, also function like a museum, where objects within society present a narrative of diversity (that is, change and conflict) but usually through now fixed notions of that history.

Perhaps it is a bit of a stretch to consider the idea of the nation akin to a museum. But it is interesting that the museum rose to prominence in tandem with the nation-state, and the objects that represent Japan—Buddhist statues, ink paintings, scenes of nature—are also the material of East Asian museums.[1] The utility of objects to the nation-state is in the power to convey meaning. Daniel Miller writes, "Material culture studies derive their importance from this continual simultaneity between the artefact as the form of natural materials whose nature we continually experience through practices, and also as the form through which we continually experience the very particular nature of our cultural order" (1987, 105). In this sense, it is not surprising that Okakura and Tagore turned their attention to art objects to "experience" their ideal of the new cultural order. The reconfiguration of artifacts as a component of the newly historicized Japan suggests the possibility that Japan itself (or any nation-state) functions in similar ways to a museum. Just as the museum is historical but displays artifacts as if it is presenting history, thereby occluding its historicity, the nation-state has managed to replace its historicity with various objects that present the chronology of a national history as if it is natural.

The danger of this reinscription of the past is to rigidify the present according to the codes of the past. To examine this socialization of nature, I will discuss two modern timeforms—architecture and childhood—that embed chronological development (progress) while at the same time presenting themselves as if they have always been immanent to Japan. These are two of many timeforms that resolve a contradistinction of modernity that is central to a temporal transformation, that between mobility and stability. While the process of change raises questions about what is, or even whether anything is, different or unique about oneself, childhood and architecture are objects that have an existence that is seemingly "real" and apart from the variability of meaning systems. In different ways they are constant reminders of the past: temples have a materiality; childhood is the perpetual presence of our past. But in both cases they become timeforms that embed a particular meaning that also provide guidance to society. We

---

[1] Okakura's famous statement come to mind: "Thus Japan is a museum of Asiatic civilization" (1970, 7). For studies on early collectors of East Asian art, see Cohen (1992) and Chen (2000).

have tended to call this relation of these pasts to the present "tradition." This is true. But I use the term timeforms because I see these objects as constitutive of modern society. The past is returned not as the celebration (invention) of a past in the present, but as a modern form that uses a reflexivity to perpetually reiterate the modern. It is not something separable as "tradition" but is embodied in the very fabric of modern society.

FRAMES

Today, the Hōryūji, one of the oldest extant building complexes on the archipelago, has become synonymous with beginnings, origins, oldest, and so forth that establish its authenticity and importance as an archetypical Buddhist temple in Japanese architectural history. But in earlier years, prior to the Meiji *Ishin*, it was a lesser temple, known among its neighbors as the *binbōdera* (poor temple).[2] As I have suggested in chapter 1, the Hōryūji experienced several discoveries during the early Meiji period, and interestingly, in each of these discoveries antiquarians, government officials, and Western scholars removed (that is, preserved) its contents. These artifacts, now constituted as art, were emptied of previous meanings and became important historical data; this is the destruction of "the life of history and culture" that critics of early European museums lament (Maleuvre 1999, 1). But these acts of "preservation" did not yet extend to ancient architecture, especially shrines and temples, such as Hōkōji, Shitennōji, Hōrinji, and the Hōryūji, that predate extant written records. In contrast to the recognition increasingly accorded to selected statues and paintings, these old structures, though no longer being torn down, sold, or burned, were suffering from considerable neglect. Indeed, in the case of the Hōryūji, the poor condition of buildings was cited as a reason to remove more artifacts to the Imperial Household than originally planned.

In the 1890s, temples, too, became objects of a reoriented past. But because of their permanence of place, this renewed attention, "preservation," returned the national exhibit of the museum to the locales. A key event in this changing configuration of old buildings occurred in October 1893 when Itō Chuta announced his "discovery" of the Hōryūji in a lecture on its architectural significance.[3] Of course, he was not the first to see it; the destruction of Buddhist icons

---

[2] It was in dilapidated condition in 1868 as a result of relative insignificance. As early as the eighth century, though it was still listed as one of the seven great temples of Nara, the prestige and patronage of the Hōryūji was declining, having been eclipsed by the Tōdaiji and Kōfukuji. After the cadastral survey in 1585, Hideyoshi reduced the Hōryūji's annual stipend to 1,000 *koku*. In comparison, the Kōfukuji received over 15,160 *koku*, the Tōdaiji, 2,115 *koku*, and the Tōshōdaiji, Saidaiji, and Yakushiji, 300 *koku* each (Takada 1993, 19–20, 22).

[3] Itō published this lecture in the November issue of the journal *Kenchiku zasshi*; it was revised in 1898, and I have relied on this latter version.

in the initial years of Meiji; the *Jinshin* survey in 1872, which catalogued its contents; the Nara exhibition held on the grounds of the Tōdaiji, which displayed some of its objects; and the excavation of the Yumedono Kannon by Okakura and Fenollosa all preceded Itō. But with the exception of the last, these discoveries served as originary moments for narratives that have not lasted. Itō's discovery gains further authority because it parallels the historical narrative of Japanese art history, outlined by Okakura and Fenollosa.

Itō investigated the Hōryūji as a graduate student at Tokyo Imperial University under the supervision of Tatsunō Kingo. He proclaimed the Hōryūji the most important historical complex in Japan: "When searching for the most remarkable lineage, the oldest, and most superb construction among our country's architecture, without hesitation, the first which should be mentioned is the Hōryūji *garan* [the western complex comprising of the main hall, pagoda, cloister, and gate] in Yamato. It is certainly no exaggeration to declare the Hōryūji *garan* as this country's most valuable ancient architecture" (1898, 1). The significance of Itō's discovery is in the incorporation of architecture into the narrative of Japanese history and art history: the temple complexes that had been the sites of the spiritual abode of kami and bodhisattva were turned into evidence of key historical events; the progressive narrative of architectural history repeated, thus further authorizing, the developmental narratives of Okakura and Fenollosa; and, those denigrated local sites were returned to the social orbit, but now as sites that remind viewers of a key moment in a history of Japan.

Itō's discovery situates the Hōryūji as a material object that depicts the originary moment of a narrative of Japanese architectural history. Pearce describes, indirectly, this transformation of the Hōryūji from *binbōdera* to the origin of a glorious history, "The real time from which the objects came no longer exists, and lumps of time have been lifted out to be offered as commodities, as available activities. We are offered not experience of the past, but a sequence of timeless myths abstracted from the past" (1992, 209). The object gains a materiality that presents a certitude that overcomes the variability of meanings attached over time. In this objectification, the artifact operates simultaneously in both the past and the present. As the past, it is an object that depicts a part of that prior age; as the present, it is a representation that brings that earlier moment into a meaningful relationship with the present. While it is the representation that recovers the past for the present and gives it life, it is the certitude presented by the object that facilitates a reading in which the meaning ascribed is conflated with it as if an innocent fact. Miller writes, "The artefact, on the other hand, tends to imply a certain innocence of facticity; it seems to offer the clarity of realism, an assertion of certainty against the buffeting of debate, an end or resting point which resolves the disorder of uncertain perspectives" (1987, 106). In short, the artifact, though of the past, is shorn of a part of its historicity. This atemporality, using objects to represent historical moments, is an important part of the modern nation-state, which through a fixation of past ideals immobilizes social relations.

Itō recognized that he was not the first to bring the temple to the attention of the modern public. Though in a rather backhanded way, he acknowledges the contributions of foreigners such as Fenollosa and Bigelow; he says that the temple's fame rose "in part from a strange interpretation produced from their curiosity, and in part from careful examination of their new discovery" (1898, 1). This fame, he argues, results from attention accorded to the extraordinary sculptures, but also exhibits a devaluation of the temple itself. This devaluation is evident in Itō's first encounter, quite a contrast to Fenollosa's impression:

> When one arrives at Hōryūji and first faces the south gate (*nandaimon*), there is a dignity that has not succumbed to the deep wounds from battling hundreds of years of rain and dew. The roof is like the open wings of a phoenix and its curve resembles the powerful footprint of a lion. But upon entering the gate and visiting the office, its considerable dilapidation appears. Floors are rotten and weeds are sprouting up; pillars are decayed and a strange fungus is apparent. The kind head priest, Chihaya, is blind in both eyes and greeted us upon the rotting floors. The haggard monks cheerlessly defend the desolate temple. When one enters the compound (*garan*), the unparalleled craftsmanship of long ago, the Asuka (Suiko) period, is relived: the wonderful beauty of the layout of the gate, corridors, main hall, and pagoda tower; the indescribably noble style of that form; and the remarkable design of the columns, bracketing, rafters, curved railing, etc. But, unless one seriously undertakes repairs, the damage will lead to a sorrowful state—the columns will bend and lean, the main hall will fall into ruins, sacred objects will scatter, and the tower will collapse—like when the cranes leave. (1982, 6:642)

We should remember that when Itō visited the temple, Chihaya had already embarked on repairs, using the funds from the donation of artifacts to the Imperial Household and from the Ministry of Home Affairs. This was the condition of the temple after some repairs!

Its condition notwithstanding, Itō argued that the Hōryūji was believed to be the oldest complex to have survived relatively intact; temple accounts claimed that the main complex was original as built in 607. (It was not the first Buddhist temple built, nor, at that time, was it the oldest extant building.) Now, originality and authenticity become key determinants for granting historical significance. Itō writes, "Only our Hōryūji has not altered its old appearance; thus we can experience the beauty of over 1,000 years, come to understand the ancient sages, and discover the true beauty in the relationship between the antique patina, the novel forms, and original methods" (1898, 175–76). Such an importance of originality, built upon a distinct (and dead) past, now presents the modern nation as if it has always been, "a sequence of timeless myths abstracted from the past." Here, it is important to remember that prior to Meiji the most powerful temples and shrines, such as the Kōfukuji and Ise, were rebuilt periodically as an indication of their power, wealth, and importance.

Subsequently, in December 1897, a commission on the preservation of old buildings identified twenty buildings of the temple complex for preservation and recorded sixty objects as national treasures (NKH100, 126–27; also see Aoi 2002, 16–33). This, however, was not the first recognition or attempt to preserve buildings; in 1880 the Ministry of Home Affairs established a capital fund for the preservation of cultural resources (*bunkazai*) and old things. Most temples and shrines received small grants, hardly enough to begin basic repairs let alone restoration. The longevity of Itō's discovery over previous ones, however, is in the congruence of his classificatory system with the modern temporal order. Like Okakura and Fenollosa, Itō suggested a Eurasian connection as far west as ancient Greece. Itō is one of the new modern researchers whose work brings out the physical properties of objects, offers a biography of a Japanese style (in 1902 he began a three-year journey from Peking to Istanbul to trace this development, specifically of Buddhist architecture), and explains its place (spatial). It is an act of bringing out similarities and differences: he compared the temple to the Parthenon of ancient Greece. And like his predecessors, he used a developmental structure that fits within Hegel's notion of aesthetic progress while both naturalizing the nation (similarities) and showing interaction with the continent (differences).

Itō's interpretation gains its power from the reintegration of nature (as environment) into this history. In other words, architecture provides that object through which one can "see" the reintegration of space, as a stable form in the mobility of time—progress. On the one hand, it is evidence that antedates the extant histories, *Kojiki* (712) and the *Nihon shoki* (720). Moreover, he acknowledges over a thousand years of rule since the age of the gods, but he complains that this society lived in darkness: "everything, everyone was in a perpetual sleep as if dead." This condition is evident in architecture (more accurately, what he imagined it to be). In its primitive state, architecture in Japan reflected a simple society, the "perpetual sleep as if dead." Buildings only warded off the rain and dew; materials were natural, wood and bamboo. On the one hand, this originary state reiterates an increasingly common trope of a Japanese love of nature. The shrines of Ise and Izumo are the closest to this early, primitive state. On the other hand, it serves as the origin, the zero point from which Japan progresses: "Like a flash of lightening from the west, this darkness was lifted, and the realm for the first time became light. Everywhere, people rose from their slumber and became active. This was the arrival of Buddhism" (1898, 174). This is a comparable moment to Hegel's development of aesthetics (and mind)—the advance to shelter from caves. At the end of the nineteenth century, it was not yet embarrassing, as it would become later, to admit that early inhabitants, indeed, the mythical imperial rulers, were primitive.

With the introduction of Buddhism, architecture, and society more broadly, changed: "In our country architecture (*kenchikujutsu*) actually began after the arrival of Buddhism, and we can say that the Suiko style is the origin of our country's architecture" (175). Buildings were larger, materials were also manufactured, and colors (ornamentation) were added. The imposing structures created a sense of adoration and admiration well beyond their functional requirements (174–75). As in art, the architecture of Suiko became that originary moment, now as the first architectural style (*ryūha*) or the origin (*hekitō*) of Japanese architectural history that demonstrates transformation and immanence. (Interestingly, the Shinto shrines, Ise and Izumo, are omitted.)[4] Like Okakura the central premise of Itō's narrative of progress is the need for occasional interchange with outside cultures. His history fits within the increasingly common trope of Japan's acceptance and adaptation of external stimuli—from India, China, and eventually the West—without upsetting its essence.

Itō acknowledges the superiority of Chinese culture (Six Dynasties) over Japanese. But this superior culture is turned around to indicate connection and difference: "However, we should observe that the aesthetics of Oriental architecture has opened up one type of universe (heaven and earth—*kenkon*), and within the architectural world demonstrates a new art form" (176). The "Oriental" is never really defined; it is "real" because of the presence of a West. In addition, Chinese culture now stands in for Buddhist forms and ideas. That new art form is that of Japan; in the process of adaptation, it took a middle path, not opting for the grand, ornate, or an esoteric transformation. In other words, "Japan" took the best of the Orient and adapted it to its needs. But this is not an innocent exercise in self-understanding; it also entails possession of connections and relations with others. Itō writes:

In tracing far back for the origins: the temples of Paekche, Koguryō, and Silla have been destroyed and none remain today; the region of Inner Asia is desert and now only has the name of ancient sites; and Greek and Indian styles are too varied in their connection. Fortunately today, Suiko architecture, which reached the pinnacle of the eave style, is isolated gloomily in a cold village named Hōryūji in the region of the old capital, Nara. The village received its name from this complex. In other words, the true value for the architectural world is actually here in Hōryūji. In its form, the desires of the Chinese style are clearly evident, there are faint reminders of the traditions of an Indian style, and the vestiges of a Greek style remain; thus interest [in the temple] is gradually increasing. Clearly, this is the role of the Hōryūji in the architectural world. (9)

This delineation of interaction refines the notions of inside and outside and of change and immanence; it distances Asia as like and as foreign. Itō uses the analogy of child-rearing to naturalize categories of indigenous, Chinese, and

[4] Isozaki Arata (1996) argues that Ise, as we know it today, is not an example of some pure Japanese architecture prior to the influence of Buddhism. He points out that the rituals that connect the imperium and the gods were established around the late seventh and early eighth centuries.

Western. The child, he argues, learns much from teachers and friends, not just from parents. If only from the latter, then there would be little change in one's character, that is, little development. Teachers and friends represent the outside world. Without education, one is always a child. Without the outside world, architecture does not change, proven in Itō's mind by looking at the structures of African aborigines and Eskimos—always the child. In architecture it means to use the supply of materials, to adopt what is suitable using the "knowledge and natural talents of nationals (*kokumin*)," and to gain new skills through training (1934, 18). As the metaphor of the child suggests, there is also something essential and unique to the child. He states,

> It goes without saying that architecture, the architecture of a certain country, emerges from the conditions of that country's geography (*tochi*)—in other words, what I call the national land (*kokudo*)—and the needs of the humans that live in that land—what I call the nationals (*kokumin*). Of course, in each region of the world there is no place where the conditions of the national land are the same. To use a metaphor of human life, children are born from a father and mother, and no child is exactly the same. The architecture, the baby, which is born from the national land as mother and the nationals as father is different throughout the world, and none are the same. . . . In other words, in Japan there is what one calls a unique Japanese architecture, and naturally (*tōzen*) it is different from the architecture of China and the architecture of Europe. . . . this is the way the gods have made us. In other words, Japanese architecture is eternally Japanese architecture; it will not turn into foreign architecture. (1934, 6–7)

The similarities to Okakura's history are obvious, and this similitude enhances the power of Hōryūji as a mnemonic of ancient Japan. The Hōryūji is less about its past than a foundational moment in Japan's past. The argument is circular, but because it is located in an unquestioned chronological narrative, the symbolic interpretation is conflated with the material object in a way where the former defines the latter. Near the end of the nineteenth century, an understanding of a historical past was emerging, one that made good use of tropes of modernity that occlude its own historicity. The idea of the nation is naturalized in several ways. First, the idea of Nature became that antithesis from which early "Japanese" developed artifacts and that empty space within which Japan emerged. The Hōryūji becomes an originary moment, grounded in connections to (and the separation from) the natural world, that serves as material evidence, prior to history, of that emergence. But this change and these very aspects facilitate the naturalization of a space endowed with certain immutable characteristics that are removed from the realm of history. As in the power of icons, the truth resides in an abstraction that gives meaning to what is readily visible.

In this narrative the Hōryūji undergoes another transformation, as the model of Suiko architecture. The bulk of Itō's article discusses in detail the key architectural features that identify the Hōryūji as characteristic of the Suiko style. He lists twenty-four features that set it off from other temples that are representative of later styles in the Tenji and Tenpyō eras. Though beginning in the seventh century (645), Tenji was indicative of a changing influence, from the Six Dynasties to Tang culture. The temples of this period reflect a more open, ornate, and refined style that punctuates an important development in Japanese architectural history. When Itō discusses other temples of Suiko, the three-story pagodas of the Hōrinji and the Hōkiji, an interesting shift occurs: the Hōryūji becomes that standard by which these earlier temples are judged. There was some uncertainty at this time whether these pagodas were originally five stories or three. Nevertheless, Itō says that the form and techniques place them on the same plane as the Hōryūji. He also mentions the Shitennōji (built by Shōtoku) as clearly in the style of Suiko, but he ends by saying that some parts, the overall form, and details were changed by later generations. Interestingly, the Hōryūji becomes the standard by which the other, earlier temples of Suiko are measured. Even though the pagodas were built prior to the Hōryūji, the latter is the standard for comparison, and Itō also describes in a note the layout of the Shitennōji as very strange (1898, 169–70). In other words, the Hōryūji has been transformed from datum to model.

Up until 1938, scholars often heatedly debated in which period the existing *garan* of the Hōryūji was actually built. Contradictory evidence existed that the main temple complex had been destroyed by a fire in the seventh century and rebuilt. Up until the Meiji period, most people accepted (if they cared at all) the official temple account that the *garan*, though repaired and restored, was original. Yet numerous textual accounts suggest conflagration; for example, a passage in the *Nihon shoki* mentions that a temple at Hōryūji was completely burned down in 670, while a biography of Shōtoku Taishi reported a fire at Ikaruga-dera in 610.[5] Around the Meiji 20s (1887–96), scholars such as Suga Masatomo and Okakura argued that the *Nihon shoki* could not be ignored, and most agreed that the temple did burn down and was probably rebuilt around 707. Yet architectural evidence suggested that the temple, clearly different from the temples of Tenji and Tenpyō, could not have been rebuilt in what would have been an anachronistic style, and in 1905 two scholars, Sekino Tadashi and Hirako Takurei, separately wrote essays arguing that the Hōryūji is indeed original and could not have been rebuilt. One of the strongest points of Sekino's arguments was the use of the *koma shaku* (a unit of measure from Koguryō, one of the ancient kingdoms on the Korean peninsula) in the existing structure. He argued that because the principal unit of measure was changed to the Tang *shaku* in the Taika reforms (645), the Hōryūji could not have burned down and been rebuilt with an anachronistic measure.

---

[5] That biography is the *Jōgū Shōtoku Taishi-den Hoketsuki*. I have reduced this rather heated and complex debate to very basic components. For more detailed information, see Murata (1949); and in English, see Soper (1978) and Machida (1968).

In 1938 archaeological evidence uncovered the remains of the Wakagusa-dera. For decades scholars had debated, ignored, and conflated the names used for the Hōryūji, Wakagusa-dera, Ikaruga-dera, and Hōryū gakumonji. Texts are ambiguous and often merit their conflation. The discovery of the remains of the *garan* of the Wakagusa-dera to the southeast of the present *garan*, however, proved the existence of an earlier temple that was destroyed by fire. Interestingly, the layout of this temple is the same as the Shitennōji, called strange by Itō when comparing it to the Hōryūji. Since this discovery (as well as evidence found during the restoration project in the 1930s), few dispute the notion that the *garan* of the Hōryūji does not date back to 607. Current scholarship dates rebuilding near the end of the seventh century.

Interestingly, this locates the architecture of the Hōryūji in the Tenji, not Suiko, period. Indeed, today there is no extant temple complex of Suiko architecture. Yet many books still describe it as an example of Suiko style; the originary role of the temple lives on. Now, it is important because it is old, very old. It rightfully belongs in the earliest moments of narratives of Buddhist architecture. But these narratives are interesting: while the text often acknowledges this archaeological evidence, the overall narrative maintains the position of Hōryūji as a Suiko style, as if it were built in 607. The power or "true" is in the connection to what is not seen, as a likeness of an ideal, rather than to material data. In short, the idea has taken precedence over the material object, which then "proves" that idea.

NOSTALGIA

In a sense, we have examined the transformation of the Hōryūji into a ghost town: it is shorn of its spirits and powers and now symbolizes a dead, but valued, complex of buildings. This shift where the idea gives meaning to the object is common within history, but it changes the relationship between individuals and the object; the object is also an actor in history (Pearce 1992, 211). The object, though built, and then given new meaning, by humans, too, serves to perform a function by reminding citizens of their connection to Japan's past. But this performance of the object is a complement, not a replacement to the text. Miller suggests its role in directing people toward certain feelings and experience. He writes that "the object tends toward presentational form, which cannot be broken up as though into grammatical sub-units, and as such it appears to have a particularly close relation to emotions, feelings and basic orientations to the world" (1987, 107). This ability to affect emotion and feelings is powerful, but for a scholar, very discomforting for its imprecision. Yet it is remarkable in the context of discussions on the nation where beliefs about the nation often persist despite empirical data to the contrary. This is true of the Hōryūji: we now know that the current structures were not built during the Suiko period; indeed, they are not even on the original site, nor the same layout as the original. Yet the temple retains its position as the founding moment of a Japanese culture.

The objectification of the Hōryūji in this museum/Japan can be examined in Watsuji Tetsurō's ruminations and impressions of a pilgrimage to Nara. But unlike the pilgrims of the Edo period, this visit was to connect with Japan's history; Hōryūji has become an important tourist destination. Watsuji published *Koji junrei*, the account of this sojourn, in 1919. This text proved to be immensely popular and, as if produced in the modern-day advertising offices of Tsukiji, generated ridership for the new railway lines in Yamato.[6] Watsuji's text achieved the early aspirations of Ninagawa and Machida in the 1870s, but with an accumulation of knowledge and repetition of narrative framework these early Meiji antiquarians did not have. His description is filled with by now familiar comparisons—the columns whose entasis is similar to Greek temples, the distinct curve of the roof when compared with temples of Tenpyō (such as the Tōshōdaiji), the statues of Suiko in comparison with those of the Fujiwara period and with the Mona Lisa.

Watsuji's discussion of Fenollosa is instructive. It exhibits his acceptance of the hagiography that has emerged of Fenollosa (Watsuji did not mention Okakura) as the discoverer of the Guze (Yumedono) Kannon and savior of Japanese art. The repetition, the narrative of art history codified by Fenollosa, is evident, as is the struggle for possession. Watsuji does not agree with Fenollosa's analogies; in particular, he is wont to point to the complexity and physicality of the West evident through the Mona Lisa in comparison with the simplicity and transcendence of the Kannon. He writes that the Mona Lisa, produced in a climate of spiritual unrest and fear where there is a separation of body and mind, expresses human hope and darkness, whereas the Kannon, produced in a climate of simple spiritual needs where body and mind were unified, expresses a freedom produced from deep meditation. Context, the specific history within which these artifacts were produced, has become fixed: the West and the East; the Kannon is more transcendent and closer to some kind of purity, "a mysteriousness difficult to describe" (286).

Watsuji questions other comparisons in Fenollosa's moment of discovery; he denies any connection to Egyptian sculpture, accepts an eery similarity between the Gothic statues of Amiens and the Kannon, which he attributes to a religiosity of a *young nation* (*wakai minzoku*), and he virtually denies the Korean influence in this early art and architecture. Watsuji's passage shows the further domestication of the temple. He is removing it from direct comparisons with the West, instead retaining (and relying upon) an implicit otherness. The Kannon is more simple, meditative, transcendent than any comparison in Europe.

By 1919 the Hōryūji had come full circle: from a temple in support of the political elite, to a relatively forgotten regional place, and, by the Taisho period,

[6] For a recent campaign to attract tourists, see Ivy (1995).

having survived the ravages of the destruction of bodhisattva, as a spiritual site as the origin of an interpretive structure of the nation-state that could be experienced through the growing tourist industry. This site has become an archetype of the spirituality of the national past so stable that data that contradict it cannot destabilize it. Perhaps now, in an age of constantly shifting meanings and forms, the temple has attained a stability beyond any period when it possessed a function as a religious site. Watsuji begins his encounter with the Hōryūji:

> On the following day Mr. F. and I set out in the morning for the Hōryūji. The weather was beautiful and we were in good spirits. From the stop for the Hōryūji we proceeded about a mile to the village along a farm road, and as we got closer we could clearly see the five-roofed pagoda. Our hearts danced and we became happier and happier; it was an exhilarating feeling. (253)

Watsuji's exhilaration suggests the power of an object and symbol to elicit feelings for the nation. His joy was in "experiencing" what Pearce (1992) describes as a timeless myth abstracted from the past. It is the antithesis of the modern, rational society; the Hōryūji, now on display as if in a museum, has endowed that myth with a materiality that demonstrates a Japanese identity that has existed since the seventh century. But this passage also recalls Tagore's lament of an "all-pervading mental slavery" among the masses in Japan accepted "with cheerfulness and pride."

CHILDHOOD

Itō's use of the metaphor of children to describe the history of Japanese architecture turns us to the modern idea of childhood. While at first glance the combination of architectural history and childhood seems odd, it is a combination that appears in several studies that are concerned with the constitution of modern society. In addition to the passage from Pearce cited in the epigraph, Daniel Miller, in his examination of material culture, turns to ontogenesis as "a process [that] always results in a socialized subject existing within the objective structures of a particular cultural order" (1987, 86). As Watsuji so joyfully indicated, the Hōryūji gives material form to the socialized subject. In our museum/Japan, childhood, I believe, operates in a similar way to immobilize social relations. It is a timeform of the past that brings meaning to the present, the nation-state, and provides guidance for social relations; it embodies the perpetual reproduction of these socialized subjects.

Many might object to the idea of describing childhood, for many the site of freedom and liberation from their present, as a participant in the petrifaction of life. But we must remember that the notion of childhood—the idealized past— is always imposed on the present, stabilizing the ever-changing modern society. Feelings that the object elicit are now embodied within the viewer, who has passed through childhood. This power results from the elevation of childhood over the child, and the simultaneous conflation of the idea and being into the child. As a temporal category, childhood is useful in facilitating the synchronization of different temporalities, what Ernst Bloch calls nonsynchronism, that "not all people exist in the same Now," into an orderly, usually hierarchical form (1977, 22). By turning the child into the focus of a developmental notion of human life, intellectuals merged ontogeny and phylogeny as if they were an "underlying essence," the mysterious and hidden, now placed in the realm of science rather than that of the supernatural (ghosts).

But the child is, of course, human and only exists through the body of one's society, "Japanese." Far from being universalistic, the constant birth of children provides that synchrony of nation, the same passage of all Japanese since the beginning of time. It brings a certainty to society as a site for an experience that "everyone" shares, regardless of their differences—age, region, occupation, class, and so forth. This perpetual metamorphosis of the child out of childhood overlays the otherness of childhood with another temporality, that of an idealized past. The child also serves as the embodied site for the future of the nation; it reminds adults of what is wrong with the present and provides the possibility for reform. In this case it is a hope for improvement—progress—but improvement based on an imagined experience. Carolyn Steedman states, "In this way, childhood as it has been culturally described is always about that which is temporary and impermanent, always describes a loss in adult life, a state that is recognised too late" (1992, 140). Here, the child plays an interesting role—it is to be something that does not exist and is based on an idealization of past experience.

This hope, embedded in childhood, is evident in the rise of children's literature around 1890. The magazine *Shōkokumin* (Young [lit. "small"] Citizen) and the series *Shōnen bungaku* (children's literature) were filled with historical stories of exemplary figures and rarely included folk stories (such as *Kogane maru*, often considered the first children's story). The main themes were effort and proper moral and ethical behavior. For example, Ogawa Mimei, whose *Akai fune* is often considered the beginning of modern children's literature, feels the need to instruct children into his imaginary world of children—naivete, sensitivity, gentleness, and honesty. The child becomes the object of instruction to reality, that is, hard work, study, obedience, and filiality. But that reality is always the imagination of adults. Inokuma Yōko criticizes Mimei: "Mimei needed the imaginary world of children's stories in order to describe his own inner world, and once he gave up 'my unique form of poetry' in order to try writing 'for the sake of' children, he instructed them, from the viewpoint of adults, on how to live harmoniously in the real world" (quoted in Karatani 1993, 115). Inokuma's perceptive critique brings out the "complex mechanism" of the child as the socialized subject existing within the "objective structures of a particular cultural order." Mimei's imaginary child's world is that other, a primitive condition, upon which the adult world (modern and mature) conceives of itself. But the adult then guides the child so that it can function in the "real" world, that is, that of the adult. But because childhood is a past that everyone has "experienced," like the temples, it helps to stabilize the constantly changing modern society. On the one hand, Mimei's child's world hints at a fantastic time into which one can temporarily escape. But this picture of innocence and naivete, too, is the imagination of an adult world. The child rescues one from the present, the problems, corruption, and alienation of modern society (Maeda 1982, 284–85). It is an escape to a past, both a past of exploration and restlessness, where one can vicariously escape the limits of "mature" behavior.

This interplay between childhood and adult experience raises a fascinating question about the extent to which pasts are embodied in our everyday activity. A wide range of scholars have sought to understand this interaction. De Certeau writes about ways users operate, the "innumerable practices by means of which users reappropriate the space organized by techniques of sociocultural production" (1984, xiv). Paul Connerton examines performance, the transmission of pasts through bodily movements, habits, and nonformal means of education, in his argument that "our experiences of the present largely depend upon our knowledge of the past, and that our images of the past commonly serve to legitimate a present social order" (1989, 3). An example of childhood as a "reservoir of meanings" is in a wonderful passage in a history of children's songs (shōka). Anzai Aiko describes their efficacy: "When leaving Japan and stepping on foreign soil, I somehow realize that Japan is a beautiful country. Home of green mountains, home of clear water" (1977, 7). Clearly she is reiterating the song "Kokyō" (My Old Village), written in 1888: "Home where mountains are green / Home where water is clear / Someday after realizing my dreams / I will return home." Matsunaga Gōichi points out that this song appeared just before the promulgation of the Constitution (1889) and connects it to the emerging bourgeois, national society (1975, 83–90).[7]

Anzai's memories of childhood echo the quote from Daniel Miller used at the outset of this chapter, about a "simultaneity between the artefact as the form of natural materials whose nature we continually experience through practices, and also as the form through which we continually experience the very particular nature of our cultural order" (1987, 105). The seduction is that one's childhood past becomes a site of experience, obfuscating the historicity of the particular meanings that have objectified the idea of childhood. Like Anzai's feelings about Japan (elicited when in the West), they are "real" because they were experienced. But that reality, the chosen characteristics, is part of a coherent image that reoriented society around those abstract forms of knowledge, that

---

[7] "Kokyō no sora" (The Skies of Home) was written by Owada Kenji in 1888 using the melody of the Scottish tune "Comin' through the Rye."

cultural order that provides a point of sameness to all people of the archipelago. Like the Hōryūji, the child becomes a symbol—not an object of display and tourism, but daily evidence of the nation-state.[8]

It is at this point that we can see the importance of the difference between object (child) and representation (childhood). Children are natural beings, clear for everyone (with the proper knowledge) to see, that become the metonym for a childhood that seeks monopoly over experience itself. But children also embody instability; like ghosts who constantly threaten to create mischief or conflagration, children constantly pose the threat that they might rebel or not mature and turn into productive citizens. The conflation of childhood and children seemingly resolves this instability; as the specific idea of childhood became increasingly common, the artificiality of this new ethical system waned and became "natural."[9] Everyday life—indeed, the body—becomes a repository for the codes of behavior of the nation-state. Inner time, while believed to be "natural" time embedded in everyday habits or bodily rhythms, is meaningful only as socially objectified norms. This embodiment of the idea pushes the function of objects of pasts, like childhood and the Hōryūji, from identification to the nation to identity with it.[10] This shift from identification to identity is the problem indicated by Tagore: he applauds the desire for identification but is disturbed by the dictatorial and homogenizing tendency of identity, that is, Japanese who meet their "mental slavery with cheerfulness and pride."

THE TUTELARY COMPLEX

To ensure that children fulfill this hope (or, probably more accurately, to reduce the instability presented by children), they became a "socialized subject existing within the objective structures" of the nation-state. Childhood locates children as an antithesis—an other located in a prior time—that confirms the process of socialization as knowledge acquisition. As an empty vessel in need of edification and discipline, children are those in need of direction (in little bits and pieces) before becoming participating members. Successful internalization of the

---

[8] Steedman describes this role: "Developments in scientific thought in the 19th century showed that childhood was both a stage of growth and development common to all of us, abandoned and left behind, but at the same time, a core of the individual's psychic life, always immanent, waiting there be drawn on in various ways" (1992, 129).

[9] This naturalization is made painfully evident in Norma Field's (1995) essay that points to the further reduction of this temporal category in Japan to that of laborer and consumer of the educational system that must give them the knowledge to become good citizens.

[10] Maleuvre writes, "Identification entails the mimetic absorption of the individual into an ideal image of the group, the prototype, the ancestor, the father. Conceived as identification, that is, as power gathering, identity entails repression: it groups and categorizes and therefore eliminates and coerces" (1999, 109).

proper codes—learning—allows the child to leave that temporary site for the "mature" condition of citizenship. Inoue Tetsujirō writes in his commentary to the Imperial Rescript on Education, "The virtues that were established when our imperial founder and ancestors founded the country are very deep. Thus, when the citizens become unified and strive to be loyal and filial, the prestige of our country will rise above all other countries. Thus, to achieve this education about our country must serve as the foundation" (1974a, 158). The world of the child is a mirror to the future, a desire in the guise of guidance that imposes restrictions on actions based on the present. Ontology presents the child as a blank slate that needs to be educated into a contributing member of the nation-state. For Inoue, the purpose of education was that all citizens have an understanding of "public affairs" (seimu). But his notion of seimu was quite specific: attentiveness, law-abiding, and punctuality (the latter, he laments, is particularly lacking among common Japanese) (1974b, 500). In Inoue's discussion on ethics, he uses an ambiguous word, shōnin (lit. "small person"), for child; it suggests both the child and the uneducated. Through edification (the context of his discussion is the efficacy of humiliation), "even the child changes, becomes a man of character (kunshi), and this man [only males could become citizens at this time] of character has an ethical conscience (ryōshin)" (1974b, 493). In other words, all people are first childlike; citizens must learn to behave and act in a certain way. This is one of the ostensible differences between children and temples; the child represents the individual and collective hope for the future. This possibility of a horizon of expectations further distinguishes childhood from temples and other material things; the child provides the opportunity to perpetuate, correct, or improve the present. The ontogeny of the child raises a demand to instruct children into the world that they make possible.

This orientation toward the future is managed by what Jacques Donzelot calls a tutelary complex. Miller's "objective structures of a particular cultural order" lead to a paradoxical condition where children have been liberated from society (bodily) into the time of childhood, but within that space tutelary authority is strengthened and national codes are embodied. Donzelot writes, "The new landscape of supervised education is here given in its entirety: a gradual dilution of the spatial structures of correction, impelled by an educative desire which endeavors to be free of any hindrance, but which can accomplish this only by replacing the coercion of bodies with control over relations" (1978, 145). Donzelot describes this control over relations as a series of concentric circles around the child: the family, technicians, and social guardians.

The most obvious part of this complex is the educational structure that emerged after the Fundamental Code of Education of 1872. This early law included compulsory education through six grades and textbooks that emphasized gradual, developmental learning. Subsequent debates focused on content; while early curriculum stressed knowledge acquisition and cognitive development, later reforms emphasized morals to cultivate social character. A revision in 1890, corresponding to the rescript, went one step further, emphasizing "education for citizenship." By 1912, the end of the Meiji period, the Ministry of Education boasted of an attendance rate of 98.2 percent of Japanese children in compulsory education (Kami 1989, 506). A number of historians have written fine works that describe the connection of this educational system to the emperor system.[11]

These statistics encapsulate many of the problems of a facile overlay of modern cultural norms over a non-Western one. The description ends with the celebration of the transformation—the liberation of the socialized child into the productive world of modern society. Childhood, as an association based on common interests—age-based categories of various early levels of intellectual development—becomes a temporal category that reinforces the social rationalization and fragmentation that is part of modern society. The history of this reconfiguration of the child has been occluded in the naturalness of the developmental child and the institutions that are established to support that process. We must remember that the tutelary complex is just that, a complex. It is more than the educational edifice, but incorporates a whole series of circles that envelop the child. There are a number of institutions to which one can turn—governmental programs, local aid groups, and social reformers. Here, I would like to continue along the lines of the embodiment of the past and turn to the modern family, the innermost circle of this tutelary complex.

The idea of the family, as Philippe Aries has pointed out, rose in tandem with the idea of childhood, and indeed, it is difficult if not impossible for the idealized family to exist without the child (1962, 353). Again, we must be careful not to conflate the reproductive system with the conceptual family.[12] The family of course existed in pre-Meiji Japan, and many travelers commented on the extent of affection parents had for their children. But the newly defined modern family replaced former intermediary organizations—village or neighborhood—now emplotted into secondary categories.[13] In their place, some ideas and institutions that had been a part of the local are elevated to a transhistorical status that dictates relations of the local in the name of society. Inoue Tetsujirō's connection of the family to the nation-state is an example:

> The relation between the ruler (*kokkun*) and subjects is like that between parents and offspring (*shison*). In other words, a country is like an expanded family, and there is no difference between the leader of a country who commands his subjects

[11] See, for example, Irokawa (1985); Gluck (1985); Kawashima (1957); Bernstein (1991); Garon (1997); and Uno (1999). For an essay that examines the relation between the family and state in the United States, see Mintz (2001).

[12] For a study that argues that the family system has been the defining unit of Japanese society throughout history, see Murakami (1984).

[13] For an interesting essay showing the relation of the space of the home and the changing modern family, see Sand (1998).

and parents of a family who benevolently direct their offspring. Thus, today, when our emperor calls upon all throughout the land, these subjects must listen attentively and reverently as do all offspring to their honored father and affectionate mother. (1974a, 159)

Inoue employs the metaphor of the organism to obscure the tenuous connection of family and nation-state (1911, 1–18). Ideas of growth, development, and nurturing suggest an inner time of the nation, but one that while connected to, indeed formed by, the historical is also timeless. The appeal to the nation-state as an organism blurs the distinction between the past and future, or experience and expectation. The convergence of family and nation-state valorizes the private of the family but only as the everyday subject to the public of the nation-state. Ostensibly the everyday is separate from the nation-state, connected only when participating in its "important" events (such as holidays). But by constituting the everyday as proper behavior of nationals, the family is simultaneously political — the materiality of the state — for its activities are now framed by the responsibility to train and oversee the maintenance of good citizens.

To ignore this conflation returns the historian to an ahistorical position where the abstract time of modern society determines the concrete time of everyday life (as they are today) as the common sense of the nation-state.[14] The notion of nation as an organism turns an idea, the *ethnos*, into a natural, prepredictive category. Because the "natural" time of everyday habits and bodily rhythms is understood through family interaction, Inoue has shifted the family and the nation-family into that transhistorical realm. It allows claims to a new experience despite conceptual gaps. Inoue does not claim a logical relation: "Those who exist in one country are all interconnected. Why? Because the interests (*rigai*) of one person become the interests of the nation-state, and its influence extends to all nationals" (1974a, 177). (We must remember that these ideas were being formulated at the same time intellectuals were concerned about the "social problem" that was rooted in the individuation of liberal-capitalist society.) In his argument for unity, Inoue mentions the variation, diversity, and disagreement within the archipelago. Yet difference is blurred in this appeal to the *ethnos*, a leap of faith (the "because") in the nation as the origin. While this is evident in his 1891 official commentary to the Imperial Rescript on Education, Inoue is much more explicit on the relation between individual and nation in his 1899 revision: "Each person (*kakuji*) is one element of the nation (*kokumin*) and the nation is made up of each person. There is no person outside the nation; there is no nation outside of each person. For this reason, the fortunes of the nation influence each person and the fortune of each person influences the nation. Individuals and the nation are indivisibly bound together. In other

---

[14] For a criticism of this conflation of loyalty and filiality as a strategy that occludes the historicity of Japan, see Tsuda (1938).

words, the individual is the small ego and the nation is the big ego."[15] Here the word *kakuji* for person refers to the individual of the nation but also connotes an abstract and interchangeable unit. Importantly, it depicts the growing abstraction of individuals within the confines of the nation-state. While individuals become abstract units, their relations are increasingly organized through embodied practices. "The Japanese *ethnos* draws upon the lineage from the same ancient texts, has resided on the same territory for thousands of years, and possesses the same language, habits, customs, history, etc. . . . Thus, those who are part of the Japanese *ethnos*, just like a member of a family, are related by blood" (1974b, 509). Inoue's turn to the past as the accumulation of practices that give form to the nation is similar to Takayama's (or more accurately, Takayama is similar to Inoue). The difference, though, is crucial; Inoue turns these accumulated practices into the collective body of the Japanese, fixing those practices as transhistorical characteristics of the nation.

The child validates this social notion of organic community, one of growth, continuity, and posterity. Inoue writes, "In the first place, the special kind of affection the child feels for its parents, originally emerges from a relation of flesh and bones, and is a thoroughly natural (*shizen*) feeling. . . . Thus, one has to say that the filiality of the child toward its parents is this inevitable force" (1974a, 159). Furthermore, the race is tied to the deeds of all ancestors, who had a spirit that is passed on to descendants; this is historical thought. Inoue conflates the biological and the social—birth and filiality are the same. The blood family becomes the primary social unit (itself problematic as many families used adoption to perpetuate their line), and the child, a future citizen, reminds of continuity and the future. But now, history guised as the experience of the past dictates those norms codified by the modern state, extracting from the past.

Inoue hints at this new notion of experience in his analogy of child and parent to citizen and emperor. The social idea increasingly assumes a normative status. This experience becomes natural as filiality and loyalty are conflated, combining the family with the national past: "Our Japanese nation-state long ago formed the family system: the country is an expanded family, and the family is a contracted country. . . . Thus in the family children obey the head, and in the country, through the spirit of obedience toward this family head, they obey the monarch. In other words, it is the extension of filiality directly to loyalty" (1974b, 513). Such passages make clear that he understands that part of the transformation of society is changing the way people think and the way their lives are oriented, from the local to the nation. To do so it is necessary to create different reasons, an ideology, apprehended through everyday experience to tie

[15] In this revised and enlarged version, Inoue more clearly articulates the position of the individual in the nation-state. I have used passages from the revised version, which is often not differentiated from the original. The 1899 version, I believe, indicates a greater concern for articulating the contemporary indigenous sites for unity, rather than arguing for unity to avoid the atomization of modern/Western society (1974b, 509).

them to the whole. The family becomes a caricature of the various units that were part of a local economy; it is now the primary site that specifies, on an everyday level, the roles of good citizens.

The analogy between filiality and loyalty further binds citizens to the nation by locating childhood as the moment citizens become indebted to the nation-state. Inoue writes,

> People receive protection of the country (*honkoku*), develop in safety, and receive education in the schools of the country, thereby refining their abilities, developing their knowledge, and acquiring skills. Because of these the great obligation (*daion*) to the country, being profound and superior to all other obligations (*onkei*), must obviously be requited, and more important, the peace and prosperity of the whole country must not be damaged for one or a few persons. (1974a, 168)

Here, the child is the focal point of that matrix of relations that mediates the interaction of the individual to the nation-state. By receiving something from superiors—protection, knowledge, guidance, etc.—it incurs an obligation that should be returned in the future. The subject shifts first from the individual to the family and then to the nation-state.

The transformation of childhood is one example of the reintegration of abstractions of the social, through the family, back into the lives of people. In this sense, even though families have probably occurred throughout humankind, the modern family should not be conflated with the family as a reproductive unit. Instead, the family has become the chief agent for the socialization of children as both productive members of society as well as obedient citizens of the nation-state. Importantly, the family, here, is a singular idea, common to all. This uniformity homogenizes the possible range of experiences according to one national ideal type. The family has gained new importance, now as a public institution that mediates between individual desires and national proscriptions. Here, the family, not labor, as the central institution of Japan, has objectified social relations.

Even though the family became a key institution in the formulation of a Japanese society, interestingly, its influence over its members was weakened rather than strengthened. In his discussion of pre–World War II Japan, Kuno Osamu has described society as containing exoteric and esoteric ideologies. The exoteric (*kenkyō*) was the public ideology proffered to most citizens in which the authority of the emperor, thus the state that governed for him, was absolute. In other words, it was a system based on belief. In contrast, the esoteric (*mikkyō*) served as the canon of the ruling elite, which recognized the limitations of the emperor within a constitutional system predicated on rationality—the mechanism and rationale for (and against) rule (1978, 60–80). This system could easily be described through the metaphor of childhood where citizens are infantilized and the state apparatus becomes the adult, the possessor of knowledge to rule. Importantly, the chief role of parents is reproduction of the components of the nation-state—to provide a nurturing environment, not the transmission of social knowledge. Education, formerly, a process of socialization by members of the community, regardless of age, now became the obligation of the state. Public schools take on the role of education shifting learning from integration into the local society to becoming good and productive citizens. Indeed, here, too, parents were considered children.

The decline of family influence was furthered in this functionalization of daily habits. Here, the family is better considered in terms of an economy of the family. Each part of the unit was to act within proper, or assigned roles and rules. Tasks that had been shared were increasingly assigned to specific people (Edelstein 1983; Liljestrom 1983). Inoue was quite aware of this change: "When they form a family unit, it leads, without fail, to the separation of work between husband and wife. In other words, the husband exists outside and works, while the wife remains and tends to the house; by planning together and helping each other, in hopes for future prosperity, they must work for their mutual development and progress" (1974a, 163). Prior to the Meiji period, roles of individual family members, especially among the nonsamurai, were not as restrictive (see, e.g., Uno 1991). The bourgeois ideal establishes complementary roles for each member that fosters an interchangeability across the nation within their respective roles: work becomes a male endeavor, separate from the household and housework, and reproduction becomes gendered, the now devalued role of the wife. Moreover, it also ties labor to abstract gratification, some nonexperiential "reward" in the future. Implicit in the deferred gratification, "hopes for future prosperity," is the child, the one who will improve upon current conditions and perpetuate the family line. The child as rescuer contributes to a resignation to one's present conditions. Moreover, this economy also penetrates to the individual roles within the family. The father must bring his pay home (rather than gamble or drink); the mother takes care of the household, monitoring its finances and hygiene; and the child goes to school, both preparing to become a future worker and allowing the parents to fulfill their roles.

This relation of the family to the state is a central part of Maruyama's analysis of Japanese society and the relative absence of individuation. He writes: "The Meiji leaders zealously injected national consciousness by a full-scale mobilization of irrational attachments to the primary group. Above all, this meant that feudal loyalty and traditional devotion to the father as family head were centralized in the Emperor, the concrete manifestation of Japan's national unity" (1963, 145). My difference with Maruyama is not in the centrality of the family, but that it is less a remnant from the past than a reconfiguration of an idea from the past into a modern mechanism. If we accept the arguments of Donzelot, the centrality of the family in the articulation of society was also part of, not a hindrance to, the process of becoming modern. In this instance, we must consider law and culture together; an ethical idea of the family is imbricated into the Old Civil Code (1889) and the Civil Code (1898), which legalized a patriarchal system that connected the hierarchy of the family to the nation (Kawashima 1957;

Nolte and Hastings 1991). This does not mean that the Japanese family is the same as that of France and England; to be sure, Japan formulated this tutelary complex differently, but in these three nation-states, we must first consider the family as the rearticulation of the past to support the modern. Donzelot writes:

> This is the advanced liberal family, then: a residue of feudalism whose internal and external contours are blurred through the effect of an intensification of its relations and a contractualization of its bonds; a sort of endless whirl in which the standard of living, educational behavior, and the concern with sexual and emotional balance lead one another around in an upward search that concentrates the family a little more on itself with every turn; an unstable compound that is threatened at any moment with defection by its members, owning to that relational feverishness which exposes them to the temptations of the outside, as well as to that overvaluing of the inside which makes escape all the more necessary; a half-open place, constantly obsessed with the desire for a withdrawal into itself that would restore its old power at the cost of the individual integrity of its members, or—inversely— obsessed with the temptation of a renunciation that would deprive them of that last vestige of identity which it secures for them outside the sphere of social discipline. (1978, 228–29)

The re-emplotment of the family as a "residue of feudalism" is a powerful method of eliding this institution, as culture, from modernity. At this point Lewis Mumford's comment on the museum is apt: "[The public museum] gave modern civilization a direct sense of the past and a more accurate perception of its memorials than any other civilization had, in all probability, had. Not alone did they make the past more immediate: they made the present more historic by narrowing the lapse of time between the actual events themselves and their concrete record" (1934, 244). If we return to the notion of Japan as a museum, it is without doubt true that the archipelago has had a better sense of its past, memorials, and sense of the present as historic than any earlier period. But the danger of this museum is to conceive of the past as fixed. Maruyama is consistent in attributing to the family a transhistorical status; it is an indication of the successful internalization of the notions of childhood and family as a transhistorical cultural form that is separate from politics. Maruyama's Japanese family is a continuation of an anachronistic institution, the traditional opposed to the modern that must eventually be overcome by the modern. His family in Europe, however, is not subject to the same analytical framework; instead, it gains a normative status. The difficulty here is to forget that, in the incessant professions to and search for the new, modernity is built upon a transmuted past, that functions as a dead, inert past. In the end, the family and childhood, too, are frozen in the past, natural materials whose nature we continually experience through the everyday, but transhistorical forms through which the very particular nature of our cultural order becomes internalized as daily habit and practices.

When its history is recovered, we can see that the family becomes the mechanism that transfers codes of behavior (the delimitation of desire) from the ideal of the nation-state to the everyday. We might be able to recover the politicality of culture, in this case a naturalized time of modernity that binds its members to the economy as well as the norms of society, but without calling attention to itself as a mechanism of the nation-state.

This, of course, raises the dilemma of the non-West in becoming modern. Can the Orient become modern when the idea of the modern is constructed upon the Orient, as past? The difference, I believe, is the way that culture is reinscribed into the social, especially in the non-West. In both Japan and Europe, the family played an important role in the constitution of the social. But in Japan, the pasts that constitute the social turned into ahistorical ideas, whereas the pasts of the European family tend to stay in the past. In other words, in Japan, the process of historicization of society returns the past into the present as a way of maintaining some distinction from the social, that, when connected to the mechanistic process, is conflated with Westernization. This past is relegated to culture, those remnants that have defied the full implementation of modernity. It distinguishes a Japan from the West, but it also organizes that society within a straitjacket of identity, that is, reinforced by mnemonic objects such as architecture and childhood.

GHOSTLY REMNANTS?

Interestingly, this notion of childhood and modern historical practices reinforce each other. History, too, through its narratives of the nation-state, is removed from society. Both history and childhood reinforce diachrony as if it is natural time; history as chronology and childhood as ontogeny. But the collective children—childhood—conflates the relation of the individual to the social unit, the nation-state. History, then, need not consider its relation to that nation-state; that is, the way that certain pasts have been removed from history and transformed into immanent characteristics of that nation-state.

The specters of the past are apparent in the tools the intellectuals, educators, and political leaders used to map out what citizens/children should experience. For example, a modern adaptation of the story of Shuten dōji for children is an example of this desire for certainty amid other temporalities. Iwaya Sazanami seeks to quell the ghosts and spirits by reminding his young readers that they are not real. He writes in the postscript:

> In the story, Mt. Oe's Shuten dōji is a demon, but there were no demons in that world; being an allegory, it was actually a big thug, scary like a demon and his followers, who hid in the mountains. Raiko, along with the Shitennō [four kings] and Hōjō [Yasutomo], received orders from the emperor (okami) and masterfully subdued them. Stories are stories, reality is reality. Children, you must not mix them up. (Quoted in Satake 1977, 189–90)

Oeyama was the sixth volume of his series of children's books, *Nihon mukashi-banashi* (Old Tales of Japan), an important series in the rise of a children's literature that emerged in the 1890s. Iwaya's version is a more ethical (than mystical) tract that emphasized the gods (Shinto), order, and police/military. But this postscript makes clear the discomfort with the unstable signifiers; Iwaya silences both ghosts and children. Ghosts are located in the imaginations of a primitive past, and children become the hope and fantasy for Japan's future. The earlier forms of transmitting the past are denigrated; history is absent; folk stories like Shuten dōji become evidence of an ahistorical Japanese character. Yet Iwaya's warning suggests that the alternate temporality of the child remains. Just as Donzelot points to family stability as always threatened from within, the child, too, is always around to haunt the imagined certainty of the modern.

Just because children were told how to think does not mean that they internalized it. If experience is socially constituted—which I believe it is—then on one level Agamben's warning falls back to an Enlightenment ideal, that there can be a pure experience. When we recognize the historicity of the social, then we can also recognize the various socials that constitute experiences. The monological claims of science and nation-state are one, albeit predominant, of those socials. In the case of Japan, the common sense of the nation is that "orderly or coherent mental representation—the urge in reflection to *command a clear view*—[that] in fact *prevents* us from achieving a proper grasp of the pluralistic, non-orderly nature of our circumstances" (Shotter 1993, 19). Nevertheless, even though a nation-state like Japan implies a rather thorough internalization of codes that suggest a common belief, our archive today is rich with evidence of a great variety of experiences beyond what has been described through History. Indeed, there are many socials that guide individual experiences, and the ambiguity of categories, such as childhood, also creates spaces, albeit rather narrow, for individuals to act autonomously.

One also can find many different types of experiences throughout pre–World War II Japan. I will cite two from the 1930s that suggest that even during the height of Japan's fascism, multiple temporalities existed. As late as 1938 a teacher riding home on his bicycle in a remote farm village in Yamagata (northern Japan) recalled an encounter with a small farmer. He described the child's appearance, commenting that he looked just like an adult: "He wore straw sandals quite skillfully. Even his way of walking was that of an adult; . . . It was the image of a laborer, a small peasant." But beyond the lack of distinction between child and farmer/laborer, the conversation raised questions of utility and the category of the child.

> I asked suspiciously, aren't you Shun'ichi who, even though now in the fourth grade, was scolded for not knowing your multiplication tables. Well, wonderful. I had to reconsider that I scolded, again today, such a useful fellow for not being able to read. He laughed, "sensei [honorific for teacher], today I've tilled three fields.

Hey, I've even developed blisters." . . . Then whenever I saw him I wondered, what
am I doing when he is working in the fields? I'm recording detailed lesson plans
and buried among countless, worthless reports. (Kokubun 1972, 220)

At least in this case the teacher was reflexive enough to question his modern
temporality. It was quite the opposite in a different incident; in 1930 villagers in
Takagami village in Chiba rose up against those who symbolized the nation-
state—the police, teachers, and wealthy, functionaries of the tutelary complex.[16]
Children recalled, "By yelling at the bushy-faced thugs (police) who tried to
drive us off and by showing resistance as much as we, the smallest, could, we
wanted to show again and again that we knew. It was they who oppressed our fathers; they squeezed everyone for as many as twenty years" (Seki 1972, 473–74).
The children obviously did not directly experience the twenty years of embezzlement, but they were part of a community that transmitted what it considered
knowledge necessary to function within the village. Indeed, this socialization for
village life conflicted with the socialization for the nation-state: "At school the
teacher taught us: it was bad to create such trouble, etc. etc. But that? No one is
that tight: those who made our fathers suffer so; those thugs who oppressed those
who have endured in silence. How can we remain silent to the words of the government teacher? To his eyes that still see this as proper? That's why we yelled
and threw rocks; we wanted to attack again and again" (474).

These incidents indicate that for the members of the tutelary complex, the
children, though treated as such, were not innocents: "No matter how much
those thugs told us that we could not watch and tried to chase us away, we always
returned, yelling" (473). These children indicate the presence of different social
knowledges, that of a local, participatory form which, in this case, remained separate from the homogenization to a national, abstract form. These events can be
described as local vs. national, but they are not dialectical categories, but varied,
coexisting, and conflicting forms of knowledge. These children were not uninformed about changes brought about by the new government; they possessed
several voices. On the one hand, they were heard by authorities only through
the monological codes of the nation-state—they were unruly, delinquent, and
uneducated. But on the other hand, they also had a different knowledge (more
sophisticated than authorities believed) about the relation between power and
individuals. While learning (but differentially internalizing) the codes of the
nation-state, they were also defending their world, a space of experience, which
included, but were not incorporated by, the hierarchical horizons of the nation-
state. Indeed, the farmer/child even caused the teacher to question his own
modernness. But lest we romanticize these moments as resistance, they are reminders that specters of instability are an ingrained, though suppressed, part of
the very constitution of modern society.

---

[16] Takagami was a combined farming and fishing village not far from Tokyo. It was not impoverished.
The riot was precipitated by discovery of embezzlement of public funds by the mayor and an increase in local taxes.

EPILOGUE

Time is no longer simply the medium in which all histories
take place; it gains a historical quality. Consequently, history
no longer occurs in, but through, time. Time becomes a dynamic and historical force in its own right.

—Koselleck (1985)

ON SATURDAY, September 1, 1923, at 11:58'44," a violent earthquake shook the
Tokyo/Yokohama region. The epicenter was in Sagami Bay, northeast of Oshima, the island that John Milne (and others) visited in 1880. The amplitude of
this earthquake was greater than the 1855 Ansei earthquake. The destruction
was catastrophic: over 100,000 were killed by the falling buildings and the fires
that raged afterwards; of the 2.4 million inhabitants of Tokyo, less than 800,000
still had a roof over their head. Virtually all of Yokohama's 71,000 buildings had
been destroyed. Communications systems were destroyed; telephone and telegraph lines were down, and newspaper offices (and plants) collapsed. Estimates
of damage were as high as $5 billion (Jaggar 1923, 124–46).

Otis Manchester Poole, then working at Dodwell & Co., Ltd in the Foreign
settlement, wrote not long after leaving his office building (which was damaged
but still standing):

> It was here that the full measure of the catastrophe came home to us. What seemed
> most terrible was the quiet. A deathly stillness had fallen, in which the scraping of
> our own feet sounded ghostly. Shattered fragments of buildings rose like distorted
> monuments from a sea of devastation beyond belief. Over everything had already
> settled a thick, white dust, giving the ruins the semblance of infinite age; and
> through the yellow fog of dust, still in the air, a copper-coloured sun shone upon this
> silent havoc in sickly unreality. Not a soul but our own small group was to be seen
> anywhere. It was as if life had been blotted out—the end of the world. (1968, 37)

The description of Saturday afternoon is one of shock and survival. People trying to survive, find their family members and friends, and escape from the fires
that erupted soon after the first tremors. But the shaking was only the beginning.
An unseasonably strong wind also blew that day; fires quickly erupted, probably
from the stoves lit to prepare lunch, and continued until Monday, when most of
Tokyo had been destroyed. As many as 100,000 Japanese died; approximately
32,000 were burned seeking refuge from the fire at the Army Clothing Department in Honjō, east of the palace. Then, sometime on Saturday, rumors began

to spread that Koreans were setting fires, poisoning wells, looting buildings, and raping women. In the violence against Koreans that followed, well over 6,000 were murdered.

The earthquake leveled the buildings and forms that were a remnant of Edo and made possible a rebuilding of the city. It punctuated the demise of *shitamachi*, the eastern part of the city that Ogi studied to examine the transition of Edo to Tōkei to Tokyo, and catalyzed the move of the city center toward the west. Jinnai Hidenobu (1995) describes the 1920s as the third phase of the history of Tokyo, when its framework changed to the modern city we know today. Edward Seidensticker, too, writes, with both nostalgia and celebration: "Fires raged through it for two days following high noon of September 1, 1923, and left almost nothing behind save modern buildings along the western fringes. . . . The great shift to the High City [west of the castle] was already in process and would have occurred even without the disaster, but the disaster sped it along. . . . It is an extreme instance, but symbolic of what happened to the whole Low City. The sites were there, but denuded, stripped of history and culture" (1990, 5–6). In this sense, the earthquake became a momentary disaster in the procession of Japan as a liberal-capitalist nation-state.

For others, the earthquake ruptured the certainty of modern society built upon the separation of nature and history and suggested that they should be recombined in some way. Gonda Yasunosuke describes life after the earthquake as worse than human: it "sunk beyond human consciousness" (1989, 69). For many contemporaries and historians of Tokyo, the earthquake was a watershed event; it was a reminder that time, too, is "a dynamic and historical force in its own right." The earthquake jolted many to recognize that society had forgotten that time had been dynamic before receding into the historical consciousness of modern Japanese. The rupture of time jolted many into the possibility of a new time; for someone like Gonda, the edifice, that truth, that had been destroyed is history, that is the historicization of society, that had ordered Japan. In his quest to identify the basis of a national life that was not determined by the materialism of modernity, the return to a primordial condition, though momentary, brought hope—hope that Japan might rebuild where the culture of the nation-state did not determine experience.

Gonda envisioned the potential for a different future, the second phase of modern life. He identified a different permanence that, like Miyake and Takayama before him, found a permanence within the people of the nation, rather than an idea of the nation. He argued that pleasure (*goraku*) refocused people away from the empty quest for material objects that characterized modern life before the earthquake. The Tokyo that was destroyed was a part of the first phase, indeed, at that time, the only phase of capitalist development. People who functioned in this system sought merely material things, "ornaments" of life. His description of people's modern lives echoes the comments of Tagore that Japanese have become slaves of the nation-state. Gonda writes, "For the sake of the edict 'increase national wealth,' all things [unity of] have been forgotten, all things have been fixed, all things have been authorized, all things have been coopted and then accepted. And even those who live feel no guilt whatsoever that it has been taken" (5). For Gonda, the hope rested in the destruction of this edifice that supported a society that had been fixed and channeled desire toward shallow material objects.

In this sense, for Gonda, who considered his research a science of the everyday, the earthquake became that millenarian (now, revolutionary) moment that, like the catfish that appeared after the Ansei earthquake, brought destruction as well as retribution, correcting for all the evils of history (that is, as devolution). In general, catfish did not appear as they did after the Ansei earthquake (Ouwehand 1964, 42–43). Stories did emerge, but they are interesting in their reflection of the transmutation of the past. In a recollection about the earthquake, Tōma Wataru, then living in a farming village near Hiratsuka, recalls the unusual activity of catfish before and after the earthquake. He believes his experience is proof of the old tale that catfish go into a frenzy before an earthquake (1977, 18). Ouwehand found a few similar stories. Tōma's awareness of the activity of catfish continues the tale of the connection of the catfish to earthquakes. But now, catfish have some kind of extrasensory capability that enables them to sense an impending earthquake. Today, scientific research is being conducted to determine whether catfish serve as a predictor.[1] The catfish has transmuted from a ghostly force to an animal that can predict. The connection of the catfish can be understood only in some temporal horizon.

It is at this point that we confront an absence within the abstract system that history establishes to ameliorate the absolutism of reality. What/who caused the earthquake? William James, the great American psychologist and leader of the Pragmatist movement, similarly questioned the abstract codes that organize modern life after his reaction to the 1906 San Francisco earthquake:

> First, I personified the earthquake as a permanent individual entity. . . . Animus and intent were never more present in any human action, nor did any human activity ever more definitely point back to a living agent as its source and origin. . . . But what was this "It?" . . . I realize better now than ever how inevitable were men's earlier mythological versions of such catastrophes, and how artificial and against the grain of our spontaneous perceiving are the later habits into which science educates us." (quoted in Ouwehand 1964, 244–45)

The cause, explained by Imamura Akitsune, geophysicist at Tokyo Imperial University, would certainly not satisfy James. Imamura writes, "The enormous depression and elevation of the sea-bottom in the heart of the Sagami Bay indicate

---

[1] One can imagine the scepticism among geophysicists. For research conducted at the National Research Institute for Earth Science and Disaster Prevention in Japan, see Fujinawa and Takahashi (1994, 145–46). See also Ouwehand (1964, 56–57).

that this area was the seat of the extraordinary commotion which took place thereabout at a certain depth" (1924, 147). Yet Joseph Dahlmann combines causation with the desire for personification in a passage that stands out because he so assiduously avoids attribution throughout his rather thorough description of the destruction of the earthquake and fire: "The capital was unhappily pre-eminent in the extent of the losses, chiefly because it is the capital and offered to the monsters of the deep an incalculable number of structures on which to vent their fury." The "monsters of the deep" resonates with the catfish that appeared in the nineteenth century (1924, 106).

In his analysis of the people, Gonda locates this animus and fear in a primordial moment. He writes, "In the first week after the earthquake people worried about eating; the faces of strangers appeared to be Korean; trails of slugs seemed like threatening code; loud voices seemed to upset the public order; parents even worried that crying babies would disturb neighbors. Even after this when worries about food and false rumors declined, the spirits of people still could not think of pleasure" (1989, 69). The strangers, those *ijin* that haunted pre-Meiji society, have transmuted from outsiders and apparitions to foreigners, Koreans. The written word was on people's minds, even though it was in the form of snail trails, and what had been the principal form of communication, talking, is a potential source of disturbance of harmony. In short, Gonda's primordial is strangely modern—it is imagined from an idea of Japan that was formulated in the earlier decades.

Whereas James's desire for personification is a primordial sense, Gonda's primordial was an originary society, that raw human existence prior to history. This return to the primordial is akin to Agamben's return to infancy, as if that moment of birth is the only possible site of experience, prior to the imposition of those cultural and social codes that determine how people experience. Such a return is impossible, but Gonda identified the rupture of time created by the earthquake as that return: it dislodged people's spirits from their foundation, and the fire wiped out a sense of balance. He writes, "The civilized twentieth century people who experienced the earthquake were threatened by the uncertainty of starvation and the danger of tribal conflict. They did not look to the past, they did not consider the future; they had only a painful awareness of life that was the same as uncivilized barbarian tribes that can only live for the present" (63).

The hope of this moment was in the momentary rupture of the predictable linearity of progressive time; it was a moment possibly to establish a different horizon, a new future. Gonda sought out the various experiences as they changed in the days and weeks immediately after the earthquake. One could experience the history that led to the first stage in a hypercompressed span of time: "Actually, the residents of Kantō who survived this disaster returned to a barbaric, low-class of peoples still without economy or culture; then they experienced the approximately 2,500-year social development of the race to the so-called civilized life of the twentieth century (to the condition of capitalist economic life) in only sixty days" (55). Gonda is not alone in this assessment of the possibility of actually experiencing a past. Florence Wells, an American teacher who was in the Mitsui Bank building in the center of Tokyo, writes, "In a single day we rushed back into the civilization of three hundred years ago, but during this week we have begun to return to the present day. On Thursday night we had city water again . . . , on Friday electric lights, on Saturday the first street car started running, and on that day we could mail letters going north" (quoted in Jaggar 1923, 142). Of course, the moment of the primordial as well as the horizon of expectation are quite different between Gonda, a critic of modernity, and Wells, who was steeped in it. Yet both saw a compressed experience of the past centuries of development. For Wells, the experience brought a welcome relief and a reaffirmation of civilization, but for Gonda, it was an opportunity to tweak the trajectory of development. His hope, of course, was that having experienced various forms of "pleasure," from the primordial euphoria of finding food or water, to the gradual quest for music, stories, and so forth, people would now develop what he believed was a national character that was not circumscribed by a national culture.[2] Like earlier intellectuals, such as Miyake and Takayama, Gonda turns to the body, the pleasures of fulfilling basic bodily needs, for a permanence that does not privilege the transhistorical culture of the nation-state.

We know that the Tokyo of a modern, civilized nation-state enjoyed by Wells and Seidensticker prevailed. The new temporality that Gonda had hoped for was superceded by a modern form of renewal, the continued razing of the old. Seismologists, architects, and engineers analyzed the damaged (and undamaged) buildings to prescribe better construction techniques, that is, more modern buildings. The new governor, Gotō Shimpei, best known for his colonial leadership in Taiwan and the South Manchurian Railway Company, envisioned grand boulevards, perhaps on the lines of Haussman's Paris. Though only *Shōwa dōri* was built, at half his desired width, *shitamachi* lost its luster, and much of the life of the city moved to the west—in short, to the newer, more modern areas.

Yet Gonda was right to seize this rupture as an opportunity to question the very constitution of the modern individual and the edifice that organizes human lives. Even though a nation-state like Japan today suggests a rather thorough internalization of codes that enforce a common belief, our archive is rich with evidence of a great variety of experiences beyond what has been described through History. Indeed, there are many socials that guide individual experiences, and the ambiguity of categories, such as childhood, also creates spaces, albeit rather narrow, for individuals to act autonomously (Herzfeld 1992). Gonda sought to identify within modern life the potential for an alternate time in their everyday lives. It does not mean that the everyday, itself, is a site of resistance or autonomous

[2] He writes, "I carry doubts toward considerations of 'national culture' [because] it imparts fixed, unchanging conditions from the beginning of national life down to the present" (quoted in Harootunian 2000, 149).

from the confines of modernity. Gonda finds in the popular the uncanny, those sites where the past is not separated from the present, that is, something that is discovered, defined, and categorized. It is in this potential, which he sees as pleasure, that he finds the second phase of modern Japanese society.

But to discuss the problem of the modern apart from the nation-state that frames the unit of analysis is to overlook a critical part of the modern. During the 1930s Gonda, too, turned away from this atomized notion of a national character in favor of a more unified national culture.[3] In Gonda's analysis of rumors we can see a will to ignore one of the most troubling aspects of this new modernity, the use of timeforms to demonize difference. In this case it is in the statement, "the faces of foreigners looked like Koreans." In his essay on nonsynchronism written in 1932, Ernst Bloch points out the tendency of the immiserated middle class to romanticize some better time, but it is one that usually (in 1930s Germany) leads to a "primitive-atavistic 'participation mystique'" where the "ignorance of the white-collar worker as he searches for past levels of consciousness, transcendence in the past, increases to an orgiastic hatred of reason"(26). In nonmodern Japan, ghosts, catfish, and demons bore the brunt of that irrationality, but now that they have been relegated to the stable past of superstition and folklore, foreigners who are assigned to some temporality of the inferior or the "not yet," become convenient targets (thereby reinforcing the transhistorical temporality of the idea of the nation or nation-state) that fill James's desire for some human agent to blame.

Beginning sometime Saturday, while fires were still raging and aftershocks numerous (there were over 114 aftershocks on Saturday, 88 on Sunday, and 60 on Monday), Japanese rumors began that Koreans were about to revolt, were poisoning wells, and were starting the fires. They spread quickly on Sunday, being fueled by authorities. Martial law was declared at 4:00 P.M., for the first time since the Hibiya riots in 1905, which began as a celebration of Japan's victory over Russia. Reserves, firefighters, and youth groups were mobilized to aid police against this rumored violence of Koreans, in essence, creating vigilante groups. Poole describes one scene:

> A stream of people were flowing along the Bluff Road towards Camp hill and the waterfront, urged on by police and ugly rumours of an uprising of Koreans. True, there were many Korean convicts in Negishi jail; also hundreds of Korean labourers in the industrial strip between Yokohama and Tokyo, all malcontents; but these alarming tales of an uprising were a figment of panicky imagination. What unhappily seems true is that the police, fired by these tales, dealt summarily with any Koreans acting at all supiciously, as well as all looters, Korean or Japanese, caught in the act, stringing some of them up to telegraph poles and shooting or executing others. (1968, 91)

---

[3] See Harootunian's analysis of Gonda (2000, 149–77).

Clearly Poole was not well disposed toward the Korean laborers in his vicinity. Yet he brings out the spuriousness of the rumors. It is unclear exactly who started the rumors, but most historians today argue that they were spread, if not started, by the police and other authorities, possibly even Mizuno Rentarō, the home minister.[4] Without doubt, this was an egregious moment in the history of race relations in Japan. It is even worse, as many are now pointing out, that such incidents have been ignored, papered over, and even denied. In part we can blame the censorship imposed under martial law, but even after it was lifted, the Japanese press, if critical at all, blamed the vigilante groups as those who had not yet learned the restraint and composure of civilized people (Matsuo 1963–64, 116). I bring this up here, though, not to join the chorus pointing to another moment of historical amnesia in Japan. (There are several fine, critical accounts written by major Japanese historians up to the mid-1960s. We should ask why such accounts have been ignored since then.)[5] Instead, it points to the transmutation of the past where the new temporality alters the notion of otherness from an alien-I to an I-Thou relationship.

In accounts of the riots, historians bring up the fear of Mizuno and Akaike Atsushi, the inspector general of the Tokyo Metropolitan Police Department, of domestic disorder. The massive destruction revived fears of the rice riots of 1918 and the labor activism that revived after World War I. In 1921 the Japanese Federation of Labor (*Nihon rōdō sōdōmei*) was founded, and the Japan Farmers' Union (*Nihon nōmin kumiai*) came into being a year later. Throughout the industrial world, the post–World War I years brought on considerable angst among the leaders that the capitalist system was about to implode. Historian Arno J. Mayer (1970) long ago described this as a contestation between forces of movement and forces of order. The forces of order soon seized the moment, not so much to reestablish order as to further the range of what I have been calling the materiality of the state. When martial law was declared over Tokyo on September 2, troops were mobilized to protect order. In addition to arrests of Koreans, socialist leaders were also arrested. For example, the social activist Ōsugi Sakae, his wife, the writer Itō Noe, and his nephew were arrested and murdered by police. One week later, after many services and order were restored, the Kantō Martial Law Headquarters (also formed on September 2) issued the following celebratory statement: "Koreans and Bolsheviks did their best to incite riots by disquieting speeches, but the prevalence of such outrages has been kept down by the presence of soldiers, police, army reservists, and members of Young Men's Associations" (quoted in Weiner 1989, 168–69).

[4] Matsuo (1963–64) has a fine analysis trying to trace the origins. See also Kang (1963); in English, see Weiner (1989, esp. 164–200).

[5] In commemoration of the fortieth anniversary of the incident, Hani Gorō (1963) introduced a symposium on the riot and earthquake in which he emphasized the need to discuss this aspect of the past to improve Japan-Korea relations, and international relations more broadly.

The combination of labor activism, sedition, and Koreans is another example of the transformation of Japan brought about by the new time of modernity.[6] The animate beings—catfish and ghosts—were no longer effective sources to which to attribute calamities. But if Bloch, James, and Gonda are correct that such a catastrophic event returns us to some form of precivilized form where there is a desire to personify blame, then the state went after the threats to the stability of the system: Koreans became that other, the outsider that brings calamity (but not retribution) as had the catfish; socialists offered an alternate idea of society where labor, not culture, objectified the social.

As pasts became domesticated as earlier moments of the same, that is, Japan's past, an important realm to which people had turned to explain disaster had been eliminated. Instead, a desire for personification turned to outsiders, now foreigners. The alien-I form of alterity that is unstable because one can always become the other (i.e., a ghost) is replaced by an I-Thou form of otherness; Koreans became a modern category of *ijin*, a stranger or outsider, who reinforce the security of being Japanese. Various non-Japanese were attacked as being Korean. Otis Poole writes, "Bill Blatch of the Rising Sun (Shell Oil) . . . was attacked by a mob in Kamakura village, mistaking him for a Korean suspect, and was being bludgeoned to death when saved by the timely appearance of a Japanese cavalry officer" (1968, 102).[7] But Korean also served as that category personified. Koreans became the people who reinforced the unity of a Japan and Japanese. It is an argument that uses the body (race) to mark a cultural, that is, national, difference. This is the obverse of the role of the child in marking the unity of a Japan. The child confirms the "we" of Japanese and becomes the object through which a horizon of expectations (future) becomes reality. Koreans, too, reinforce the modernness of being Japanese; they are both of the past (temporally behind) and outside, demarcating the difference between us and them throughout history.

While Koreans helped to reinforce the idea of a Japan, the purge of socialists reduced the threat to the recently historicized society. In the formulation of society in the 1890s, the child and family formed the basis of society by providing norms that ameliorated the social problem. They provided an alternative to that of a society objectified by labor, one that provided both a chronology of change and a transhistorical stability. In the fear of social unrest during the early 1920s,

---

[6] For an essay connecting Koreans and the labor movement, see Abe (1983).

[7] Interestingly the reports of the first day are virtually the antithesis of these rumors. For example, an American professor at Keio University, D. B. Langford, writes, "The very striking thing was the stoicism with which they viewed the disaster and their wonderful self-control. Not a single complaint was heard on the journey from Manazuru to Yokohama nor an instance noted of exhibition of grief or despair. No instance of selfishness was seen on the part of the Japanese, although some foreigners whom we met behaved disgracefully. Each individual had, to all appearances, put away all thought of his own trouble and was making every effort possible to help others and make them also forget the horror" (Poole 1968, 137).

labor was further marginalized by being grouped with Koreans (Koreans were brought in as inexpensive labor, especially during the boom years fueled by World War I). What is implicit is that having established the content of being Japanese, in the child and the family, outsiders (Koreans) help demarcate dissension as also outside the norm (but if, like the vigilantes, people acted for the state, it became a case of overexuberance or evidence of their need for further refinement). In the end, this violence returned time to "simply the medium in which all histories take place." That is, the timeforms that had come to regulate society returned as if they alone represented time. Japanese culture becomes reified, maintained from within, through the reproduction of each child, and from without, the threat to the order (in this case imagined but no less effective) of the national body.

In the end, the world of rationality and science professes certainty and predictability, but that understanding deadens the past and, in this fixation of fluid processes, establishes categories of sameness and difference that render understanding of outsiders possible only through rigid categories. This is not an appeal to return to some premodern epistemology, but to question our modern forms of knowledge, to remember that time, too, is a "dynamic and historical force." At this point, in the case of Japan, an essay by Masao Miyoshi, "Japan Is Not Interesting" (2000), comes to mind. It is not that Japan is uninteresting, but that life has become so controlled, predictable (these are the tools for certainty), and banal that Japanese themselves utter the equivalent in Japanese, "Nihon wa tsumaranai." We need to question to what extent the modern amelioration of the absolutism of reality has brought us so much certainty that we now manufacture threats, like the ghosts that haunted premodern Japan, using the category of outsider.

WORKS CITED

Abe, Kazuhiro. 1983. "Race Relations and the Capitalist State: A Case Study of Koreans in Japan, 1917 through the mid-1920s." *Korean Studies* 7:35–60.

Abe, Stanley K. 1995. "Inside the Wonder House: Buddhist Art and the West." In Donald S. Lopez, Jr. ed. *Curators of the Buddha: The Study of Buddhism under Colonialism.* Chicago: University of Chicago Press.

Addiss, Stephen. 1985. *Japanese Ghosts and Demons.* New York: George Braziller.

Agamben, Giorgio. 1993. *Infancy and History.* Translated by Liz Heron. London: Verso.

Amino Yoshihiko. 1992. "Deconstructing 'Japan.'" Translated by Gavan McCormack. *East Asian History* 3:121–42.

Ankersmit, F. R. 2001. *Historical Representation.* Stanford: Stanford University Press.

Anzai Aiko. 1977. "Shōka o tataeru." In Kindaichi Haruhiko and Anzai Aiko, eds. *Nihon no shōka (jō) Meiji hen.* Tokyo: Kodansha bunko.

Aoi Tetsubito. 2002. "Hōryūji to sekai kenchikushi—Itō Chuta 'Hōryūji kenchikuron' no nijūsei to sono kisū." In Yonekura Michio, ed. *Nihon ni okeru bijutsushigaku no seiritsu to tenkai.* Tokyo: Tokyo bunkazai kenkyūjo.

Aries, Philippe. 1962. *Centuries of Childhood: A Social History of Family Life.* Translated by Robert Baldick. New York: Vintage.

Asad, Talal. 1993. *Genealogies of Religion: Discipline and Reasons of Power in Christianity and Islam.* Baltimore: Johns Hopkins University Press.

Barry, Andrew, Thomas Osborne, and Nikolas Rose. 1996. "Introduction." In Andrew Barry, Thomas Osborne, and Nikolas Rose, eds. *Foucault and Political Reason.* Chicago: University of Chicago Press.

Bartholomew, James R. 1989. *The Formation of Science in Japan.* New Haven: Yale University Press.

Bartky, Ian R. 2000. *Selling the True Time: Nineteenth-Century Timekeeping in America.* Stanford: Stanford University Press.

Baudrillard, Jean. 1994. "The System of Collecting." In John Elsner and Roger Cardinal, eds. *The Cultures of Collecting.* Cambridge: Harvard University Press.

Baxter, James C. 1994. *The Meiji Unification through the Lens of Ishikawa Prefecture.* Cambridge: Harvard East Asian Monographs.

Beauchamp, Edward R., and Akira Iriye, eds. 1990. *Foreign Employees in Nineteenth-Century Japan.* Boulder: Westview Press.

Bender, John, and David Wellbery, eds. 1991. *Chronotypes: The Construction of Time.* Stanford: Stanford University Press.

Benjamin, Walter. 1968. *Illuminations.* New York: Harcourt, Brace and World, Inc.

Berman, Marshall. 1982. *All That Is Solid Melts into Air.* New York: Penguin.

Bernstein, Gail L. 1991. *Recreating Japanese Women, 1600–1945.* Berkeley: University of California Press.

Bialock, David T. 1999. "Nation and Epic: *The Tale of the Heike* as a Modern Classic." In Haruo Shirane and Tomi Suzuki, eds. *Inventing the Classics: Modernity, National Identity, and Japanese Literature.* Stanford: Stanford University Press.

Bird, Isabella. 1984[1880]. *Unbeaten Tracks in Japan*. Boston: Beacon Press.

Bleed, Peter. 1986. "Almost Archaeology: Early Archaeological Interest in Japan." In Richard J. Pearson, ed. *Windows on the Japanese Past: Studies in Archaeology and Prehistory*. Ann Arbor: Center for Japanese Studies.

Bloch, Ernst. 1977. "Nonsynchronism and the Obligation to Its Dialectics." *New German Critique* 11:22–38.

Blumenberg, Hans. 1985. *Work on Myth*. Translated by Robert M. Wallace. Cambridge: MIT Press.

Blussé, Leonard. 1979. "Japanese Historiography and European Sources." In P. C. Emmer and H. L. Wesseling, eds. *Reappraisals in Overseas History*. Leiden: Leiden University Press.

Borst, Arno. 1993. *The Ordering of Time: From the Ancient Computus to the Modern Computer*. Chicago: University of Chicago Press.

Bowen, Roger W. 1980. *Rebellion and Democracy in Meiji Japan: A Study of Commoners in the Popular Rights Movement*. Berkeley: University of California Press.

Braisted, William R., trans. 1976. *Meiroku Zasshi: Journal of Japanese Enlightenment*. Cambridge: Harvard University Press.

Bramsen, William. 1880. *Japanese Chronological Tables, Showing the Date, according to the Julian or Gregorian Calendar, of the First Day of Each Japanese Month*. Tokio: Seishi bunsha.

Brownlee, John S. 1997. *Japanese Historians and the National Myth: 1600–1945*. Vancouver: UBC Press.

Brownstein, Michael C. 1987. "From Kokugaku to Kokubungaku: Canon-Formation in the Meiji Period." *Harvard Journal of Asiatic Studies* 47.2:435–60.

Buckle, Henry Thomas. 1908. *History of Civilization in England*. London: Longmans, Green.

Buck-Morss, Susan. 1989. *The Dialectics of Seeing*. Cambridge: MIT Press.

Burchell, Graham. 1996. "Liberal Government and Techniques of the Self." In Andrew Barry, Thomas Osborne, and Nikolas Rose, eds. *Foucault and Political Reason*. Chicago: University of Chicago Press.

Carruthers, Mary. 1990. *The Book of Memory*. Cambridge: Cambridge University Press.

Castoriodis, Cornelius. "Time and Creation." In John Bender and David E. Wellbery, eds. *Chronotypes: The Construction of Time*. Stanford: Stanford University Press.

Certeau, Michel de. 1983. "History: Ethics, Science, and Fiction." In Norma Haan et al., eds. *Social Science as Moral Inquiry*. New York: Columbia University Press.

———. 1984. *The Practice of Everyday Life*. Translated by Steven F. Rendall. Berkeley: University of California Press.

———. 1988. *The Writing of History*. Translated by Tom Conley. New York: Columbia University Press.

Chakrabarty, Dipesh. 2000. *Provincializing Europe: Postcolonial Thought and Historical Difference*. Princeton: Princeton University Press.

Chandler, Alfred D. 1977. *The Visible Hand: The Managerial Revolution in American Business*. Cambridge: Belknap Press.

Chen, Constance. 2000. "From Passion to Discipline: East Asian Art and the Culture of Modernity in the United States, 1893–1944." Ph.D. dissertation. University of California, Los Angeles.

Cohen, Warren. 1992. *East Asian Art and American Culture*. New York: Columbia University Press.

Collingwood, R. G. 1960[1945]. *The Idea of Nature*. Oxford: Oxford University Press.

Connerton, Paul. 1989. *How Societies Remember*. Cambridge: Cambridge University Press.

Cranston, Edwin A., trans. 1993. *A Waka Anthology*. Volume 1: *The Gem-Glistening Cup*. Stanford: Stanford University Press.

Dahlman, Joseph. 1924. *The Great Tokyo Earthquake*. Translated by Victor F. Gettleman. New York: The America Press.

Dan, Ino. 1931. "Art." In Inazo Nitobe et al. *Western Influences in Modern Japan*. Chicago: University of Chicago Press.

Daston, Lorraine, and Katherine Park. 1998. *Wonders and the Order of Nature, 1150–1750*. Cambridge: MIT Press.

Davidson, Arnold. 2001. *The Emergence of Sexuality*. Cambridge: Harvard University Press.

Davis, F. Hadland. 1992[1913]. *Myths and Legends of Japan*. New York: Dover Publications.

Davison, Charles. 1927. *The Founders of Seismology*. Cambridge: Cambridge University Press.

De Bary, William Theodore, Wing-tsit Chan, and Burton Watson. 1969. *Sources of Chinese Tradition*. New York: Columbia University Press.

Diamond, Stephen A. 1996. *Anger, Madness, and the Daimonic: The Psychological Genesis of Violence, Evil, and Creativity*. Albany: State University of New York Press.

Dohrn-van Rossum, Gerhard. 1996. *History of the Hour: Clocks and Modern Temporal Orders*. Translated by Thomas Dunlap. Chicago: University of Chicago Press.

Donzelot, Jacques. 1978. *The Policing of Families*. Translated by Robert Hurley. New York: Pantheon Books.

Droysen, Johann Gustav. 1967. *Outline of the Principles of History*. Translated by E. Benjamin Andrews. New York: Howard Fertig.

Duus, Peter. 1974. "Whig History, Japanese Style: The Min'yūsha Historians and the Meiji Restoration." *Journal of Asian Studies* 33:415–36.

Eagleton, Terry. 1990. *The Ideology of the Aesthetic*. Oxford: Blackwell.

———. 2000. *The Idea of Culture*. Oxford: Blackwell.

Earhart, H. Byron. 1989. "Mount Fuji and Shugendō." *Japanese Journal of Religious Studies* 16:205–26.

Edelstein, Wolfgang. 1983. "Cultural Constraints on Development and the Vicissitudes of Progress." In Frank S. Kessel and Alexander W. Siegel, eds. *The Child and Other Cultural Inventions*. New York: Praeger.

Elias, Norbert. 1985. *The Loneliness of the Dying*. Translated by Edmund Jephcott. Oxford: Blackwell.

———. 1992. *Time: An Essay*. Oxford: Blackwell.

Escobar, Arturo. 1995. *Encountering Development*. Princeton: Princeton University Press.

Faulds, Henry. 1973[1885]. *Nine Years in Nipon: Sketches of Japanese Life and Manners*. New York: Scholarly Resources.

Fenollosa, Ernest F. 1911. *Epochs of Chinese and Japanese Art*. New York: Frederick A. Stokes Co.

Field, Norma. 1995. "The Child as Laborer and Consumer: The Disappearance of Childhood in Contemporary Japan." In Sharon Stephens, ed. *Children and the Politics of Culture*. Princeton: Princeton University Press.

Figal, Gerald. 1999. *Civilization and Monsters: Spirits of Modernity in Meiji Japan*. Durham: Duke University Press.

Foucault, Michel. 1973. *The Order of Things: An Archeology of the Human Sciences*. New York: Vintage Books.

———. 1979. *Discipline and Punish: The Birth of the Prison*. Translated by Alan Sheridan. New York: Vintage Books, 1979.

Fujinawa Yoshio and Takahashi Kōzō. 1994. "A Relation among Earthquakes, Japanese Catfish and Electric Field Changes." *Jishin yōchi renrakukai kaihō* 52 (August): 145–46.

Fujitani, Takashi. 1996. *Splendid Monarchy: Power and Pageantry in Modern Japan*. Berkeley: University of California Press.

Fukuzawa Yukichi. 1973. *An Outline of a Theory of Civilization*. Translated by David A. Dilworth and G. Cameron Hurst. Tokyo: Sophia University Press.

Garon, Sheldon. 1987. *The State and Labor in Modern Japan*. Berkeley: University of California Press.

———. 1997. *Molding Japanese Minds*. Princeton: Princeton University Press.

Geary, Patrick. 2002. *The Myths of Nations: The Medieval Origins of Europe*. Princeton: Princeton University Press.

Gluck, Carol. 1978. "The People in History: Recent Trends in Japanese Historiography." *Journal of Asian Studies* 38:25–50.

———. 1985. *Japan's Modern Myths: Ideology in the Late Meiji Period*. New York: Columbia University Press.

Gonda Yasunosuke. 1989[1931]. *Minshū gorakuron*. Tokyo: Ōzorasha.

Gordon, Andrew. 1991. *Labor and Imperial Democracy in Prewar Japan*. Berkeley: University of California Press

Grapard, Allan G. 1984. "Japan's Ignored Cultural Revolution: The Separation of Shinto and Buddhist Divinities in Meiji (*shimbutsu bunri*)." *History of Religions* 23, 3:240–65.

———. 1992. *Protocol of the Gods*. Berkeley: University of California Press.

Gurevich, A. J. 1985. *Categories of Medieval Culture*. Translated by G. L. Campbell. London: Routledge and Kegan Paul.

Haga Yaichi and Tachibana Sensaburō. 1989. *Kokubungaku dokuhon shoron*. In Hisamatsu Senichi, ed. *Ochiai Naobumi, Ueda Kazutoshi, Haga Yaichi, Fujioka Sakutaro shū*. Tokyo: Chikuma shobō.

Hani Gorō. 1963. "Kantō daishinsai chōsenjin kyōsatsu jiken: yonjū shūnen o mukaeru ni atatte." *Rekishi hyōron* 157:1–8.

Hanley, Susan B., and Kozo Yamamura. 1977. *Economic and Demographic Change in Preindustrial Japan*. Princeton: Princeton University Press.

Hardacre, Helen. 1989. *Shinto and the State, 1868–1945*. Princeton: Princeton University Press.

Harootunian, Harry. 1974. "Between Politics and Culture: Authority and the Ambiguities of Intellectual Choice in Imperial Japan." In Bernard S. Silberman and H. D. Harootunian, eds. *Japan in Crisis: Essays on Taishō Democracy*. Princeton: Princeton University Press.

———. 2000. *Overcome by Modernity*. Princeton: Princeton University Press.

Harvey, David. 1996. *Justice, Nature and the Geography of Difference.* Oxford: Blackwell.

Haryū Kiyohito. 1987. "Meiji tetsugaku no kaihi." In *Inoue Enryō senshū.* Volume 1. Tokyo: Tōyōgaku.

Hashikawa Bunsō. 1962. "Takayama Chogyū," *Asahi Janaru* 4(9–16): 387–93

Hattori, I. 1878. "Destructive Earthquakes in Japan." *Transactions of the Asiatic Society of Japan* 6:249–75.

Hearn, Lafcadio. 1971. *Kwaidan: Stories and Studies of Strange Things.* Rutland, VT: Charles E. Tuttle Company.

Hegel, Georg W. F. 1956. *Philosophy of History.* Translated by J. Sibree. New York: Dover Publications.

———. 1975. *Aesthetics: Lectures on Fine Art.* Translated by T. M. Knox. Oxford: Clarendon Press.

Herbert-Gustar, A. L., and P. A. Nott. 1980. *John Milne: Father of Modern Seismology.* Tenterden, Kent: Paul Norbury Publications.

Herzfeld, Michael. 1992. *The Social Production of Indifference: Exploring the Symbolic Roots of Western Bureaucracy.* Chicago: University of Chicago Press.

Hides, Sean. 1997. "The Genealogy of Material Culture and Cultural Identity." In Susan M. Pearce, ed. *Experiencing Material Culture in the Western World.* New York: Leicester University Press.

Hirose Hideo. 1993. *Koyomi.* Tokyo: Tokyodō shuppan.

Hisamatsu Senichi. 1957. *Nihon bungaku kenkyūshi.* Tokyo: Yamada Shoin.

Hochberg, Julian. 1972. "The Representation of Things and People." In E. H. Gombrich, Julian Hochberg, and Max Black, eds. *Art, Perception, and Reality.* Baltimore: Johns Hopkins University Press.

Hori, Ichirō. 1968. *Folk Religion in Japan: Continuity and Change.* Chicago: University of Chicago Press.

Howland, Doug. 1996. *Borders of Chinese Civilization.* Durham: Duke University Press.

———. 2002. *Translating the West: Language and Political Reason in Nineteenth-Century Japan.* Honolulu: University of Hawai'i Press.

Hughes, Peter. 1995. "Ruins of Time: Estranging History and Ethnology in the Enlightenment and After." In Diane Owen Hughes and Thomas R. Trautmann, eds. *Time: Histories and Ethnologies.* Ann Arbor: University of Michigan Press.

Iida Nagao. 1883. "Honyaku kojiki sōron." *Shigaku kyōkai zasshi* 4:47–52.

Imamura, A. 1924. "Preliminary Note on the Great Earthquake of Southeastern Japan on September 1, 1923." *Bulletin of the Seismological Society of America* 14:136–49.

Inoue Enryō. 1902. "Yōkaigaku to shinrigaku to no kankei." In *Hosui Ronshu.* Tokyo: Fukuon insatsu.

———. 1979[1896]. *Yōkaigaku kōgi.* Tokyo: Kokusho kankōkai.

———. 1991. "Shinri tekiyō." In *Inoue Enryō senshū.* Volume 9. Tokyo: Tōyō daigaku.

———. 1992. "Shinkiokujutsu." In *Inoue Enryō senshū.* Volume 10. Tokyo: Tōyō daigaku.

Inoue Tetsujirō. 1891–92. "Tōyōshigaku no kachi." *Shigakkai zasshi* 2:709–17, 788–98.

———. 1911. "Waga kokutai to kazoku seido." *Tōa no hikari* 6–9:1–18.

———. 1915. "Shizen to dōtoku." In *Shakai to dōtoku.* Tokyo: Kodōkan.

———. 1974a[1891]. "Chokugo engi." In Katayama Seiichi, ed. *Shiryō, chokugo engi: kappatsuji oyobi kanrensho shiryō.* Tokyo: Kōryōsha shoten.

——. 1974b. *Zōtei chokugo engi.* In Furuta Shōkin, ed. *Kyōiku chokugo kankei shiryō.* Tokyo: Nihon daigaku seishin bunka kenkyūjo.

Irokawa Daikichi. 1985. *The Culture of the Meiji Period.* Translation edited by Marius Jansen. Princeton: Princeton University Press.

Ishida Ryūjirō. 1984. *Nihon ni okeru kindai chirigaku no seiritsu* Tokyo: Omeido.

Ishiguro, Yoshiaki. 1998. "A Japanese National Crime: The Korean Massacre after the Great Kantō Earthquake of 1923." *Korea Journal* 38 (Winter): 331–54.

Ishikawa Chiyomatsu. 1967. "Professor Edward Sylvester Morse." In Edward Sylvester Morse. *Ōmori kaizuka.* Tokyo: Tokyo-to ōmori kaizuka hozonkai.

——. 1968. "Mōsu sensei." In *Meiji bungaku zenshū.* Volume 49. Tokyo: Chikuma shobō.

Isozaki Arata. 1996. "Ise: shigen no modoki." In *Shigen no modoki.* Tokyo: Kagoshima shuppankai.

Itō Chuta. 1982. "Hōryūji homonki." In *Itō Chuta chōsakushū* 6:642.

——. 1898. "Hōryūji kenchikuron." *Tokyo teikoku daigaku kiyo* 1:1–176.

——. 1934. *Nihon kenchiku no hensen.* Tokyo: Keimeikai.

Ivy, Marilyn. 1995. *Discourses of the Vanishing: Modernity, Phantasm, Japan.* Chicago: University of Chicago Press.

Iwai Tadakuma. 1963. "Nihon kindai shigaku no keisei." *Iwanami kōza nihon rekishi* (bekkan 22). Tokyo: Iwanami shoten.

Jaggar, T. A. 1923. "The Yokohama-Tokyo Earthquake of September 1, 1923." *Bulletin of the Seismological Society of America* 13, 4 (December): 124–46.

Jansen, Marius, ed. 1965. *Changing Attitudes toward Modernization.* Princeton: Princeton University Press.

Jinnai Hidenobu. 1995. *Tokyo: A Spatial Anthropology.* Translated by Kimiko Nishimura. Berkeley: University of California Press.

Jones, Hazel J. 1980. *Live Machines: Hired Foreigners and Meiji Japan.* Vancouver: University of British Columbia Press.

Kami Shōichirō. 1989. *Nihon jidōshi no kaitaku.* Tokyo: Komine shoten.

——. 1994. "Jidō bungaku: Edo kara Meiji e." In Inagaki Shinichi, Kami Shōichirō, and Kuroda Hideo, eds. *Ukiyoe no kodomotachi.* Tokyo: Tōbu bijutsukan.

Kanai Noburu. 1893. "Shakai mondai no kenkyū." *Rikugo zasshi* 152:8–25.

Kang Tok-sang. 1963. "Tsukuri dasareta ryūgen: Kantō daishinsai ni okeru chōsenjin kyōsatsu ni tsuite." *Rekishi hyōron* 157:9–22.

Karatani Kōjin. 1993. *Origins of Modern Japanese Literature.* Translation edited by Brett de Bary. Durham: Duke University Press.

Katō Hiroyuki. 1890. "Hakubutsugaku to rekishigaku: Natural history and the history." *Shigakkai zasshi* 4:1–9.

——. 1912. *Shizen to rinri.* Tokyo: Jitsugyō no nihonsha.

——. 1959. *Hiroyuki jiden.* Tokyo: Chōryo shōrin.

Katō Minoru. 1977. "Aru mōsu hihan: Matsumori Taneyasu *Roseki Yodan* kara." *Kōkogaku kenkyū* 24:86–89.

Katō Shūichi and Maruyama Masao. 1991. *Honyaku no shisō.* Tokyo: Iwanami shoten.

Katsumata Shizuo with Martin Collcutt. 1981. "The Development of Sengoku Law." In John Whitney Hall, Nagahara Keiji, and Kozo Yamamura, eds. *Japan before Tokugawa: Political Consolidation and Economic Growth, 1500–1650.* Princeton: Princeton University Press.

Kawamura Kunimitsu. 1990. *Genshi suru kindai kūkan: meishin, byōki, zashikiro, aruiwa rekishi no kioku.* Tokyo: Seikyūsha.

Kawashima Takeyoshi. 1957. *Ideorogii to shite no kazoku seido.* Tokyo: Iwanami shoten.

Keene, Donald. 1969. "Japanese Aesthetics." *Philosophy East and West* 19, 3:293–306.

Keirstead, Thomas. 1998. "Inventing Medieval Japan: The History and Politics of National Identity." *The Medieval History Journal* 1, 1:47–71.

Kelly, William W. 1985. *Deference and Defiance in Nineteenth-Century Japan.* Princeton: Princeton University Press.

Kessen, William. 1979. "The American Child and Other Cultural Inventions." *American Psychologist* 34:815–20.

Ketelaar, James. 1990. *Of Heretics and Martyrs in Meiji Japan: Buddhism and Its Persecution.* Princeton: Princeton University Press.

Kigu Yasuhiko. 1937. "Nihon shinsaishi gaisetsu." *Shakaishi kenkyū* 10, 4:1–17.

Kokubun Ichitarō. 1972. "Kodomo zuihitsu: mura no kodomo." In Matsunaga Gōichi, ed. *Kindai minshū no kiroku: nōmin.* Tokyo: Shinjinbutsu ōraisha.

Komatsu Kazuhiko. 1995. *Nihon yōkai ibunroku.* Tokyo: Shogakkan raiburarii.

Konakamura Kiyonori. 1889. "Rekishi no hanashi." *Shigakkai zasshi* 1:5–10.

Kornicki, P. F. 1994. "Public Display and Changing Values: Early Meiji Exhibitions and Their Precursors." *Monumenta Nipponica* 49, 2:167–96.

Koselleck, Reinhardt. 1985. *Futures Past: On the Semantics of Historical Time.* Translated by Keith Tribe. Cambridge: MIT Press.

Kublin, Hyman. 1964. *Asian Revolutionary: The Life of Sen Katayama.* Princeton: Princeton University Press.

Kume Kunitake. 1991a. "Rekishigaku no susumi." In Tanaka Akira and Miyachi Masato, eds. *Rekishi ninshiki.* Tokyo: Iwanami shoten.

——. 1991b. "Shūshi ikensho." In Tanaka Akira and Miyachi Masato, eds. *Rekishi ninshiki.* Tokyo: Iwanami shoten.

Kuno Osamu. 1978. "The Meiji State, Minponshugi, and Ultranationalism." In J. Victor Koschmann, ed. *Authority and the Individual in Japan.* Tokyo: University of Tokyo Press.

Kuroda Hideo. 1989. *'Emaki' kodomo no tōjō: chūsei shakai no kodomozō.* Tokyo: Kawade shobō shinsha.

——. 1994. "Edoki no kodomo o shakai shiteki ni miru." In Inagaki Shinichi, Kami Shōichirō, and Kuroda Hideo, eds. *Ukiyoe no kodomotachi.* Tokyo: Tōbu bijutsukan.

Latour, Bruno. 1986. "Visualization and Cognition: Thinking with Eyes and Hands." *Knowledge and Society* 6:1–40.

Leeds, Eric J. 1991. *The Mind of the Traveler: From Gilgamesh to Global Tourism.* New York: Basic Books.

Lefebvre, Henri. 1995. "What Is Modernity?" In *Introduction to Modernity.* London: Verso.

Liljestrom, Rita. 1983. "The Public Child, The Commercial Child, and Our Child." In Frank S. Kessel and Alexander W. Siegel, eds. *The Child and Other Cultural Inventions.* New York: Praeger.

Lincicome, Mark. 1995. *Principle, Praxis, and the Politics of Educational Reform in Meiji Japan.* Honolulu: University of Hawai'i Press.

Lovejoy, Arthur O. 1948. "'Nature' as Aesthetic Norm." In *Essays in the History of Ideas.* Baltimore: Johns Hopkins University Press.

Lowell, Percival. 1894. *Occult Japan*. Boston: Houghton Mifflin.

Lowenthal, David. 1985. *The Past Is a Foreign Country*. Cambridge: Cambridge University Press.

Luckmann, Thomas. 1991. "The Constitution of Human Life in Time." In John Bender and David E. Wellbery, eds. *Chronotypes: The Construction of Time*. Stanford: Stanford University Press.

Lukacs, Georg. 1971. *History and Class Consciousness: Studies in Marxist Dialectics*. Translated by Rodney Livingstone. Cambridge: MIT Press.

Lyman, Benjamin Smith. 1877. *Geological Survey of Hokkaido: A General Report on the Geology of Yesso*. Tōkei: Kaitakushi.

Mabuchi Akiko. 1997. *Japonisumu: gensō no nihon*. Tokyo: Brucke.

Machida Kōichi. 1968. "A Historical Survey of the Controversy as to Whether the Hōryūji Was Rebuilt or Not." *Acta Asiatica* 15:87–115.

Maeda Ai. 1982. *Toshi kūkan no naka no bungaku*. Tokyo: Chikuma shobō.

———. 1989. "Inoue Tetsujirō to Takayama Chogyū." In *Maeda Ai chosakushū*. Volume 4. Tokyo: Chikuma shobō.

Maher, John C., and Gaynor McDonald. 1995. *Diversity in Japanese Culture and Language*. London: Kegan International.

Maleuvre, Didier. 1999. *Museum Memories: History, Technology, Art*. Stanford: Stanford University Press.

Maruyama Masao. 1963. *Thought and Behavior in Modern Japanese Politics*. Edited by Ivan Morris. New York: Oxford University Press.

Maruyama Sakura. 1883. "Shigaku kyōkai sōritsu no shushi." *Shigaku kyōkai zasshi* 1:2–8.

Matsumoto Gōichi. 1975. "Monbusho shōka no giman." In *Furusato kō*. Tokyo: Kōdansha.

Matsuo Takayoshi. 1963–64. "Kantō shinsai shita no chōsenjin kyōsatsu jiken." *Shisō* 471:1218–35 and 476:246–56.

Mayer, Arno J. 1970[1959]. *Political Origins of the New Diplomacy, 1917–1918*. New York: Vintage Books.

McCullough, Helen Craig, trans. 1959. *The Taiheiki: A Chronicle of Medieval Japan*. Wesport, CT: Greenwood Press.

McManners, Keith. 1981. *Death and the Enlightenment*. New York: Oxford University Press.

Mehl, Margaret. 1998a. *History and the State in Nineteenth-Century Japan*. New York: St. Martin's Press.

———. 1998b. "The Mid-Meiji 'History Boom': Professionalization of Historical Scholarship and Growing Pains of an Emerging Academic Discipline." *Japan Forum* 10, 1:67–83.

Mehta, Uday Singh. 1999. *Liberalism and Empire: A Study in Nineteenth-Century British Liberal Thought*. Chicago: University of Chicago Press.

Merchant, Carolyn. 1980. *The Death of Nature: Women, Ecology and the Scientific Revolution*. New York: HarperCollins.

Mikami Sanji. 1992. *Meiji jidai no rekishi gakkai*. Tokyo: Yoshikawa kobunkan.

Mikami Sanji and Takatsu Kuwasaburo. 1982[1890]. *Nihon bungakushi*. Tokyo: Nihon tosho senta.

Miller, Daniel. 1987. *Material Culture and Mass Consumption*. Oxford: Blackwell.

Mills, D. E. 1970. *A Collection of Tales from Uji: A Study and Translation of Uji shūi monogatari*. Cambridge: Cambridge University Press.

Milne, John. 1877. "A Visit to the Volcano of Oshima." *Geological Magazine*. New Series (May) 2.4.

———. 1878. "On the Form of Volcanos." *Geological Magazine* 2.5.

———. 1881. "The Stone Age in Japan." *Journal of the Anthropological Institute of Great Britain and Ireland* 10:389–423.

———. 1886. *Earthquakes and Other Earth Movements*. New York: D. Appleton.

Milne, John, and W. K. Burton. ca1894. *The Great Earthquake in Japan, 1891*. Yokohama: Lane, Crawford.

Mintz, Steven. 2001. "Regulating the American Family." In Joseph M. Hawes and Elizabeth I. Nybakken, eds. *Family and Society in American History*. Chicago: University of Chicago Press.

Miura Hiroyuki. 1930. *Nihonshi no kenkyū*. Volume 2. Tokyo: Iwanami shoten.

Miyake Setsurei. 1931a. *Shinzenbi nihonjin*. In *Miyake Setsurei shū, Gendai nihon bungaku zenshū*. Volumr 5. Tokyo: Kaizōsha.

———. 1931b. *Giakushū nihonjin*. In *Miyake Setsurei shū, Gendai nihon bungaku zenshū*. Volume 5. Tokyo: Kaizōsha.

Miyata Noboru. 1990. *Yōkai no minzokugaku: Nihon no mienai kūkan*. Tokyo: Iwanami shoten.

Miyoshi, Masao. 2000. "Japan Is Not Interesting." In *Re-mapping Japanese Culture*. Victoria: Monash Asia Institute.

Mizuchi Toshio. 1994. "Chiri shisō to kokumin kokka keisei." *Shisō* 845:75–94.

Mizuki Yōtaro. 1921. "Meiji shonen no nanto dandaiji." In Murakami Senjō, Tsuji Zennosuke, and Washio Junkei, eds. *Meiji ishin shinbutsu bunri shiryō*. Volume 2. Tokyo: Tōhō shoin.

Morris, Dana, and Thomas C. Smith. 1985. "Fertility and Mortality in an Outcaste Village in Japan, 1750–1869." In Susan B. Hanley and Arthur P. Wolf. *Family and Population in East Asian History*. Stanford: Stanford University Press.

Morris-Suzuki, Tessa. 1998. *Reinventing Japan: Time, Space, Nation*. Armonk, NY: M. E. Sharpe.

Morse, Edward Sylvester. 1879. "Traces of an Early Race in Japan." *Popular Science Monthly* 14 (January): 257–66.

———. 1917. *Japan Day by Day, 1877, 1878–79, 1882–83*. Boston: Houghton Mifflin.

———. 1967. *Ōmori kaizuka*. Tokyo: Tokyo-to Ōmori Kaizuka Hozonkai.

———. 2539(1879). "Shell Mounds of Omori." *Memoirs of the Science Department, University of Tokio, Japan* 1:1–8.

Moscovici, Serge. 1993. *The Invention of Society*. Translated by W. D. Halls. Cambridge: Polity Press.

Mumford, Lewis. 1934. *Technics and Civilization*. New York: Harcourt, Brace.

Murakami Senjō, Tsuji Zennosuke, and Washio Junkei. 1921. *Meiji ishin shinbutsu bunri shiryō*. Volume 2. Tokyo: Tōhō shoin.

Murakami Yasusuke. 1984. "Ie Society as a Pattern of Civilization." *Journal of Japanese Studies*. 10:281–363.

Murata Jirō. 1949. *Hōryūji no kenkyūshi*. Tokyo: Mainichi shimbunsha.

Najita, Tetsuo. 1974. *Japan*. Englewood Cliffs: Prentice Hall.

Naka Michiyo. 1897. "Joseinenki kō." *Shigaku zasshi* 8:747–78, 884–910, 997–1021, 1206–31.

——. 1991[1878]. *Jōko nendai kō*. In Tanaka Akira and Miyachi Masato, eds. *Rekishi ninshiki*. Tokyo: Iwanami shoten.

Nakae Chōmin. 1984. *A Discourse by Three Drunkards on Government*. Translated by Nobuko Tsukui. New York: John Weatherhill.

Nakayama, Shigeru. 1969. *A History of Japanese Astronomy: Chinese Background and Western Impact*. Cambridge: Harvard University Press.

Nandy, Ashis. 1995. "History's Forgotten Doubles." *History and Theory* 34:44–66.

Nara Kokuritsu Hakubutsukan. 1996. *Nara kokuritsu hakubutsukan hyakunen no ayumi*. Nara: Nara kokuritsu hakubutsukan.

NHK Shōsōin Purojekuto. 1990. *Dokumento Shōsōin: 1200 nen no tobira ga hirakareta*. Tokyo: Nihon hōsō shuppan kyōkai.

Nishioka Hideo. 1989. *Minzoku kōkogaku*. Tokyo: Nyū saienshusha.

Nolte, Sharon H. 1983. "Ōnishi Hajime and the Imperial Rescript on Education." *Monumenta Nipponica* 38:283–94.

Nolte, Sharon H., and Sally Hastings. 1991. "The Meiji State's Policy toward Women, 1890–1910." In Gail L. Bernstein, ed. *Recreating Japanese Women, 1600–1945*. Berkeley: University of California Press.

Noma Seiroku. 1967. *The Arts of Japan*. Volumes 1 and 2. Translated by Glenn T. Webb. Tokyo: Kodansha International.

Nora, Pierre. 1989. "Between Memory and History: *Les Lieux des Memoire*." *Representations* 26:7–25.

Norman, E. H. 1945. *Soldier and Peasant in Japan: The Origins of Conscription*. New York: Institute for Pacific Relations.

Norton, Robert E. 1991. *Herder's Aesthetic and the European Enlightenment*. Ithaca: Cornell University Press.

Notehelfer, F. G. 1975. "Japan's First Pollution Incident." *Journal of Japanese Studies* 1, 2:351–83.

Numata Jirō. 1961. "Shigeno Yasutsugu and the Modern Tokyo Tradition." in W. G. Beasley and E. G. Pulleyblank, eds. *Historians of China and Japan*. London: Oxford University Press.

O'Brien, Jay, and William Roseberry, eds. 1991. *Golden Ages, Dark Ages: Imagining the Past in Anthropology and History*. Berkeley: University of California Press.

Ōeyama no shuten dōji. 1990. Kyoto: ōeyama oni denstetsu issennensai jikko iinkai.

Ogawa Masako and Watanabe Masao. 1976. "E.S. Mōsu to Ōmori kaizuka." *Seibutsu-gakushi kenkyū* 29:1–12.

Ogi Shinzō. 1980. *Tōkei jidai: Edo to Tokyo no aida de*. Tokyo: NHK Books.

Okada Yoshirō. 1994. *Meiji kaireki: 'toki' no bunmei kaika*. Tokyo: Dashūkan shoten.

Okada Yoshirō and Akune Suetada, eds. 1993. *Gendai koyomi yomitoki jiten*. Tokyo: Kashiwa shōbo.

Okakura, Kakuzō. 1922[1904]. "Modern Art from a Japanese Point of View." In *The Heart of Heaven*. Tokyo: Nippon bijutsuin.

——. 1939. *Nihon bijutsushi*. In *Okakura Tenshin zenshū*. Volume 4. Tokyo: Rokugeisha

——. 1956[1906]. *The Book of Tea*. Rutland, VT: Charles E. Tuttle.

——. 1970[1904]. *The Ideals of the East*. Rutland, VT: Charles E. Tuttle.

Onda Akira. 1991. "Kaisetsu." In *Inoue Enryō senshū*. Volume 9. Tokyo: Tōyōgaku.

Ono Yōjirō. 1894. "Shakai mondai no shōrai." *Rikugo zasshi* 158:1–11.

Oreskes, Naomi. 1999. *The Rejection of Continental Drift: Theory and Method in American Earth Science*. Oxford: Oxford University Press.

Osborne, Peter. 1995. *The Politics of Time: Modernity and the Avant-Garde*. London: Verso.

Ōta Yūzō. 1988. *E. S. Mosu: "furuki nihon" o tsutaeta shinnichi kagakusha*. Tokyo: Riburopōto.

Ouwehand, C. 1964. *Namazu-e and Their Themes*. Leiden: E. J. Brill.

Pearce, Susan M. 1992. *Museums, Objects, and Collections*. Washington, DC: Smithsonian Institution Press.

Philippi, Donald, trans. 1967. *Kojiki*. Tokyo: University of Tokyo Press.

Pierson, John D. 1980. *Tokutomi Sohō, 1863–1957: A Journalist for Modern Japan*. Princeton: Princeton University Press.

Polanyi, Karl. 1944. *The Great Transformation: The Political and Economic Origins of Our Time*. Boston: Beacon Press.

Poole, Otis Manchester. 1968. *The Death of Old Yokohama*. London: George Allen and Unwin.

Poole, Robert. 1998. *Time's Alteration: Calendar Reform in Early Modern England*. London: UCL Press.

Postone, Moishe. 1993. *Time, Labor, and Social Domination*. Cambridge: Cambridge University Press.

Poulantzas, Nicos. 2000[1978]. *State, Power, and Socialism*. London: Verso.

Pratt, Mary Louise. 1992. *Imperial Eyes: Travel Writing and Transculturation*. London: Routledge.

Price, Sally. 1989. *Primitive Art in Civilized Places*. Chicago: University of Chicago Press.

Pyle, Kenneth B. 1970. *The New Generation in Meiji Japan*. Stanford: Stanford University Press.

Richards, E. G. 1998. *Mapping Time: The Calendar and Its History*. Oxford: Oxford University Press.

Richards, Thomas. 1993. *The Imperial Archives: Knowledge and the Fantasy of Empire*. London: Verso.

Roberts, Luke. 1998. *Mercantilism in a Japanese Domain*. Cambridge: Cambridge University Press.

Rochberg-Halton, Eugene. 1986. *Meaning and Modernity: Social Theory in the Pragmatic Attitude*. Chicago: University of Chicago Press.

Rose, Nikolas. 1996. "Governing 'Advanced' Liberal Democracies." In Andrew Barry, Thomas Osborne, and Nikolas Rose, eds. *Foucault and Political Reason*. Chicago: University of Chicago Press.

——. 1999. *Powers of Freedom: Reframing Political Thought*. Cambridge: Cambridge University Press.

Rosenstone, Robert A. 1998. *Mirror in the Shrine: American Encounters with Meiji Japan*. Cambridge: Harvard University Press.

Ross, Dorothy. 1991. *The Origins of American Social Science*. Cambridge: Cambridge University Press.

Rostow, W. W. 1990[1960]. *The Stages of Economic Growth: A Non-Communist Manifesto*. 3rd edition. Cambridge: Cambridge University Press.

Rydell, Robert W. 1984. *All the World's a Fair: Visions of Empire at American International Exhibitions, 1876–1916*. Chicago: University of Chicago Press.

Sack, Robert David. 1980. *Conceptions of Space in Social Thought*. Minneapolis: University of Minnesota Press.

———. 1986. *Human Territoriality: Its Theory and History*. Cambridge: Cambridge University Press.

Said, Edward. 1978. *Orientalism*. New York: Pantheon Books.

———. 1993. *Culture and Imperialism*. New York: Alfred A. Knopf.

Sand, Jordan. 1998. "At Home in the Meiji Period: Inventing Japanese Domesticity." In Stephen Vlastos, ed. *Mirror of Modernity: Invented Traditions of Modern Japan*. Berkeley: University of California Press.

Sansom, Sir George. 1958. *A History of Japan to 1334*. Stanford: Stanford University Press.

Sasaki Yōichirō. 1985. "Urban Migration and Fertility in Tokugawa Japan: The City of Takayama, 1773–1871." In Susan B. Hanley and Arthur P. Wolf, eds. *Family and Population in East Asian History*. Stanford: Stanford University Press.

Satake Akihirō. 1977. *Shuten dōji ibun*. Tokyo: Heibonsha.

Satō Doshin. 1999. *Meiji kokka to kindai bijutsu: bi no seijigaku*. Tokyo: Yoshikawa kobunkan.

Schivelbusch, Wolfgang. 1977. *The Railway Journey: The Industrialization of Time and Space in the 19th Century*. Berkeley: University of California Press.

Seidensticker, Edward. 1990. *Tokyo Rising: The City since the Great Earthquake*. New York: Alfred A. Knopf.

Seife, Charles. 2000. *Zero: The Biography of a Dangerous Idea*. New York: Viking Penguin.

Seki Genkichi. 1972. "Kodomotachi." In Matsunaga Gōichi. *Kindai minshū no kiroku: nōmin*. Tokyo: Shinjinbutsu ōraisha.

Serres, Michel, with Bruno Latour. 1995. *Conservations on Science, Culture, and Time*. Translated by Roxanne Lapidus. Ann Arbor: University of Michigan Press.

Shapin, Steven. 1996. *The Scientific Revolution*. Chicago: University of Chicago Press.

Shigeno Yasutsugu. 1991a. "Kokushi hensan no hōhō o ronzu." In Tanaka Akira and Miyachi Masato, eds. *Rekishi ninshiki*. Tokyo: Iwanami shoten.

———. 1991b. "Sejō rufu no shiden oku jijutsu o ayamaru." In Tanaka Akira and Miyachi Masato, eds. *Rekishi ninshiki*. Tokyo: Iwanami shoten.

———. 1991c. "Shi no hanashi." In Tanaka Akira and Miyachi Masato, eds. *Rekishi ninshiki*. Tokyo: Iwanami shoten.

Shimao, Eikoh. 1981. "Darwinism in Japan, 1877–1927." *Annals of Science*. 38:93–102.

Shimoyama Kanichirō. 1889. "Shigakushi." *Shigakkai zasshi* 1.

Shirane, Haruo, and Tomi Suzuki, eds. 2000. *Inventing the Classics: Modernity, National Identity, and Japanese Literature*. Stanford: Stanford University Press.

Shotter, John. 1993. *The Cultural Politics of Everyday Life: Social Constructionism, Rhetoric and Knowing of the Third Kind*. Toronto: University of Toronto Press.

Smith, Jonathan Z. 1991. "A Slip in Time Saves Nine: Prestigious Origins Again." In John Bender and David E. Wellbery, eds. *Chronotypes: The Construction of Time*. Stanford: Stanford University Press.

Sohn-Rethel, Alfred. 1975. "Science as Alienated Consciousness." *Radical Science Journal* 2, 3:65–101.

Soper, Alexander Coburn III. 1978[1942]. *The Evolution of Buddhist Architecture in Japan*. New York: Hacker Art Books.

Soper, Kate. 1995. *What Is Nature?* London: Blackwell.

Spaulding, Robert M. 1967. "The Intent of the Charter Oath." In Richard K. Beardsley, ed. *Studies in Japanese History and Politics*. Ann Arbor: Center for Japanese Studies.

Squires, Graham. 2001. "Yamaji Aizan's *Traces of the Development of Human Rights in Japanese History*." *Monumenta Nipponica* 56, 2:139–71.

Steedman, Carolyn. 1992. *Past Tenses: Essays on Writing, Autobiography and History*. London: Rivers Oram Press.

Strong, Kenneth. 1977. *Ox against the Storm*. Tenterden: Paul Norbury Publications.

Tagore, Rabindranath. 1917. *Nationalism*. New York: MacMillan.

Takada Ryōshin. 1987. *Hōryūji, I: rekishi to kobunken*. Osaka: Hoikusha.

———. 1993. *Hōryūji no nazo to hiwa*. Tokyo: Shōgakkan.

———. 1994. *Hōryūji senyonhyakunen*. Tokyo: Shinchosha.

Takayama Chogyū. 1914a[1893]. "Hibijutsuteki nihonjin." In *Chogyū zenshū*. Volume 1. Tokyo: Hakubunkan.

———. 1914b. "Rekishi o daimoku to seru bijutsu." In *Chogyū zenshū*. Volume 1. Tokyo: Hakubunkan.

———. 1970a[1897] "Nihonshugi." In *Takayama Chogyū, Saitō Nonobito, Anesaki Chōfū, Tobari Chikufu*. Volume 40. Tokyo: Chikuma shobō.

———. 1970b[1900]. "Bikan ni tsuite no kansatsu." In *Takayama Chogyū, Saitō Nonobito, Anesaki Chōfū, Tobari Chikufu*. Volume 40. Tokyo: Chikuma shobō.

———. 1970c[1901]. "Bunmei hihyōka to shite no bungakusha." In *Takayama Chogyū, Saitō Nonobito, Anesaki Chōfū, Tobari Chikufu*. Volume 40. Tokyo: Chikuma shobō.

———. 1970d[1901]. "Biteki seikatsu o ronzu." In *Takayama Chogyū, Saitō Nonobito, Anesaki Chōfū, Tobari Chikufu*. Volume 40. Tokyo: Chikuma shobō.

———. 1970e[1902]. "Kangai issoku." In *Takayama Chogyū, Saitō Nonobito, Anesaki Chōfū, Tobari Chikufu*. Volume 40. Tokyo: Chikuma shobō.

———. 1970f[1902]. "Mudairoku." In *Takayama Chogyū, Saitō Nonobito, Anesaki Chōfū, Tobari Chikufu*. Volume 40. Tokyo: Chikuma shobō.

Tanaka, Stefan. 1993. *Japan's Orient*. Berkeley: University of California Press.

———. 1994. "Imaging History: Inscribing Belief in the Nation." *Journal of Asian Studies* 53:24–44.

Tanaka Akira and Miyachi Masato, eds. 1991. *Rekishi ninshiki*. Tokyo: Iwanami shoten.

Taylor, Charles. 1975. *Hegel*. Cambridge: Cambridge University Press.

Theunissen, Michael. 1984. *The Other*. Translated by Christopher Macann. Cambridge: MIT Press.

Thomas, Julia. 2001. *Reconfiguring Modernity: Concepts of Nature in Japanese Political Ideology*. Berkeley: University of California Press.

Thomas, Keith. 1971. *Religion and the Decline of Magic*. New York: Charles Scribner's Sons.

Thompson, E. P. 1967. "Time, Work-Discipline and Industrial Capitalism." *Past and Present* 38:56–97.

Tobari Chikufu. 1970. "Kaichō." In *Takayama Chogyū, Saitō Nonobito, Anesaki Chōfū, Tobari Chikufu*. Volume 40. Tokyo: Chikuma shobō.

Toby, Ronald P. 1986. "Carnival of the Aliens: Korean Embassies in Edo-Period Art and Popular Culture." *Monumenta Nipponica* 41, 4:415–56.

Tokunō Ryōsuke, ed. 1880. *Kokka yohō*. 5 vols. Museo d'Arte Orientale (Genoa), acq. nos. 3264–3268.

Tokyo kokuritsu hakubutsukan. 1959. *Hōryūji kennō homotsu mokuroku*. Tokyo: Tokyo hakubutsukan.

———. 1973. *Tokyo kokuritsu hakubutsukan hyakunenshi*. Volume 1. Tokyo: Tokyo kokuritsu hakubutsukan.

Tokyo teikoku daigaku gojūnenshi. 1932. Tokyo: Tokyo teikoku daigaku.

Tōma Wataru. 1977. "Jishin no mae ni namazu ga nanpiki mo." *Kanagawa-ken onsen chigaku kenkyūjo hōkoku* 9, 3:18.

Torii Ryūzō. 1967[1925]. "Yushi izen no nihon." In Edward Sylvester Morse. *Ōmori kaizuka*. Tokyo: Tokyo-to ōmori kaizuka hozonkai.

———. 1974. "Nihon kōkogaku no hattatsu." In *Nihon kōkogaku senshū*. Volume 6. Tokyo: Tsukiji shokan.

Totman, Conrad. 2000. *A History of Japan*. Malden, MA: Blackwell Publishers.

Toulmin, Stephen, and June Goodfield. 1965. *The Discovery of Time*. Chicago: University of Chicago Press.

Tozawa Mitsunori. 1977. "Nihon kōkogaku ganen o ōtta kuroi kage: Mōsu no shokujin-setsu o megutte." *Kōkogaku kenkyū* 24:97–102.

Tsuda Sōkichi. 1938. *Shina shisō to nihon*. Tokyo: Iwanami shinsho.

Ueda Kazutoshi. 1989. "Kokubungaku shōgen." In Hisamatsu Senichi, ed. *Ochiai Naobumi, Ueda Kazutoshi, Haga Yaichi, Fujioka Sakutaro shū*. Tokyo: Chikuma shobō.

Umegaki Michio. 1986. "From Domain to Prefecture." In Marius B. Jansen and Gilbert Rozman, eds. *Japan in Transition: From Tokugawa to Meiji*. Princeton: Princeton University Press.

Uno, Kathleen S. 1991. "Women and Changes in the Household Division of Labor." In Gail Lee Bernstein, ed. *Recreating Japanese Women, 1600–1945*. Berkeley: University of California Press.

———. 1999. *Passages to Modernity: Motherhood, Childhood, and Social Reform in Early Twentieth Century Japan*. Honolulu: University of Hawaii Press.

Vico, Giambattista. 1990. *On the Study Methods of Our Time*. Translated by Elio Gianturco. Ithaca: Cornell University Press.

Viswanathan, Gauri. 1989. *Masks of Conquest: Literary Study and British Rule in India*. New York: Columbia University Press.

Watsuji Tetsurō. 1953[1919]. *Koji junrei*. Tokyo: Iwanami shoten.

Wayman, Dorothy G. 1942. *Edward Sylvester Morse: A Biography*. Cambridge: Harvard University Press.

Weiner, Michael. 1989. *The Origins of the Korean Community in Japan, 1910–1925*. Manchester: Manchester University Press.

Williams, Raymond. 1976. *Keywords: A Vocabulary of Culture and Society*. New York: Oxford University Press.

Wilson, George Macklin. 1980. "Time and History in Japan." *American Historical Review* 85:557–71.

———. 1992. *Patriots and Redeemers in Japan: Motives in the Meiji Restoration*. Chicago: University of Chicago Press.

Winchester, Simon. 2001. *The Map That Changed the World: William Smith and the Birth of Modern Geology*. New York: HarperCollins.

Yabe, H. 1917. "Problems Concerning the Geotectonics of the Japanese Islands: Critical Reviews of Various Opinions Expressed by Previous Authors on the Geotectonics." *Science Reports of the Tohoku Imperial University*. Second series, 4:75–104.

Yamaji Aizan. 1965a. "Genji no shakai mondai oyobi shakaishugisha." In *Meiji bungaku zenshū*. Volume 35. Tokyo: Chikuma shobō.

———. 1965b. "Nihon gendaishi no shigaku." In *Meiji bungaku zenshū*. Volume 35. Tokyo: Chikuma shobō.

———. 1985. "Kokkashakaishugi to shakaishugi." In Oka Toshirō, ed. *Yamaji Aizan shū*. Volume 2. Tokyo: San'ichi shobō.

Yamashita Noboru. 1992. "Nauman no kaseki kenkyū: Nauman no nihon chishitsu e no kōken, 4." *Chishitsugaku zasshi* 98:791–809.

Yamashita Shigekazu. 1975. "Fenorosa no Tokyo daigaku kyōju jidai." *Kokugakuin hōgaku*. 12, 4:121–63.

Yanagita Kunio, ed. 1957. *Japanese Manners and Customs in the Meiji Era*. Translated by Charles S. Terry. Tokyo: Obunsha.

Yashiro Yukio. 1987. "Jo—bijutsushi to bijutsu." *Nihon bijutsu no saikentō*. Tokyo: Perikansha.

Yoshiaki Ishiguro. 1998. "A Japanese National Crime: The Korean Massacre after the Great Kantō Earthquake of 1923." *Korea Journal* 38:331–54.

Yoshida Toshihiro. 1982. "Shigaku chirigaku kōza ni okeru kindai jinbun chirigaku dōnyū no keiken." In Kyoto daigaku bungakubu chirigaku kyōshitsuhen. *Chiri no shisō*. Kyoto: Chijin shobō.

Yoshimi Shunya. 1992. *Hakurankai no seijigaku: manazashi no kindai*. Tokyo: Chūō kōronsha.

Yoshioka Ikuo. 1987. *Nihon jinshu ronsō no yoake: Mōsu to ōmori kaisuka*. Tokyo: Kyōritsu shuppan.

Young, John. 1958. *The Location of Yamatai*. Baltimore: Johns Hopkins University Press.

Yuasa, Mitsutomo. 1976. "Principal Stages of the History of Science in Japan." In *Proceedings, XIVth International Congress of the History of Science*. Tokyo.

Yumoto Kōichi. 1999. *Meiji yōkai shinbun*. Tokyo: Kashiwa shobō.

Yutani, Eiji, trans. 1985. "Nihon no kaso shakai of Yokoyama Gennosuke." Ph.D. dissertation, University of Washington.

INDEX

"absolutism of reality," 22, 28, 53, 71, 74, 76, 84, 86, 140, 158, 195, 201
Adwaita ideal, the, 106n, 142n
"Aesthetic Life, An" (Takayama), 154, 158, 159
aesthetics, 36, 85n, 92–93, 102, 158; Greek, 106; Hegelian, 128, 173
Agamben, Giorgio, 145, 191, 196
Ainu and pre-Ainu peoples, 41, 41n. 17, 44, 46, 83, 97
Akai fune (Mimei), 180
Akaike Atsushi, 199
Akazome Emon, 130
alien-I relationship, 23, 199, 200
All That Is Solid Melts into Air (Berman), 86
Amino Yoshihiko, 91
Ankersmit, F. R., 85
Arai Hakuseki, 29
Aries, Philippe, 184
art history, 102, 102n, 126–33, 139–40, 178. *See also* Japanese art
Ashio, 65
Azuma kagami, 81, 119

Bacon, Francis, 82
Baelz, Erwin, 1
Bain, Alexander, 72
Baishōron, 80
Benjamin, Walter, 1, 2, 3, 8, 38
Berman, Marshall, 86
Bigelow, William S., 96
Bird, Isabella, 41n. 17
Bloch, Ernst, 180, 198
"blood tax," 67–68
Blumenberg, Hans, 22, 28, 56, 66, 66n. 21, 118, 126, 158
Brentano, Lujo, 150
Brownlee, John, 124, 138
Buck-Morss, Susan, 38
Buckle, Henry Thomas, 99
Buddhism, 30nn. 2 and 3, 56, 106, 109; and architecture, 173–74, 174n; Buddhist art, 36, 140–41
bunmeikaika, 2, 20, 69, 129

cannibalism, 42–47, 69
capitalism, 19, 20, 32, 96, 145, 146–47, 146n
caricature, 108, 110, 142, 187
Carruthers, Mary, 143
catfish, 61, 65, 66, 74, 75, 195
Certeau, Michel de, 21, 22, 29, 92–93, 111, 125–26, 181
Chakrabarty, Dipesh, 88
Chamberlain, Basil, 117
Chihaya Jōchō, 36–37, 172
childhood, 26, 59, 59n. 7, 133–37, 145–46, 182–84, 197; divisions of, 136–37n. 28; and the idea of family, 184–85; and Japanese architecture, 179–82; and reorientation of locales into the nation, 141, 142; spirit of, 152; utility of, 191–92
China, 119
"*chokugo engi*," 135
Christianity, 45, 89, 90, 156, 161
chronology, 112–14, 118–26, 142; and art history, 128; and national literature, 129–30; naturalization of, 137–38. *See also* time: chronological
clocks, 11–12, 23; and divisions of the day, 12–13
Collingwood, R. G., 89n, 91
Confucianism, 156, 161; idols of, 69
Connerton, Paul, 181

Dahlmann, Joseph, 196
Dai nihon komonjo, 139
Dai nihon shiryō (Chronological Source Books of Japanese History), 139
Dai nihonshi, 78, 79, 81
Davidson, Arnold, 17, 24
Department of Topography, 50n. 32
Donzelot, Jacques, 145, 183, 188–89, 191
Droysen, Johann, 87, 122n. 13
Dupront, Alphonse, 22
Duus, Peter, 125

Eagleton, Terry, 85, 85n, 108
Earthquake (Milne), 63–64
earthquakes, 61, 63–64, 74–75, 74n, 199n. 5. *See also* Tokyo: and 1923 earthquake